A CENTURY OF PARODY AND IMITATION

JAMES AND HORACE SMITH

A
CENTURY OF PARODY
AND IMITATION

EDITED BY

WALTER JERROLD

AND

R. M. LEONARD

'No author ever spared a brother,
Wits are gamecocks to one another.'
GAY

OXFORD UNIVERSITY PRESS
LONDON, EDINBURGH, GLASGOW
NEW YORK, TORONTO, MELBOURNE, BOMBAY
1913

REPUBLISHED BY GALE RESEARCH COMPANY, BOOK TOWER, DETROIT, 1968

Library of Congress Catalog Card Number 68–30585

PREFATORY NOTE

THE object of this compilation is to provide a corpus of
representative parodies and imitations of a century,
beginning with *Rejected Addresses* (1812), which practi-
cally marked the birth of modern parody, and are here
printed in their entirety. Prose parodies, excepting
those in *Rejected Addresses*, have been excluded; the
derivation of the word 'parody' may be referred to in
justification. Emerson wrote in his 'Fable'

> '——all sorts of things and weather
> Must be taken in together
> To make up a year
> And a sphere;

so in this volume will be found all forms of imitations
from, in Mr. Owen Seaman's words, ' the lowest, a mere
verbal echo, to the highest, whère it becomes a department of pure criticism.'

It is quite unnecessary to add to the published mass
of writing, wise and foolish, on the art and ethics of
parody. Some of the pieces in this book are included
chiefly because they have an historical place in the
development of parody to its present high standard of
execution and good taste.

Isaac D'Israeli asserted that ' unless the prototype
is familiar to us a parody is nothing.' As a matter of
fact some of the best work is that of which the originals
have been forgotten long since; although, of course,
when the poets and the poems imitated are familiar
the art of the imitator can be better appreciated.

The word ' century ' has been interpreted with some
licence. The work of living parodists does not fall

within the scope of this collection, and it is a real self-denying ordinance which forbids the inclusion of triumphs by Sir Frederick Pollock, Mr. Owen Seaman, Sir Arthur Quiller-Couch, Mr. Barry Pain, the Rev. Anthony Deane, and others who, in their undergraduate days, enlivened the periodicals of Oxford and Cambridge, or to-day show their dexterity in the pages of *Punch*. By way of recompense, the volume contains parodies by some, still living in 1812, whose work was published before *Rejected Addresses*. The parodies which follow therefore range from George Ellis, who was born in 1753, to Andrew Lang, who died in 1912. Very sparing use has been made of anonymous work, and in this connexion it may be well to explain that ' Adolphus Smalls of Boniface ' is ruled out, because, although published anonymously, it is known to be the joint composition in their Balliol days of Dr. W. W. Merry, the Rector of Lincoln College, Oxford, and Alfred Blomfield, afterwards Bishop of Colchester.

With regard to *Rejected Addresses,* the publication of which may be said to have revived and established the art of parody, the genesis of the work is sufficiently explained in the authors' prefaces and notes. There were parodists before the Brothers Smith, yet their topical little volume has a lasting value, not only because of its inherent excellence, but also because it struck the note which the best later exponents of the art have followed. Published in the autumn of 1812, the book reached its fifteenth edition within two years, and its success led to the publication of a volume of certain of the *Addresses* that had really been sent to Drury Lane for competition. The one hundred and fifteen such Addresses which were actually submitted are, with one or two exceptions, preserved in the Manuscript Department of the British Museum.

The compilers' best thanks are due to those who

have kindly allowed the use of copyright parodies or imitations—namely, to the following: Sir Herbert Stephen (and Messrs. Bowes and Bowes) for parodies by his brother J. K. Stephen ; Mr. Theodore Watts-Dunton and Messrs. Chatto and Windus for Swinburne's parodies; Mr. W. M. Rossetti and Messrs. Ellis for those by Dante Gabriel Rossetti; Messrs. G. Bell and Sons for the copyright pieces by C. S. Calverley in *Fly-Leaves ;* Messrs. Blackwood and Sons for Sir Theodore Martin's ' Lay of the Lovelorn ' and H. D. Traill's parodies; Messrs. Bradbury, Agnew and Co. for R. F. Murray's ' Tennysonian Fragment ' from *Punch ;* Messrs. Burns and Oates for Francis Thompson's imitation of Omar Khayyam ; Messrs. Chatto and Windus, and, for the American rights, the Houghton, Mifflin Company, for the parodies by Bret Harte and Bayard Taylor ; the Editor of the *Journal of Education* for ' A Girtonian Funeral ' by an unknown author, presumably deceased; Messrs. Longmans, Green and Co. for the parodies by Andrew Lang; Messrs. J. MacLehose and Sons for the additional pieces by R. F. Murray; Messrs. Metcalfe and Co. for A. C. Hilton's parodies; Messrs. Pickering and Chatto for Miss Fanshawe's pieces ; and Messrs. Charles Scribner's Sons for the variations by H. C. Bunner on the familiar theme of ' Home, Sweet Home.' The sources of the copyright work are given in the notes at the end of the volume. The footnotes are those of the writers of the parodies.

WALTER JERROLD
R. M. LEONARD.

ALPHABETICAL LIST
OF AUTHORS, WITH THEIR PARODIES
OR IMITATIONS

REJECTED ADDRESSES[1]

OR

THE NEW THEATRUM POETARUM

Fired that the House reject him!——s death!
I'll print it, and shame the fools.

POPE.

LOYAL EFFUSION.

BY W. T. F.[2]

Quicquid dicunt, laudo: id rursum si negant,
Laudo id quoque.

TERENCE.

HAIL, glorious edifice, stupendous work!
God bless the Regent and the Duke of York!
 Ye Muses! by whose aid I cried down Fox,
Grant me in Drury Lane a private box,
Where I may loll, cry bravo! and profess
The boundless powers of England's glorious press;
While Afric's sons exclaim, from shore to shore,
' Quashee ma boo!'—the slave-trade is no more!

[1] The preface is given at the beginning of the Notes on p. 393.

[2] WILLIAM THOMAS FITZGERALD. The annotator's first personal knowledge of this gentleman was at Harry Greville's Pic-Nic Theatre, in Tottenham Street, where he personated Zanga in a wig too small for his head. The second time of seeing him was at the table of old Lord Dudley, who familiarly called him Fitz, but forgot to name him in his will. The Earl's son (recently deceased), however, liberally supplied the omission by a donation of five thousand pounds. The third and last time of encountering him was at an anniversary dinner of the Literary Fund, at the Freemasons' Tavern. Both parties, as two of the stewards, met their brethren in a small room about half an hour before dinner. The lampooner, out of delicacy, kept aloof from the poet. The latter, however, made up to him, when the following dialogue took place:

B

In fair Arabia (happy once, now stony,
Since ruined by that arch-apostate Boney),
A phœnix late was caught: the Arab host
Long ponder'd—part would boil it, part would roast;
But while they ponder, up the pot-lid flies,
Fledged, beak'd, and claw'd, alive they see him rise
To heaven, and caw defiance in the skies.
So Drury, first in roasting flames consumed,
Then by old renters to hot water doom'd,
By Wyatt's trowel patted, plump and sleek,
Soars without wings, and caws without a beak.
Gallia's stern despot shall in vain advance[1]
From Paris, the metropolis of France;
By this day month the monster shall not gain
A foot of land in Portugal or Spain.
See Wellington in Salamanca's field
Forces his favourite general to yield,
Breaks through his lines, and leaves his boasted Marmont
Expiring on the plain without his arm on;
Madrid he enters at the cannon's mouth,
And then the villages still further south.
Base Buonapartè, fill'd with deadly ire,
Sets, one by one, our playhouses on fire.
Some years ago he pounced with deadly glee on
The Opera House, then burnt down the Pantheon;
Nay, still unsated, in a coat of flames,
Next at Millbank he cross'd the river Thames;

Fitzgerald (with good humour): ' Mr. ——, I mean to recite
after dinner.'
    Mr. ——: ' Do you ?'
    Fitzgerald: ' Yes; you'll have more of " God bless the Regent
and the Duke of York !" '
    The whole of this imitation, after a lapse of twenty years, appears
to the Authors too personal and sarcastic; but they may shelter
themselves under a very broad mantle:

' Let hoarse Fitzgerald bawl
His creaking couplets in a tavern-hall.'
BYRON.

[1] ' The first piece, under the name of the loyal Mr. Fitzgerald,
though as good, we suppose, as the original, is not very interesting.
Whether it be very like Mr. Fitzgerald or not, however, it must
be allowed that the vulgarity, servility, and gross absurdity of the
newspaper scribblers is well rendered in the following lines.'—
Edinburgh Review.

Thy hatch, O Halfpenny !¹ pass'd in a trice,
Boil'd some black pitch, and burnt down Astley's twice;
Then buzzing on through ether with a vile hum,
Turn'd to the left hand, fronting the Asylum,
And burnt the Royal Circus in a hurry—
('Twas call'd the Circus then, but now the Surrey).
  Who burnt (confound his soul !) the houses twain
Of Covent Garden and of Drury Lane ?
Who, while the British squadron lay off Cork
(God bless the Regent and the Duke of York !)
With a foul earthquake ravaged the Caraccas,
And raised the price of dry goods and tobaccos ?
Who makes the quartern loaf and Luddites rise ?
Who fills the butchers' shops with large blue flies ?
Who thought in flames St. James's court to pinch ?
Who burnt the wardrobe of poor Lady Finch ?—
Why he, who, forging for this isle a yoke,
Reminds me of a line I lately spoke,
' The tree of freedom is the British oak.'
  Bless every man possess'd of aught to give;
Long may Long Tilney, Wellesley, Long Pole live;
God bless the Army, bless their coats of scarlet,
God bless the Navy, bless the Princess Charlotte;
God bless the Guards, though worsted Gallia scoff,
God bless their pig-tails, though they're now cut off;
And, oh ! in Downing Street should Old Nick revel,
England's prime minister, then bless the devil !

----

¹ In plain English, the Halfpenny-hatch, then a footway through fields; but now, as the same bards sing elsewhere—

> ' St. George's Fields are fields no more,
>   The trowel supersedes the plough;
> Swamps, huge and inundate of yore,
>   Are changed to civic villas now.'

Fitzgerald actually sent in an address to the committee on the 31st of August, 1812. It was published among the other genuine *Rejected Addresses*, in one volume, in that year. The following is an extract:—

> ' The troubled shade of Garrick, hovering near,
> Dropt on the burning pile a pitying tear.'

What a pity that, like Sterne's recording angel, it did not succeed in blotting the fire out for ever ! That failing, why not adopt Gulliver's remedy ?

THE BABY'S DEBUT.

BY W. W.[1]

Thy lisping prattle and thy mincing gait,
All thy false mimic fooleries I hate;
For thou art Folly's counterfeit, and she
Who is right foolish hath the better plea:
Nature's true idiot I prefer to thee.

CUMBERLAND.

[*Spoken in the character of Nancy Lake, a girl eight years of age, who
    is drawn upon the stage in a child's chaise by Samuel Hughes,
    her uncle's porter.*]

MY brother Jack was nine in May,[2]
And I was eight on New-year's-day;
    So in Kate Wilson's shop
Papa (he's my papa and Jack's)
Bought me, last week, a doll of wax,
    And brother Jack a top.

Jack 's in the pouts, and this it is,—
He thinks mine came to more than his;
    So to my drawer he goes,
Takes out the doll, and, O, my stars :
He pokes her head between the bars,
    And melts off half her nose !

[1] WILLIAM WORDSWORTH.
[2] Jack and Nancy, as it was afterwards remarked to the Authors,
are here made to come into the world at periods not sufficiently
remote. The writers were then bachelors. One of them, unfor-
tunately, still continues so, as he has thus recorded in his niece's
album:

' Should I seek Hymen's tie,
As a poet I die—
Ye Benedicks, mourn my distresses !
For what little fame
Is annexed to my name
Is derived from Rejected Addresses.'

The blunder, notwithstanding, remains unrectified. The reader
of poetry is always dissatisfied with emendations: they sound dis-
cordantly upon the ear, like a modern song, by Bishop or Braham,
introduced in *Love in a Village.*

Quite cross, a bit of string I beg,
And tie it to his peg-top's peg,
 And bang, with might and main,
Its head against the parlour-door:
Off flies the head, and hits the floor,
 And breaks a window-pane.

This made him cry with rage and spite:
Well, let him cry, it serves him right.
 A pretty thing, forsooth !
If he's to melt, all scalding hot,
Half my doll's nose, and I am not
 To draw his peg-top's tooth !

Aunt Hannah heard the window break,
And cried, ' O naughty Nancy Lake,
 Thus to distress your aunt:
No Drury Lane for you to-day !'
And while Papa said, ' Pooh, she may !'
 Mamma said, ' No, she sha'n't !'

Well, after many a sad reproach,
They got into a hackney coach,
 And trotted down the street.
I saw them go : one horse was blind,
The tails of both hung down behind,
 Their shoes were on their feet.

The chaise in which poor brother Bill
Used to be drawn to Pentonville
 Stood in the lumber-room:
I wiped the dust from off the top,
While Molly mopp'd it with a mop,
 And brush'd it with a broom.

My uncle's porter, Samuel Hughes,
Came in at six to black the shoes,
 (I always talk to Sam :)
So what does he, but takes, and drags
Me in the chaise along the flags,
 And leaves me where I am.

My father's walls are made of brick,
But not so tall and not so thick
    As these; and, goodness me!
My father's beams are made of wood,
But never, never half so good
    As those that now I see.

What a large floor! 'tis like a town!
The carpet, when they lay it down,
    Won't hide it, I'll be bound;
And there's a row of lamps!—my eye!
How they do blaze! I wonder why
    They keep them on the ground.

At first I caught hold of the wing,
And kept away; but Mr. Thing-
    umbob, the prompter man,
Gave with his hand my chaise a shove,
And said, ' Go on, my pretty love;
    ' Speak to 'em, little Nan.

' You've only got to curtsy, whisp-
er, hold your chin up, laugh, and lisp,
    And then you're sure to take:
I've known the day when brats, not quite
Thirteen, got fifty pounds a-night;[1]
    Then why not Nancy Lake?'

---

[1] This alludes to the young Betty mania. The writer was in the stage-box at the height of this young gentleman's popularity. One of the other occupants offered, in a loud voice, to prove that young Betty did not understand Shakespeare. ' Silence !' was the cry; but he still proceeded. ' Turn him out !' was the next ejaculation. He still vociferated ' He does not understand Shakespeare;' and was consequently shouldered into the lobby. ' I'll prove it to you,' said the critic to the door-keeper. ' Prove what, sir ?' ' That he does not understand Shakespeare.' This was Molière's housemaid with a vengeance !

Young Betty may now be seen walking about town—a portly personage, aged about forty—clad in a furred and frogged surtout; probably muttering to himself (as he has been at college), ' O mihi præteritos !' &c.

But while I'm speaking, where's papa ?
And where's my aunt ? and where's mamma ?
    Where's Jack ? O, there they sit !
They smile, they nod; I'll go my ways,
And order round poor Billy's chaise,
    To join them in the pit.

And now, good gentlefolks, I go
To join mamma, and see the show;
    So, bidding you adieu,
I curtsy, like a pretty miss,
And if you'll blow to me a kiss,
    I'll blow a kiss to you.
                    [*Blows a kiss, and exit.*]

' The author does not, in this instance, attempt to copy any of
the higher attributes of Mr. Wordsworth's poetry; but has succeeded
perfectly in the imitation of his maukish affectations of childish
simplicity and nursery stammering. We hope it will make him
ashamed of his *Alice Fell*, and the greater part of his last volumes
—of which it is by no means a parody, but a very fair, and indeed
we think a flattering, imitation.'—*Edinburgh Review.*

AN ADDRESS

WITHOUT A PHŒNIX.

BY S. T. P.[1]

This was looked for at your hand, and this was balked.
                    What You Will.

WHAT stately vision mocks my waking sense ?
Hence, dear delusion, sweet enchantment, hence !
Ha ! is it real ?—can my doubts be vain ?
It is, it is, and Drury lives again !
Around each grateful veteran attends,
Eager to rush and gratulate his friends,
Friends whose kind looks, retraced with proud delight,
Endear the past, and make the future bright:
Yes, generous patrons, your returning smile
Blesses our toils, and consecrates our pile.

[1] For an account of this anonymous gentleman, see the Preface.

When last we met, Fate's unrelenting hand
Already grasped the devastating brand;
Slow crept the silent flame, ensnared its prize,
Then burst resistless to the astonished skies.
The glowing walls, disrobed of scenic pride,
In trembling conflict stemmed the burning tide,
Till crackling, blazing, rocking to its fall,
Down rushed the thundering roof, and buried all !

Where late the sister Muses sweetly sung,
And raptured thousands on their music hung,
Where Wit and Wisdom shone, by Beauty graced,
Sat lonely Silence, empress of the waste;
And still had reigned—but he, whose voice can raise
More magic wonders than Amphion's lays,
Bade jarring bands with friendly zeal engage
To rear the prostrate glories of the stage.
Up leaped the Muses at the potent spell,
And Drury's genius saw his temple swell;
Worthy, we hope, the British Drama's cause,
Worthy of British arts, and *your* applause.

Guided by you, our earnest aims presume
To renovate the Drama with the dome;
The scenes of Shakespeare and our bards of old,
With due observance splendidly unfold,
Yet raise and foster with parental hand
The living talent of our native land.
O ! may we still, to sense and nature true,
Delight the many, nor offend the few.
Though varying tastes our changeful Drama claim,
Still be its moral tendency the same,
To win by precept, by example warn,
To brand the front of Vice with pointed scorn,
And Virtue's smiling brows with votive wreaths adorn.

CUI BONO?

BY LORD B.[1]

I.

SATED with home, of wife, of children tired,
The restless soul is driven abroad to roam;[2]
Sated abroad, all seen, yet nought admired,
The restless soul is driven to ramble home;
Sated with both, beneath new Drury's dome
The fiend Ennui awhile consents to pine,

---

[1] LORD BYRON.

[2] This would seem to show that poet and prophet are synonymous,
the noble bard having afterwards returned to England, and again
quitted it, under domestic circumstances painfully notorious. His
good-humoured forgiveness of the Authors has been already alluded
to in the Preface. Nothing of this illustrious poet, however
trivial, can be otherwise than interesting. 'We knew him well.'
At Mr. Murray's dinner-table the annotator met him and Sir John
Malcolm. Lord Byron talked of intending to travel in Persia.
'What must I do when I set off?' said he to Sir John. 'Cut off
your buttons!' 'My buttons! what, these metal ones?' 'Yes;
the Persians are in the main very honest fellows; but if you go thus
bedizened, you will infallibly be murdered for your buttons.' At
a dinner at Monk Lewis's chambers in the Albany, Lord Byron
expressed to the writer his determination not to go there again,
adding, 'I never will dine with a middle-aged man who fills up his
table with young ensigns, and has looking-glass panels to his book-
cases.' Lord Byron, when one of the Drury Lane Committee of
Management, challenged the writer to sing alternately (like the
swains in Virgil) the praises of Mrs. Mardyn, the actress, who, by
the by, was hissed off the stage for an imputed intimacy, of which
she was quite innocent.
The contest ran as follows:

> 'Wake, muse of fire, your ardent lyre,
>   Pour forth your amorous ditty,
> But first profound, in duty bound,
>   Applaud the new committee;
> Their scenic art from Thespis cart
>   All jaded nags discarding,
> To London drove this queen of love,
>   Enchanting Mrs. Mardyn.

> 'Though tides of love around her rove,
>   I fear she'll choose Pactolus—
> In that bright surge bards ne'er immerge,
>   So I must e'en swim solus.

There growls, and curses, like a deadly Gnome,
Scorning to view fantastic Columbine,
Viewing with scorn and hate the nonsense of the Nine.

" Out, out, alas !" ill-fated gas,
    That shin'st round Covent Garden,
Thy ray how flat, compared with that
    From eye of Mrs. Mardyn !'

And so on.   The reader has, no doubt, already discovered ' which
is the justice, and which is the thief.'

Lord Byron at that time wore a very narrow cravat of white
sarsnet, with the shirt-collar falling over it; a black coat and waistcoat, and very broad white trousers, to hide his lame foot—these
were of Russia duck in the morning, and jean in the evening.   His
watch-chain had a number of small gold seals appended to it, and
was looped up to a button of his waistcoat.   His face was void of
colour; he wore no whiskers.   His eyes were grey, fringed with
long black lashes; and his air was imposing, but rather supercilious.
He undervalued David Hume; denying his claim to genius on
account of his bulk, and calling him from the heroic epistle,

' The fattest hog in Epicurus' sty.'

One of this extraordinary man's allegations was, that ' fat is an
oily dropsy.'   To stave off its visitation, he frequently chewed
tobacco in lieu of dinner, alleging that it absorbed the gastric juice
of the stomach, and prevented hunger.   ' Pass your hand down
my side,' said his lordship to the writer; ' can you count my ribs ?'
' Every one of them.'   ' I am delighted to hear you say so.   I called
last week on Lady ——; " Ah, Lord Byron," said she, " how fat
you grow !"   But you know Lady —— is fond of saying spiteful
things !'   Let this gossip be summed up with the words of Lord
Chesterfield, in his character of Bolingbroke: ' Upon the whole, on
a survey of this extraordinary character, what can we say but
" Alas, poor human nature !" '

His favourite Pope's description of man is applicable to Byron
individually:

Chaos of thought and passion all confused,
Still by himself abused or disabused;
Created part to rise and part to fall,
Great lord of all things, yet a slave to all;
Sole judge of truth, in endless error hurled—
The glory, jest, and riddle of the world.'

The writer never heard him allude to his deformed foot except
upon one occasion, when, entering the green-room of Drury Lane,
he found Lord Byron alone, the younger Byrne and Miss Smith the
dancer having just left him, after an angry conference about a *pas
seul*.   ' Had you been here a minute sooner,' said Lord B., ' you
would have heard a question about dancing referred to me;—me !
(looking mournfully downward) whom fate from my birth has
prohibited from taking a single step.'

II.

Ye reckless dupes, who hither wend your way
To gaze on puppets in a painted dome,
Pursuing pastimes glittering to betray,
Like falling stars in life's eternal gloom,
What seek ye here ?   Joy's evanescent bloom ?
Woe's me ! the brightest wreaths she ever gave
Are but as flowers that decorate a tomb.
Man's heart, the mournful urn o'er which they wave,
Is sacred to despair, its pedestal the grave.

III.

Has life so little store of real woes,
That here ye wend to taste fictitious grief ?
Or is it that from truth such anguish flows,
Ye court the lying drama for relief ?
Long shall ye find the pang, the respite brief:
Or if one tolerable page appears
In folly's volume, 'tis the actor's leaf,
Who dries his own by drawing others' tears,
And, raising present mirth, makes glad his future years.

IV.

Albeit, how like young Betty doth he flee !
Light as the mote that danceth in the beam,
He liveth only in man's present e'e,
His life a flash, his memory a dream,
Oblivious down he drops in Lethe's stream.
Yet what are they, the learned and the great ?
Awhile of longer wonderment the theme,
Who shall presume to prophesy *their* date,
Where nought is certain, save the uncertainty of fate ?

V.

This goodly pile, upheaved by Wyatt's toil,
Perchance than Holland's edifice[1] more fleet,
Again red Lemnos' artisan may spoil;
The fire-alarm and midnight drum may beat,

[1] ' Holland's edifice.'   The late theatre was built by Holland
the architect.   The writer visited it on the night of its opening.

And all be strewed y-smoking at your feet !
Start ye ? perchance Death's angel may be sent,
Ere from the flaming temple ye retreat;
And ye who met, on revel idlesse bent,
May find, in pleasure's fane, your grave and
  monument.

The performances were *Macbeth* and the *Virgin Unmasked*. Between the play and the farce, an excellent epilogue, written by George Colman, was excellently spoken by Miss Farren. It referred to the iron curtain which was, in the event of fire, to be let down between the stage and the audience, and which accordingly descended, by way of experiment, leaving Miss Farren between the lamps and the curtain. The fair speaker informed the audience, that should the fire break out on the stage (where it usually originates), it would thus be kept from the spectators; adding, with great solemnity—

> ' No ! we assure our generous benefactors
> 'Twill only burn the scenery and the actors !'

A tank of water was afterwards exhibited, in the course of the epilogue, in which a wherry was rowed by a real live man, the band playing—

> ' And did you not hear of a jolly young waterman ?'

Miss Farren reciting—

> ' Sit still, there's nothing in it,
> We'll undertake to drown you in a single minute.'

' O vain thought !' as Othello says. Notwithstanding the boast in the epilogue—

> ' Blow, wind—come, wrack, in ages yet unborn,
> Our castle's strength shall laugh a siege to scorn '—

the theatre fell a victim to the flames within fifteen years from the prognostic ! These preparations against fire always presuppose presence of mind and promptness in those who are to put them into action. They remind one of the dialogue, in Morton's *Speed the Plough*, between Sir Abel Handy and his son Bob:

' *Bob.* Zounds, the castle 's on fire !
Sir A. Yes.
Bob. Where's your patent liquid for extinguishing fire ?
Sir A. It is not mixed.
Bob. Then where's your patent fire-escape ?
Sir A. It is not fixed.
Bob. You are never at a loss ?
Sir A. Never.
Bob. Then what do you mean to do ?
Sir A. I don't know.'

VI.

Your debts mount high—ye plunge in deeper waste;
The tradesman duns—no warning voice ye hear;
The plaintiff sues—to public shows ye haste;
The bailiff threats—ye feel no idle fear.
Who can arrest your prodigal career?
Who can keep down the levity of youth?
What sound can startle age's stubborn ear?
Who can redeem from wretchedness and ruth
Men true to falsehood's voice, false to the voice of truth?

VII.

To thee, blest saint! who doffed thy skin to make
The Smithfield rabble leap from theirs with joy,
We dedicate the pile—arise! awake!—
Knock down the Muses, wit and sense destroy,
Clear our new stage from reason's dull alloy,
Charm hobbling age, and tickle capering youth
With cleaver, marrow-bone, and Tunbridge toy;
While, vibrating in unbelieving tooth,[1]
Harps twang in Drury's walls, and make her boards
    a booth.

VIII.

For what is Hamlet, but a hare in March?
And what is Brutus, but a croaking owl?
And what is Rolla? Cupid steeped in starch,
Orlando's helmet in Augustine's cowl.
Shakespeare, how true thine adage, 'fair is foul!'
To him whose soul is with fruition fraught,—
The song of Braham is an Irish howl,—
Thinking is but an idle waste of thought,
And nought is every thing, and every thing is nought.

IX.

Sons of Parnassus! whom I view above,
Not laurel-crown'd, but clad in rusty black;
Not spurring Pegasus through Tempè's grove,
But pacing Grub-street on a jaded hack;

[1] A rather obscure mode of expression for *Jews'*-harp; which
some etymologists allege, by the way, to be a corruption of *Jaws'*-
harp. No connexion, therefore, with King David.

What reams of foolscap, while your brains ye rack,
Ye mar to make again ! for sure, ere long,
Condemn'd to tread the bard's time-sanction'd track,
Ye all shall join the bailiff-haunted throng,
And reproduce, in rags, the rags ye blot in song.

x.

So fares the follower in the Muses' train;
He toils to starve, and only lives in death;
We slight him, till our patronage is vain,
Then round his skeleton a garland wreathe,
And o'er his bones an empty requiem breathe—
Oh ! with what tragic horror would he start,
(Could he be conjured from the grave beneath)
To find the stage again a Thespian cart,
And elephants and colts down-trampling Shakespeare's
art.

xi.

Hence, pedant Nature ! with thy Grecian rules !
Centaurs (not fabulous) those rules efface;
Back, sister Muses, to your native schools;
Here booted grooms usurp Apollo's place.
Hoofs shame the boards that Garrick used to grace,
The play of limbs succeeds the play of wit,
Man yields the drama to the Hou'yn'm race,
His prompter spurs, his licenser the bit,
The stage a stable-yard, a jockey-club the pit.

xii.

Is it for these ye rear this proud abode ?
Is it for these your superstition seeks
To build a temple worthy of a god,
To laud a monkey, or to worship leeks ?
Then be the stage, to recompense your freaks,
A motley chaos, jumbling age and ranks,
Where Punch, the lignum-vitæ Roscius, squeaks,
And Wisdom weeps, and Folly plays her pranks,
And moody Madness laughs and hugs the chain he clanks.

' The author has succeeded better in copying the moody and
misanthropic sentiments of *Childe Harold*, than the nervous and
impetuous diction in which his noble biographer has embodied them.
The attempt, however, indicates very considerable power; and the
flow of the verse and the construction of the poetical period are
imitated with no ordinary skill.'—*Edinburgh Review.*

SECRETARY OF THE MANAGING COMMITTEE OF DRURY-LANE PLAYHOUSE.

SIR,

　To the gewgaw fetters of *rhyme* (invented by the monks to enslave the people) I have a rooted objection. I have therefore written an address for your theatre in plain, homespun, yeoman's *prose;* in the doing whereof I hope I am swayed by nothing but an *independent* wish to open the eyes of this gulled people, to prevent a repetition of the dramatic *bamboozling* they have hitherto laboured under.　If you like what I have done, and mean to make use of it, I don't want any such *aristocratic* reward as a piece of plate with two griffins sprawling upon it, or a *dog* and a *jackass* fighting for a ha'p'worth of *gilt gingerbread,* or any such Bartholomew-fair non-sense.　All I ask is, that the door-keepers of your play-house may take all the *sets of my Register* now on hand, and *force* every body who enters your doors to buy one, giving afterwards a debtor and creditor account of what they have received, *post-paid,* and in due course remitting me the money and unsold Registers, *carriage-paid.*

I am, &c.

W. C.[1]

A HAMPSHIRE FARMER.

————— Rabidâ qui concitus irâ
Implevit pariter ternis latratibus auras,
Et sparsit virides spumis albentibus agros.

OVID.

MOST THINKING PEOPLE,

WHEN persons address an audience from the stage, it is usual, either in words or gesture, to say, ' Ladies and Gentlemen, your servant.'　If I were base enough,

---

[1] WILLIAM COBBETT—now M.P.

mean enough, paltry enough, and *brute beast* enough,
to follow that fashion, I should tell two lies in a
breath. In the first place, you are *not* Ladies and
Gentlemen, but I hope something better, that is to
say, honest men and women; and in the next place,
if you were ever so much ladies, and ever so much
gentlemen, I am not, *nor ever will be*, your humble servant. You see me here, *most thinking people*, by mere
chance. I have not been within the doors of a playhouse
before for these ten years; nor, till that abominable
custom of taking money at the doors is discontinued,
will I ever sanction a theatre with my presence. The
stage-door is the only gate of *freedom* in the whole edifice,
and through that I made my way from Bagshaw's[1] in
Brydges Street, to accost you. Look about you. Are
you not all comfortable ? Nay, never slink, mun; speak
out, if you are dissatisfied, and tell me so before I leave
town. You are now, (thanks to *Mr. Whitbread*,) got
into a large, comfortable house. Not into a *gimcrack
palace ;* not into a *Solomon's temple ;* not into a frost-
work of Brobdingnag filigree; but into a plain, honest,
homely, industrious, wholesome, *brown brick playhouse.*
You have been struggling for independence and elbow-
room these three years; and who gave it you ? Who
helped you out of Lilliput ? Who routed you from a
rat-hole, five inches by four, to perch you in a palace ?
Again and again I answer, *Mr. Whitbread.* You might
have sweltered in that place with the Greek name[2] till
doomsday, and neither *Lord Castlereagh, Mr. Canning,*
no, nor the *Marquess Wellesley,* would have turned a
trowel to help you out ! Remember that. Never forget
that. Read it to your children, and to your children's
children ! And now, *most thinking people,* cast your
eyes over my head to what the builder (I beg his pardon,
the architect) calls the *proscenium.* No motto, no
slang, no popish Latin, to keep the people in the dark.
No *veluti in speculum.* Nothing in the dead languages,
properly so called, for they ought to die, aye and be
damned to boot ! The Covent Garden manager tried

---

[1] Bagshaw. At that time the publisher of Cobbett's Register.
[2] The old Lyceum Theatre, pulled down by Mr. Arnold. That
since destroyed by fire was erected on its site.

that, and a pretty business he made of it ! When a man says *veluti in speculum*, he is called a man of letters. Very well, and is not a man who cries O. P. a man of letters too ? You ran your O. P. against his *veluti in speculum*, and pray which beat ? I prophesied that, though I never told any body. I take it for granted, that every intelligent man, woman, and child, to whom I address myself, has stood severally and respectively in Little Russell Street, and cast their, his, her, and its eyes on the outside of this building before they paid their money to view the inside. Look at the brick-work, *English Audience !* Look at the brick-work ! All plain and smooth like a quakers' meeting. None of your Egyptian pyramids, to entomb subscribers' capitals. No overgrown colonnades of stone, like an alderman's gouty legs in white cotton stockings, fit only to use as rammers for paving Tottenham Court Road. This house is neither after the model of a temple in Athens, no, nor a *temple* in *Moorfields*, but it is built to act English plays in; and, provided you have good scenery, dresses, and decorations, I daresay you wouldn't break your hearts if the outside were as plain as the pikestaff I used to carry when I was a sergeant. *Apropos*, as the French valets say, who cut their masters' throats[1]— *apropos*, a word about dresses. You must, many of you, have seen what I have read a description of, Kemble and Mrs. Siddons in Macbeth, with more gold and silver plastered on their doublets than would have kept an honest family in butcher's meat and flannel from year's end to year's end ! I am informed, (now mind, I do not vouch for the fact,) but I am informed that all such extravagant idleness is to be done away with here. Lady Macbeth is to have a plain quilted petticoat, a cotton gown, and a *mob cap* (as the court parasites call it;—it will be well for them, if, one of these days, they don't wear a mob cap—I mean a *white cap*, with a *mob* to look at them); and Macbeth is to appear in an honest yeoman's drab coat, and a pair of black calamanco breeches. Not *Sala*manca; no, nor *Talavera* neither, my most Noble Marquess; but plain, honest, black calamanco

---

[1] An allusion to a murder then recently committed on Barnes Terrace.

stuff breeches. This is right; this is as it should be.
Most thinking people, I have heard you much abused.
There is not a compound in the language but is strung
fifty in a rope, like onions, by the Morning Post, and
hurled in your teeth. You are called the mob; and
when they have made you out to be the mob, you are
called the *scum* of the people, and the *dregs* of the people.
I should like to know how you can be both. Take a
basin of broth—not *cheap soup*, *Mr. Wilberforce*—not
soup for the poor, at a penny a quart, as your mixture
of horses' legs, brick-dust, and old shoes, was denomi-
nated—but plain, wholesome, patriotic beef or mutton
broth; take this, examine it, and you will find—mind,
I don't vouch for the fact, but I am told—you will find
the dregs at the bottom, and the scum at the top. I
will endeavour to explain this to you: England is a large
earthenware pipkin ; John Bull is the *beef* thrown into it;
taxes are the *hot water* he boils in; rotten boroughs are
the *fuel* that blazes under this same pipkin; parliament
is the *ladle* that stirs the hodge-podge, and sometimes
——. But, hold ! I don't wish to pay *Mr. Newman*[1] a
second visit. I leave you better off than you have been
this many a day: you have a good house over your head;
you have beat the French in Spain; the harvest has
turned out well; the comet keeps its distance;[2] and red
slippers are hawked about in Constantinople for next to
nothing; and for all this, *again and again* I tell you, you
are indebted to *Mr. Whitbread ! ! !*

[1] At that time keeper of Newgate. The present superintendent
is styled governor !

[2] A portentous one that made its appearance in the year 1811;
in the midst of the war,

with fear of change
Perplexing nations.

THE LIVING LUSTRES.

BY T. M.[1]

Jam te juvaverit
Viros relinquere,
Doctæque conjugis
Sinu quiescere.

SIR T. MORE.

I.

O WHY should our dull retrospective addresses[2]
  Fall damp as wet blankets on Drury Lane fire ?
Away with blue devils, away with distresses,
  And give the gay spirit to sparkling desire !

II.

Let artists decide on the beauties of Drury,
  The richest to me is when woman is there;
The question of houses I leave to the jury;
  The fairest to me is the house of the fair.

III.

When woman's soft smile all our senses bewilders,
  And gilds, while it carves, her dear form on the heart,
What need has New Drury of carvers and gilders ?
  With Nature so bounteous, why call upon Art ?

IV.

How well would our actors attend to their duties,
  Our house save in oil, and our authors in wit,
In lieu of yon lamps, if a row of young beauties
  Glanced light from their eyes between us and the pit !

[1] THOMAS MOORE.
[2] ' *The Living Lustres* appears to us a very fair imitation of the
fantastic verses which that ingenious person, Mr. Moore, indites when
he is merely gallant, and, resisting the lures of voluptuousness, is
not enough in earnest to be tender.'—*Edinburgh Review.*

V.

The apples that grew on the fruit-tree of knowledge
  By woman were pluck'd, and she still wears the prize,
To tempt us in theatre, senate, or college—
  I mean the love-apples that bloom in the eyes.

VI.

There too is the lash which, all statutes controlling,
  Still governs the slaves that are made by the fair;
For man is the pupil, who, while her eye's rolling,
  Is lifted to rapture, or sunk in despair.

VII.

Bloom, Theatre, bloom, in the roseate blushes
  Of beauty illumed by a love-breathing smile!
And flourish, ye pillars,[1] as green as the rushes
  That pillow the nymphs of the Emerald Isle!

VIII.

For dear is the Emerald Isle of the ocean,
  Whose daughters are fair as the foam of the wave,
Whose sons, unaccustom'd to rebel commotion,
  Though joyous, are sober—though peaceful, are
    brave.

IX.

The shamrock their olive, sworn foe to a quarrel,
  Protects from the thunder and lightning of rows;
Their sprig of shillelagh is nothing but laurel,
  Which flourishes rapidly over their brows.

X.

O! soon shall they burst the tyrannical shackles
  Which each panting bosom indignantly names,
Until not one goose at the capital cackles
  Against the grand question of Catholic claims.

---

[1] This alludes to two massive pillars of verd antique which then
flanked the proscenium, but which have since been removed. Their
colour reminds the bard of the Emerald Isle, and this causes him
(more suo) to fly off at a tangent, and Hibernicise the rest of the
poem.

XI.

And then shall each Paddy, who once on the Liffey
  Perchance held the helm of some mackerel-hoy,
Hold the helm of the state, and dispense in a jiffy
  More fishes than ever he caught when a boy.

XII.

And those who now quit their hods, shovels, and
    barrows,
  In crowds to the bar of some ale-house to flock,
When bred to *our* bar shall be Gibbses and Garrows,
  Assume the silk gown, and discard the smock-frock.

XIII.

For Erin surpasses the daughters of Neptune,
  As Dian outshines each encircling star;
And the spheres and the heavens could never have kept
    tune
  Till set to the music of Erin-go-bragh !

THE REBUILDING.

BY R. S.[1]

——— Per audaces nova dithyrambos
Verba devolvit, numerisque fertur
Lege solutis.

HORAT.

[Spoken by a Glendoveer.]

I AM a blessed Glendoveer:[2]
'Tis mine to speak, and yours to hear.[3]

[1] ROBERT SOUTHEY.

[2] For the Glendoveer, and the rest of the *dramatis personæ* of this imitation, the reader is referred to the ' Curse of Kehama.'

[3] ' *The Rebuilding* is in the name of Mr. Southey, and is one of the best in the collection. It is in the style of the " Kehama " of that multifarious author; and is supposed to be spoken in the character of one of his Glendoveers. The imitation of the diction and measure, we think, is nearly almost perfect; and the descriptions as good as the original. It opens with an account of the burning of the old theatre, formed upon the pattern of the Funeral of Arvalan.'— *Edinburgh Review.*

Midnight, yet not a nose
From Tower-hill to Piccadilly snored !
Midnight, yet not a nose
From Indra drew the essence of repose !
See with what crimson fury,
By Indra fann'd, the god of fire ascends the walls of
Drury !

Tops of houses, blue with lead,
Bend beneath the landlord's tread.
Master and 'prentice, serving-man and lord,
Nailor and tailor,
Grazier and brazier,
Through streets and alleys pour'd—
All, all abroad to gaze,
And wonder at the blaze.
Thick calf, fat foot, and slim knee,
·   Mounted on roof and chimney,[1]
The mighty roast, the mighty stew
To see;
As if the dismal view
Were but to them a Brentford jubilee.

Vainly, all-radiant Surya, sire of Phaeton
(By Greeks call'd Apollo[2]),
Hollow

[1] This couplet was introduced by the Authors by way of bravado,
in answer to one who alleged that the English language contained
no rhyme to chimney.

[2] Apollo. A gigantic wooden figure of this deity was erected on
the roof. The writer (*horrescit referens !*) is old enough to recollect
the time when it was first placed there. Old Bishop, then one of the
masters of Merchant Tailors' School, wrote an epigram upon the
occasion, which, referring to the aforesaid figure, concluded thus:

'Above he fills up Shakespeare's place,
And Shakespeare fills up his below '—

Very antithetical: but quære as to the meaning ? The writer, like
Pluto, ' long puzzled his brain ' to find it out, till he was immersed
' in a lower deep ' by hearing Madame de Staël say, at the table
of the late Lord Dillon, ' Buonaparte is not a man, but a system.'
Inquiry was made in the course of the evening of Sir James Mackintosh as to what the lady meant. He answered, 'Mass ! I cannot
tell.' Madame de Staël repeats this apophthegm in her work on
Germany. It is probably understood *there.*

Sounds from thy harp proceed;
Combustible as reed,
The tongue of Vulcan licks thy wooden legs:
From Drury's top, dissever'd from thy pegs,
Thou tumblest,
Humblest,
Where late thy bright effulgence shone on high;
While, by thy somerset excited, fly
Ten million
Billion
Sparks from the pit, to gem the sable sky.

Now come the men of fire to quench the fires:
To Russell Street see Globe and Atlas run
Hope gallops first, and second Sun;
On flying heel
See Hand-in-Hand
O'ertake the band !
View with what glowing wheel
He nicks
Phœnix !
While Albion scampers from Bridge Street, Black-
friars—
Drury Lane ! Drury Lane !
Drury Lane ! Drury Lane !
They shout and they bellow again and again.
All, all in vain !
Water turns steam;
Each blazing beam
Hisses defiance to the eddying spout:
It seems but too plain that nothing can put it out !
Drury Lane ! Drury Lane !
See, Drury Lane expires !

Pent in by smoke-dried beams, twelve moons or more,
Shorn of his ray,
Surya in durance lay:
The workmen heard him shout,
But thought it would not pay,
To dig him out.
When lo ! terrific Yamen, lord of hell,

Solemn as lead,
Judge of the dead,
Sworn foe to witticism,
By men call'd criticism,
Came passing by that way:
Rise ! cried the fiend, behold a sight of gladness !
Behold the rival theatre !
I've set O. P. at her,[1]
Who, like a bull-dog bold,
Growls and fastens on his hold.
The many-headed rabble roar in madness;
Thy rival staggers: come and spy her
Deep in the mud as thou art in the mire.

So saying, in his arms he caught the beaming one,
And crossing Russell Street,
He placed him on his feet

---

[1] O. P. This personage, who is alleged to have growled like a bull-dog, requires rather a lengthened note, for the edification of the rising generation. The 'horns, rattles, drums,' with which he is accompanied, are no inventions of the poet. The new Covent Garden Theatre opened on the 18th Sept., 1809, when a cry of ' Old Prices ' (afterwards diminished to O. P.) burst out from every part of the house. This continued and increased in violence till the 23rd, when rattles, drums, whistles, and cat-calls, having completely drowned the voices of the actors, Mr. Kemble, the stage-manager, came forward and said, that a committee of gentlemen had undertaken to examine the finances of the concern, and that until they were prepared with their report the theatre would continue closed. ' Name them !' was shouted from all sides. The names were declared, viz. Sir Charles Price, the Solicitor-General, the Recorder of London, the Governor of the Bank, and Mr. Angersteen. ' All shareholders !' bawled a wag from the gallery. In a few days the theatre re-opened: the public paid no attention to the report of the referees, and the tumult was renewed for several weeks with even increased violence. The proprietors now sent in hired bruisers, to *mill* the refractory into subjection. This irritated most of their former friends, and, amongst the rest, the annotator, who accordingly wrote the song of ' Heigh-ho, says Kemble,' which was caught up by the ballad-singers, and sung under Mr. Kemble's house-windows in Great Russell Street. A dinner was given at the Crown and Anchor Tavern in the Strand, to celebrate the victory obtained by W. Clifford in his action against Brandon the box-keeper, for assaulting him for wearing the letters O. P. in his hat. At this dinner Mr. Kemble attended, and matters were compromised by allowing the advanced price (seven shillings) to the boxes. The writer remembers a former riot of a similar sort at the same theatre

'Neath Covent Garden dome. Sudden a sound,
    As of the bricklayers of Babel, rose:
Horns, rattles, drums, tin trumpets, sheets of copper,
  Punches and slaps, thwacks of all sorts and sizes,
From the knobb'd bludgeon to the taper switch,[1]
  Ran echoing round the walls; paper placards
Blotted the lamps, boots brown with mud the benches;
    A sea of heads roll'd roaring in the pit;
        On paper wings O. P.'s
        Reclin'd in lettered ease;
        While shout and scoff,
          Ya ! ya ! off ! off !
    Like thunderbolt on Surya's ear-drum fell,
        And seem'd to paint
      The savage oddities of Saint
        Bartholomew in hell.

(in the year 1792), when the price to the boxes was raised from five
shillings to six.   That tumult, however, only lasted three nights.

  [1] ' From the knobb'd bludgeon to the taper switch.'   This image
is not the creation of the poets: it sprang from reality.   The Authors
happened to be at the Royal Circus when ' God save the King '
was called for, accompanied by a cry of ' Stand up !' and ' Hats off !'
An inebriated naval lieutenant perceiving a gentleman in an adjoin-
ing box slow to obey the call, struck his hat off with his stick, exclaiming, ' Take off your hat, sir !'   The other thus assaulted proved
to be, unluckily for the lieutenant, Lord Camelford, the celebrated
bruiser and duellist.   A set-to in the lobby was the consequence,
where his lordship quickly proved victorious.   ' The devil is not
so black as he is painted,' said one of the Authors to the other;
' let us call upon Lord Camelford, and tell him that we were witnesses
of his being first assaulted.'   The visit was paid on the ensuing
morning at Lord Camelford's lodging, in Bond Street.   Over the
fire-place in the drawing-room were ornaments strongly expressive
of the pugnacity of the peer.   A long thick bludgeon lay horizontally
supported by two brass hooks.   Above this was placed parallel one
of lesser dimensions, until a pyramid of weapons gradually arose,
tapering to a horsewhip:

  ' Thus all below was strength, and all above was grace.'

  Lord Camelford received his visitants with great civility, and
thanked them warmly for the call; adding, that their evidence would
be material, it being his intention to indict the lieutenant for an
assault.   ' All I can say in return is this,' exclaimed the peer with
great cordiality, ' if ever I see you engaged in a row, upon my soul,
I'll stand by you.'   The Authors expressed themselves thankful
for so potent an ally, and departed.   In about a fortnight afterwards Lord Camelford was shot in a duel with Mr. Best.

Tears dimm'd the god of light—
' Bear me back, Yamen, from this hideous sight;
Bear me back, Yamen, I grow sick,
Oh ! bury me again in brick;
Shall I on New Drury tremble,
To be O. P.'d like Kemble ?
No,
Better remain by rubbish guarded,
Than thus hubbubish groan placarded;
Bear me back, Yamen, bear me quick,
And bury me again in brick.'
Obedient Yamen
Answered, ' Amen,'
And did
As he was bid.

There lay the buried god, and Time
Seemed to decree eternity of lime;
But pity, like a dew-drop, gently prest
Almighty Veeshnoo's[1] adamantine breast :
He, the preserver, ardent still
To do whate'er he says he will,
From South-hill wing'd his way,
To raise the drooping lord of day.
All earthly spells the busy one o'erpower'd;
He treats with men of all conditions,
Poets and players, tradesmen, and musicians;
Nay, even ventures
To attack the renters,
Old and new:
A list he gets
Of claims and debts,
And deems nought done, while aught remains to do.
Yamen beheld, and wither'd at the sight;
Long had he aim'd the sunbeam to control,
For light was hateful to his soul:
' Go on !' cried the hellish one, yellow with spite;
' Go on !' cried the hellish one, yellow with spleen,
' Thy toils of the morning, like Ithaca's queen,
I'll toil to undo every night.'

[1] Veeshnoo.   The late Mr. Whitbread.

Ye sons of song, rejoice !
Veeshnoo has still'd the jarring elements,
The spheres hymn music;
Again the god of day
Peeps forth with trembling ray,
Wakes, from their humid caves, the sleeping Nine,
And pours at intervals a strain divine.
' I have an iron yet in the fire,' cried Yamen;
' The vollied flame rides in my breath,
My blast is elemental death;
This hand shall tear your paper bonds to pieces;
Engross your deeds, assignments, leases,
My breath shall every line erase
Soon as I blow the blaze.'
The lawyers are met at the Crown and Anchor,
And Yamen's visage grows blanker and blanker;
The lawyers are met at the Anchor and Crown,
And Yamen's cheek is a russety brown:
Veeshnoo, now thy work proceeds;
The solicitor reads,
And, merit of merit !
Red wax and green ferret
Are fixed at the foot of the deeds !

Yamen beheld and shiver'd;
His finger and thumb were cramped;
His ear by the flea in't was bitten,
When he saw by the lawyer's clerk written,
Sealed and delivered,
Being first duly stamped.
' Now for my turn !' the demon cries, and blows
A blast of sulphur from his mouth and nose.
Ah ! bootless aim ! the critic fiend,
Sagacious Yamen, judge of hell,
Is judged in his turn;
Parchment won't burn !
His schemes of vengeance are dissolv'd in air,
Parchment won't tear ! !

Is it not written in the Himakoot book,
(That mighty Baly from Kehama took)
' Who blows on pounce
Must the Swerga renounce ?'

It is ! it is ! Yamen, thine hour is nigh:
Like as an eagle claws an asp,
Veeshnoo has caught him in his mighty grasp,
And hurl'd him, in spite of his shrieks and his squalls,
Whizzing aloft, like the Temple fountain,
Three times as high as Meru mountain,
Which is
Ninety-nine times as high as St. Paul's.
Descending, he twisted like Levy the Jew,[1]
Who a durable grave meant
To dig in the pavement
Of Monument-yard:
To earth by the laws of attraction he flew,
And he fell, and he fell
To the regions of hell;
Nine centuries bounced he from cavern to rock,
And his head, as he tumbled, went nickety-nock,
Like a pebble in Carisbrook well.

Now Veeshnoo turn'd round to a capering varlet,
Arrayed in blue and white and scarlet,
And cried, ' Oh ! brown of slipper as of hat !
Lend me, Harlequin, thy bat !'
He seized the wooden sword, and smote the earth;
When lo ! upstarting into birth
A fabric, gorgeous to behold,
Outshone in elegance the old,
And Veeshnoo saw, and cried, ' Hail, playhouse mine !'
Then, bending his head, to Surya he said:
' Soon as thy maiden sister Di
Caps with her copper lid the dark blue sky,
And through the fissures of her clouded fan
Peeps at the naughty monster man,
Go mount yon edifice,
And show thy steady face

---

[1] Levy. An insolvent Israelite who threw himself from the top
of the Monument a short time before. An inhabitant of Monument
Yard informed the writer, that he happened to be standing at his
door talking to a neighbour; and looking up at the top of the pillar,
exclaimed, ' Why, here's the flag coming down.' ' Flag !' answered
the other, ' it's a man.' The words were hardly uttered when the
suicide fell within ten feet of the speakers.

In renovated pride,
More bright, more glorious than before !'
But ah ! coy Surya still felt a twinge,
Still smarted from his former singe;
And to Veeshnoo replied,
In a tone rather gruff,
' No, thank you ! one tumble's enough !'

DRURY'S DIRGE.

BY LAURA MATILDA.[1]

You praise our sires: but though they wrote with force,
Their rhymes were vicious, and their diction coarse :
We want their *strength*, agreed; but we atone
For that and more, by *sweetness* all our own.

GIFFORD.

I.

BALMY Zephyrs, lightly flitting,
Shade me with your azure wing;
On Parnassus' summit sitting,
Aid me, Clio, while I sing.

II.

Softly slept the dome of Drury
O'er the empyreal crest,
When Alecto's sister-fury
Softly slumb'ring sunk to rest.

III.

Lo ! from Lemnos limping lamely,
Lags the lowly Lord of Fire,
Cytherea yielding tamely
To the Cyclops dark and dire.

[1] The Authors, as in gallantry bound, wish this lady to continue anonymous.

IV.

Clouds of amber, dreams of gladness,
 Dulcet joys and sports of youth,
Soon must yield to haughty sadness;
 Mercy holds the veil to Truth.

V.

See Erostratus the second
 Fires again Diana's fane;
By the fates from Orcus beckon'd,
 Clouds envelop Drury Lane.

VI.

Lurid smoke and frank suspicion
 Hand in hand reluctant dance:
While the God fulfils his mission,
 Chivalry, resign thy lance.

VII.

Hark ! the engines blandly thunder,
 Fleecy clouds dishevell'd lie,
And the firemen, mute with wonder,
 On the son of Saturn cry.

VIII.

See the bird of Ammon sailing,
 Perches on the engine's peak,
And, the Eagle firemen hailing,
 Soothes them with its bickering beak.

IX.

Juno saw, and mad with malice,
 Lost the prize that Paris gave:
Jealousy's ensanguined chalice,
 Mantling pours the orient wave.

X.

Pan beheld Patroclus dying,
  Nox to Niobe was turn'd;
From Busiris Bacchus flying
  Saw his Semele inurn'd.

XI.

Thus fell Drury's lofty glory,
  Levell'd with the shuddering stones;
Mars, with tresses black and gory,
  Drinks the dew of pearly groans.

XII.

Hark ! what soft Eolian numbers
  Gem the blushes of the morn !
Break, Amphion, break your slumbers,
  Nature's ringlets deck the thorn.

XIII.

Ha ! I hear the strain erratic
  Dimly glance from pole to pole;
Raptures sweet and dreams ecstatic
  Fire my everlasting soul.

XIV.

Where is Cupid's crimson motion ?
  Billowy ecstasy of woe,
Bear me straight, meandering ocean,
  Where the stagnant torrents flow.

XV.

Blood in every vein is gushing,
  Vixen vengeance lulls my heart;
See, the Gorgon gang is rushing !
  Never, never let us part !

' " Drury's Dirge," by Laura Matilda, is not of the first quality.
The verses, to be sure, are very smooth, and very nonsensical—as:
was intended; but they are not so good as Swift's celebrated Song
by a Person of Quality; and are so exactly in the same measure,
and on the same plan, that it is impossible to avoid making the:
comparison.'—*Edinburgh Review.*

A TALE OF DRURY LANE.

BY W. S.[1]

Thus he went on, stringing one extravagance upon another, in
the style his books of chivalry had taught him, and imitating,
as near as he could, their very phrase.[2]—DON QUIXOTE.

[*To be spoken by Mr. Kemble, in a suit of the Black Prince's Armour,
borrowed from the Tower.*]

SURVEY this shield, all bossy bright—
These cuisses twain behold !
Look on my form in armour dight
Of steel inlaid with gold;
My knees are stiff in iron buckles,
Stiff spikes of steel protect my knuckles.
These once belong'd to sable prince,
Who never did in battle wince;
With valour tart as pungent quince,
　　He slew the vaunting Gaul.
Rest there awhile, my bearded lance,
While from green curtain I advance
To yon foot-lights, no trivial dance,[3]
And tell the town what sad mischance
　　Did Drury Lane befall.

The Night.

On fair Augusta's towers and trees
Flitted the silent midnight breeze,
Curling the foliage as it past,
Which from the moon-tipp'd plumage cast
A spangled light, like dancing spray,
Then re-assumed its still array;

[1] WALTER SCOTT.

[2] Sir Walter Scott informed the annotator, that at one time he
intended to print his collected works, and had pitched upon this
identical quotation as a motto;—a proof that sometimes great wits
jump with little ones.

[3] Alluding to the then great distance between the picture-frame,
in which the green curtain was set, and the band.   For a justification of this see below—DR. JOHNSON.

When, as night's lamp unclouded hung,
And down its full effulgence flung,
It shed such soft and balmy power
That cot and castle, hall and bower,
And spire and dome, and turret height,
Appeared to slumber in the light.
From Henry's chapel, Rufus' hall,
To Savoy, Temple, and St. Paul,
From Knightsbridge, Pancras, Camden Town,
To Redriff, Shadwell, Horsleydown,
No voice was heard, no eye unclosed,
But all in deepest sleep reposed.
They might have thought, who gazed around
Amid a silence so profound,
        It made the senses thrill,
That 'twas no place inhabited,
But some vast city of the dead—
        All was so hush'd and still.

Cbe Burning.

As Chaos, which, by heavenly doom,
Had slept in everlasting gloom,
Started with terror and surprise
When light first flash'd upon her eyes—
So London's sons in nightcap woke,
        In bedgown woke her dames;
For shouts were heard 'mid fire and smoke,
And twice ten hundred voices spoke—
        'The playhouse is in flames!'
And, lo! where Catherine Street extends,
A fiery tail its lustre lends
        To every window-pane;
Blushes each spout in Martlet Court,
And Barbican, moth-eaten fort,
And Covent Garden kennels sport
        A bright ensanguined drain;
Meux's new brewhouse shows the light,
Rowland Hill's chapel, and the height
        Where patent shot they sell;
The Tennis Court, so fair and tall,
Partakes the ray, with Surgeons' Hall,
The ticket-porters' house of call,

D

Old Bedlam, close by London Wall,[1]
Wright's shrimp and oyster shop withal,
    And Richardson's Hotel.
Nor these alone, but far and wide,
Across red Thames's gleaming tide,
To distant fields, the blaze was borne,
And daisy white and hoary thorn
In borrow'd lustre seem'd to sham
The rose or red Sweet Wil-li-am.
To those who on the hills around
Beheld the flames from Drury's mound,
    As from a lofty altar rise,
It seem'd that nations did conspire
To offer to the god of fire
    Some vast stupendous sacrifice !
The summon'd firemen woke at call,
And hied them to their stations all:
Starting from short and broken snooze,
Each sought his pond'rous hobnail'd shoes,
But first his worsted hosen plied,
Plush breeches next, in crimson dyed,
    His nether bulk embraced;
Then jacket thick, of red or blue,
Whose massy shoulder gave to view
The badge of each respective crew,
    In tin or copper traced.
The engines thunder'd through the street,
Fire-hook, pipe, bucket, all complete,
And torches glared, and clattering feet
    Along the pavement paced.
And one, the leader of the band,
From Charing Cross along the Strand,
Like stag by beagles hunted hard,
Ran till he stopp'd at Vin'gar Yard.

[1] Old Bedlam at that time stood ' close by London Wall.' It
was built after the model of the Tuileries, which is said to have given
the French king great offence. In front of it Moorfields extended,
with broad gravel walks crossing each other at right angles.
These the writer well recollects; and Rivaz, an underwriter at
Lloyd's, has told him, that he remembered when the merchants of
London would parade these walks on a summer evening with their
wives and daughters. But now, as a punning brother bard sings,

        ' Moorfields are fields no more.'

The burning badge his shoulder bore,
The belt and oil-skin hat he wore,
The cane he had, his men to bang,
Show'd foreman of the British gang—
His name was Higginbottom. Now
'Tis meet that I should tell you how
    The others came in view:
The Hand-in-Hand the race begun,
Then came the Phœnix and the Sun,
Th' Exchange, where old insurers run,
    The Eagle, where the new;
With these came Rumford, Bumford, Cole,
Robins from Hockley in the Hole,
Lawson and Dawson, cheek by jowl,
    Crump from St. Giles's Pound:
Whitford and Mitford join'd the train,
Huggins and Muggins from Chick Lane,
And Clutterbuck, who got a sprain
    Before the plug was found.
Hobson and Jobson did not sleep,
But ah! no trophy could they reap,
For both were in the Donjon Keep
    Of Bridewell's gloomy mound!

E'en Higginbottom now was posed,
For sadder scene was ne'er disclosed;
Without, within, in hideous show,
Devouring flames resistless glow,
And blazing rafters downward go,
And never halloo ' Heads below!'
    Nor notice give at all.
The firemen terrified are slow
To bid the pumping torrent flow,
    For fear the roof should fall.
Back, Robins, back! Crump, stand aloof!
    Whitford, keep near the walls!
Huggins, regard your own behoof,
For, lo! the blazing rocking roof
    Down, down, in thunder falls!
An awful pause succeeds the stroke,
And o'er the ruins volumed smoke,
Rolling around its pitchy shroud,
Conceal'd them from th' astonish'd crowd.

At length the mist awhile was clear'd,
When, lo ! amid the wreck uprear'd,
Gradual a moving head appear'd,
    And Eagle firemen knew
'Twas Joseph Muggins, name revered,
    The foreman of their crew.
Loud shouted all in signs of woe,
' A Muggins ! to the rescue, ho !'
    And pour'd the hissing tide :
Meanwhile the Muggins fought amain,
And strove and struggled all in vain,
For, rallying but to fall again,
    He totter'd, sunk, and died !

Did none attempt, before he fell,
To succour one they loved so well ?
Yes, Higginbottom did aspire
(His fireman's soul was all on fire),
    His brother chief to save;
But ah ! his reckless generous ire
    Served but to share his grave !
Mid blazing beams and scalding streams,
Through fire and smoke he dauntless broke,
    Where Muggins broke before.
But sulphury stench and boiling drench,
Destroying sight, o'erwhelm'd him quite,
    He sunk to rise no more.
Still o'er his head, while Fate he braved,
His whizzing water-pipe he waved;
' Whitford and Mitford, ply your pumps,
You, Clutterbuck, come, stir your stumps
Why are you in such doleful dumps ?
A fireman, and afraid of bumps !—
What are they fear'd on ? fools ! 'od rot 'em ! '
Were the last words of Higginbottom.

Uhe Revival.

Peace to his soul ! new prospects bloom,
And toil rebuilds what fires consume !
Eat we and drink we, be our ditty,
' Joy to the managing committee !'

Eat we and drink we, join to rum
Roast beef and pudding of the plum;
Forth from thy nook, John Horner, come,
With bread of ginger brown thy thumb,
    For this is Drury's gay day:
Roll, roll thy hoop. and twirl thy tops,
And buy, to glad thy smiling chops,
Crisp parliament with lollypops,
    And fingers of the Lady.

Didst mark, how toil'd the busy train,
From morn to eve, till Drury Lane
Leap'd like a roebuck from the plain?
Ropes rose and sunk, and rose again,
    And nimble workmen trod;
To realise bold Wyatt's plan
Rush'd many a howling Irishman;
Loud clatter'd many a porter-can,
And many a raggamuffin clan,
    With trowel and with hod.

Drury revives! her rounded pate
Is blue, is heavenly blue with slate;
She ' wings the midway air ' elate,
    As magpie, crow. or chough;
White paint her modish visage smears,
Yellow and pointed are her ears,
No pendant portico appears
Dangling beneath, for Whitbread's shears [1]
    Have cut the bauble off.

Yes, she exalts her stately head;
And, but that solid bulk outspread
Opposed you on your onward tread,
And posts and pillars warranted
That all was true that Wyatt said,

[1] Whitbread's shears. An economical experiment of that gentleman. The present portico, towards Brydges Street, was afterwards
erected under the lesseeship of Elliston, whose portrait in the
Exhibition was thus noticed in the *Examiner:* ' Portrait of the great
lessee, in his favourite character of Mr. Elliston.'

You might have deem'd her walls so thick
Were not composed of stone or brick,
But all a phantom, all a trick,
Of brain disturb'd and fancy-sick,
So high she soars, so vast, so quick !

' From the parody of Walter Scott we know not what to select—
it is all good.   The effect of the fire on the town, and the description
of a fireman in his official apparel, may be quoted as amusing speci-
mens of the *misapplication* of the style and metre of Mr. Scott's
admirable romances.'—*Quarterly Review.*

' " A Tale of Drury," by Walter Scott, is, upon the whole, admirably
executed; though the introduction is rather tame.   The burning
is described with the mighty minstrel's characteristic love of localities.
The catastrophe is described with a spirit not unworthy of the name
so venturously assumed by the describer.'—*Edinburgh Review.*

JOHNSON'S GHOST.[1]

[*Ghost of Dr.* JOHNSON *rises from trap-door P. S., and Ghost of*
BOSWELL *from trap-door O. P.   The latter bows respectfully to
the House, and obsequiously to the Doctor's Ghost, and retires.*]

Doctor's Ghost loquitur.

THAT which was organised by the moral ability of one
has been executed by the physical efforts of many, and
DRURY LANE THEATRE is now complete.   Of that part
behind the curtain, which has not yet been destined
to glow beneath the brush of the varnisher, or vibrate
to the hammer of the carpenter, little is thought by
the public, and little need be said by the committee.
Truth, however, is not to be sacrificed for the accom-

----

[1] ' Samuel Johnson is not so good: the measure and solemnity
of his sentences, in all the limited variety of their structure, are
indeed imitated with singular skill; but the diction is caricatured
in a vulgar and unpleasing degree.   To make Johnson call a door
" a ligneous barricado," and its knocker and bell its " frappant
and tintinnabulant appendages," is neither just nor humorous; and
we are surprised that a writer who has given such extraordinary
proofs of his talent for finer ridicule and fairer imitation, should
have stooped to a vein of pleasantry so low, and so long ago exhausted;
especially as, in other passages of the same piece, he has shewn how
well qualified he was both to catch and to render the true characteristics of his original.   The beginning, for example, we think excellent.'—*Edinburgh Review.*

modation of either; and he who should pronounce that
our edifice has received its final embellishment would be
disseminating falsehood without incurring favour, and
risking the disgrace of detection without participating
the advantage of success.

Professions lavishly effused and parsimoniously verified are alike inconsistent with the precepts of innate
rectitude and the practice of external policy: let it
not then be conjectured, that because we are unassuming,
we are imbecile; that forbearance is any indication of
despondency, or humility of demerit. He that is the
most assured of success will make the fewest appeals
to favour, and where nothing is claimed that is undue,
nothing that is due will be withheld. A swelling opening
is too often succeeded by an insignificant conclusion.
Parturient mountains have ere now produced muscipular
abortions; and the auditor who compares incipient
grandeur with final vulgarity is reminded of the pious
hawkers of Constantinople, who solemnly perambulate
her streets, exclaiming, 'In the name of the Prophet—figs!'

Of many who think themselves wise, and of some
who are thought wise by others, the exertions are directed
to the revival of mouldering and obscure dramas; to
endeavours to exalt that which is now rare only because
it was always worthless, and whose deterioration, while
it condemned it to living obscurity, by a strange obli-
quity of moral perception constitutes its title to posthu-
mous renown. To embody the flying colours of folly,
to arrest evanescence, to give to bubbles the globular
consistency as well as form, to exhibit on the stage the
piebald denizen of the stable, and the half-reasoning
parent of combs, to display the brisk locomotion of
Columbine, or the tortuous attitudinizing of Punch;—
these are the occupations of others, whose ambition,
limited to the applause of unintellectual fatuity, is too
innocuous for the application of satire, and too humble
for the incitement of jealousy.

Our refectory will be found to contain every species
of fruit, from the cooling nectarine and luscious peach
to the puny pippin and the noxious nut. There Indolence
may repose, and Inebriety revel; and the spruce apprentice, rushing in at second account, may there chatter

with impunity; debarred, by a barrier of brick and
mortar, from marring that scenic interest in others,
which nature and education have disqualified him from
comprehending himself.

Permanent stage-doors we have none. That which is
permanent cannot be removed, for, if removed, it soon
ceases to be permanent. What stationary absurdity
can vie with that ligneous barricado, which, decorated
with frappant and tintinnabulant appendages, now
serves as the entrance of the lowly cottage, and now
as the exit of a lady's bed-chamber; at one time, in-
sinuating plastic Harlequin into a butcher's shop, and,
at another, yawning, as a flood-gate, to precipitate the
Cyprians of St. Giles's into the embraces of Macheath.
To elude this glaring absurdity, to give to each respective mansion the door which the carpenter would
doubtless have given, we vary our portal with the varying scene, passing from deal to mahogany, and from
mahogany to oak, as the opposite claims of cottage,
palace, or castle, may appear to require.

Amid the general hum of gratulation which flatters
us in front, it is fit that some regard should be paid to
the murmurs of despondence that assail us in the rear.
They, as I have elsewhere expressed it, 'who live to
please,' should not have their own pleasures entirely
overlooked. The children of Thespis are general in their
censures of the architect, in having placed the locality
of exit at such a distance from the oily irradiators which
now dazzle the eyes of him who addresses you. I am,
cries the Queen of Terrors, robbed of my fair proportions.
When the king-killing Thane hints to the breathless
auditory the murders he means to perpetrate, in the
castle of Macduff, 'ere his purpose cool,' so vast is the
interval he has to travel before he can escape from the
stage, that his purpose has even time to freeze. Your
condition, cries the Muse of Smiles, is hard, but it is
cygnet's down in comparison with mine. The peerless
peer of capers and congees[1] has laid it down as a rule,
that the best good thing uttered by the morning visitor

---

[1] The celebrated Lord Chesterfield, whose Letters to his Son,
according to Dr. Johnson, inculcate 'the manners of a dancing-
master and the morals of ——,' &c.

should conduct him rapidly to the doorway, last impressions vying in durability with first. But when, on this boarded elongation, it falls to my lot to say a good thing, to ejaculate, ' keep moving,' or to chant, ' *hic hoc horum genitivo*,' many are the moments that must elapse, ere I can hide myself from public vision in the recesses of O. P. or P. S.

To objections like these, captiously urged and querulously maintained, it is time that equity should conclusively reply. Deviation from scenic propriety has only to vituperate itself for the consequences it generates. Let the actor consider the line of exit as that line beyond which he should not soar in quest of spurious applause: let him reflect, that in proportion as he advances to the lamps, he recedes from nature; that the truncheon of Hotspur acquires no additional charm from encountering the cheek of beauty in the stage-box, and that the bravura of Mandane may produce effect, although the throat of her who warbles it should not overhang the orchestra. The Jove of the modern critical Olympus, Lord Mayor of the theatric sky,[1] has, *ex cathedrâ*, asserted, that a natural actor looks upon the audience part of the theatre as the third side of the chamber he inhabits. Surely, of the third wall thus fancifully erected, our actors should, by ridicule or reason, be withheld from knocking their heads against the stucco.

Time forcibly reminds me, that all things which have a limit must be brought to a conclusion. Let me, ere that conclusion arrives, recall to your recollection, that the pillars which rise on either side of me, blooming in

---

[1] Lord Mayor of the theatric sky. This alludes to Leigh Hunt, who, in *The Examiner*, at this time kept the actors in hot water. Dr. Johnson's argument is, like many of his other arguments, specious, but untenable; that which it defends has since been abandoned as impracticable. Mr. Whitbread contended that the actor was like a portrait in a picture, and accordingly placed the green curtain in a gilded frame remote from the foot-lights; alleging that no performer should mar the illusion by stepping out of the frame. Dowton was the first actor who, like Manfred's ancestor in the *Castle of Otranto*, took the liberty of abandoning the canon. ' Don't tell me of frames and pictures,' ejaculated the testy comedian; ' if I can't be heard by the audience in the frame, I'll walk out of it !' The proscenium has since been new-modelled, and the actors thereby brought nearer to the audience.

virid antiquity, like two massy evergreens, had yet slumbered in their native quarry, but for the ardent exertions of the individual who called them into life: to his never-slumbering talents you are indebted for whatever pleasure this haunt of the muses is calculated to afford. If, in defiance of chaotic malevolence, the destroyer of the temple of Diana yet survives in the name of Erostratus, surely we may confidently predict, that the rebuilder of the temple of Apollo will stand recorded to distant posterity in that of—SAMUEL WHITBREAD.

THE BEAUTIFUL INCENDIARY.

BY THE HON. W. S.[1]

Formosam resonare doces Amaryllida silvas.—VIRGIL.

Scene draws, and discovers a Lady asleep on a couch.

Enter PHILANDER.

PHILANDER.

I.

SOBRIETY, cease to be sober,[2]
  Cease, Labour, to dig and to delve;
All hail to this tenth of October,
  One thousand eight hundred and twelve !

---

[1] WILLIAM SPENCER.

[2] Sobriety, &c. The good-humour of the poet upon occasion of this parody has been noticed in the Preface.   ' It's all very well for once,' said he afterwards, in comic confidence, at his villa at Petersham, ' but don't do it again.   I had been almost forgotten when you revived me; and now all the newspapers and reviews ring with, " this fashionable, trashy author." '   The sand and ' filings of glass,' mentioned in the last stanza, are referable to the well-known verses of the poet apologising to a lady for having paid an unconscionably long morning visit; and where, alluding to Time, he says,

> 'All his sands are diamond sparks,
> That glitter as they pass.'

Few men in society have more ' gladdened life ' than this poet. He now resides in Paris, and may thence make the grand tour without an interpreter—speaking, as he does, French, Italian, and German, as fluently as English.

Ha ! whom do my peepers remark ?
  'Tis Hebe with Jupiter's jug;
O no, 'tis the pride of the Park,
  Fair Lady Elizabeth Mugg.

II.

Why, beautiful nymph, do you close
  The curtain that fringes your eye ?
Why veil in the clouds of repose
  The sun that should brighten our sky ?
Perhaps jealous Venus has oiled
  Your hair with some opiate drug,
Not choosing her charms should be foiled
  By Lady Elizabeth Mugg.

III.

But ah ! why awaken the blaze
  Those bright burning-glasses contain,
Whose lens with concentrated rays
  Proved fatal to old Drury Lane ?
'Twas all accidental, they cry,—
  Away with the flimsy humbug !
'Twas fired by a flash from the eye
  Of Lady Elizabeth Mugg.

IV.

Thy glance can in us raise a flame,
  Then why should old Drury be free ?
Our doom and its dome are the same,
  Both subject to beauty's decree.
No candles the workmen consumed,
  When deep in the ruins they dug;
Thy flash still their progress illumed,
  Sweet Lady Elizabeth Mugg.

V.

Thy face a rich fire-place displays:
  The mantel-piece marble—thy brows;
Thine eyes, are the bright beaming blaze;
  Thy bib, which no trespass allows,

The fender's tall barrier marks;
  Thy tippet's the fire-quelling rug,
Which serves to extinguish the sparks
  Of Lady Elizabeth Mugg.

VI.

The Countess a lily appears,
  Whose tresses the pearl-drops emboss;
The Marchioness, blooming in years,
  A rose-bud enveloped in moss;
But thou art the sweet passion-flower,
  For who would not slavery hug,
To pass but one exquisite hour
  In the arms of Elizabeth Mugg?

VII.

When at court, or some Dowager's rout,
  Her diamond aigrette meets our view,
She looks like a glow-worm dressed out,
  Or tulips bespangled with dew.
Her two lips denied to man's suit,
  Are shared with her favourite Pug;
What lord would not change with the brute,
  To live with Elizabeth Mugg?

VIII.

Could the stage be a large vis-à-vis,
  Reserved for the polished and great,
Where each happy lover might see
  The nymph he adores tête-à-tête;
No longer I'd gaze on the ground,
  And the load of despondency lug,
For I'd book myself all the year round,
  To ride with the sweet Lady Mugg.

IX.

Yes, she in herself is a host,
  And if she were here all alone,
Our house might nocturnally boast
  A bumper of fashion and ton.

Again should it burst in a blaze,
  In vain would they ply Congreve's plug,[1]
For nought could extinguish the rays
  From the glance of divine Lady Mugg.

X.

O could I as Harlequin frisk,
  And thou be my Columbine fair,
My wand should with one magic whisk
  Transport us to Hanover Square:
St. George's should lend us its shrine,
  The parson his shoulders might shrug,
But a license should force him to join
  My hand in the hand of my Mugg.

XI.

Court-plaster the weapons should tip,
  By Cupid shot down from above,
Which, cut into spots for thy lip,
  Should still barb the arrows of love.
The god who from others flies quick,
  With us should be slow as a slug;
As close as a leech he should stick
  To me and Elizabeth Mugg.

XII.

For Time would, with us, 'stead of sand,
  Put filings of steel in his glass,
To dry up the blots of his hand,
  And spangle life's page as they pass.

[1] Congreve's plug. The late Sir William Congreve had made a model of Drury Lane Theatre, to which was affixed an engine that, in the event of fire, was made to play from the stage into every box in the house. The writer, accompanied by Theodore Hook, went to see the model at Sir William's house in Cecil Street. 'Now I'll duck Whitbread!' said Hook, seizing the water-pipe whilst he spoke, and sending a torrent of water into the brewer's box.

Since all flesh is grass ere 'tis hay,[1]
O may I in clover live snug,
And when old Time mows me away,
Be stacked with defunct Lady Mugg!

'"The Beautiful Incendiary," by the Honourable W. Spencer, is also an imitation of great merit. The flashy, fashionable, artificial style of this writer, with his confident and extravagant compliments, can scarcely be said to be parodied in such lines.'—*Edinburgh Review.*

FIRE AND ALE.

BY M. G. L.[2]

Omnia transformat sese in miracula rerum.—VIRGIL.

MY palate is parched with Pierian thirst,
    Away to Parnassus I'm beckoned;
List, warriors and dames, while my lay is rehearsed,
I sing of the singe of Miss Drury the first,
    And the birth of Miss Drury the second.

The Fire King, one day, rather amorous felt;
    He mounted his hot copper filly;
His breeches and boots were of tin, and the belt
Was made of cast iron, for fear it should melt
    With the heat of the copper colt's belly.

[1] See Byron, *afterwards*, in *Don Juan* :—

'For flesh is grass, which Time mows down to hay.

But, as Johnson says of Dryden, ' His known wealth was so great, he might borrow without any impeachment of his credit.'

[2] MATTHEW GREGORY LEWIS, commonly called Monk Lewis, from his once popular romance of that name. He was a good-hearted man, and, like too many of that fraternity, a disagreeable one—verbose, disputatious, and paradoxical. His *Monk* and *Castle Spectre* elevated him into fame; and he continued to write ghost-stories till, following as he did in the wake of Mrs. Radcliffe, he quite overstocked the market. Lewis visited his estates in Jamaica, and came back perfectly negro-bitten. He promulgated a new code of laws in the island, for the government of his sable subjects: one may serve for a specimen: ' Any slave who commits murder shall have his head shaved, and be confined three days and nights in a dark room.' Upon occasion of printing these parodies, Monk Lewis

Sure never was skin half so scalding as his !
    When an infant 'twas equally horrid;
For the water, when he was baptised, gave a fizz,
And bubbled and simmer'd and started off, whizz !
    As soon as it sprinkled his forehead.

Oh ! then there was glitter and fire in each eye,
    For two living coals were the symbols;
His teeth were calcined, and his tongue was so dry,
It rattled against them, as though you should try
    To play the piano in thimbles.

From his nostrils a lava sulphureous flows,
    Which scorches wherever it lingers;
A snivelling fellow he's call'd by his foes,
For he can't raise his paw up to blow his red nose,
    For fear it should blister his fingers.

His wig is of flames curling over his head,
    Well-powder'd with white smoking ashes;
He drinks gunpowder tea, melted sugar of lead.
Cream of tartar, and dines on hot spiced gingerbread,
    Which black from the oven he gnashes.

---

said to Lady H., ' Many of them are very fair, but mine is not at all
like; they have made me write burlesque, which I never do.' ' You
don't know your own talent,' answered the lady.

    Lewis aptly described himself, as to externals, in the verses
affixed to his *Monk*, as having

<blockquote>' A graceless form and dwarfish stature.'</blockquote>

He had, moreover, large grey eyes, thick features, and an inexpressive
countenance. In talking, he had a disagreeable habit of drawing
the fore-finger of his right hand across his right eyelid. He affected,
in conversation, a sort of dandified, drawling tone; young Harlowe,
the artist, did the same. A foreigner who had but a slight knowledge of the English language might have concluded, from their
cadences, that they were little better than fools—' just a born
goose,' as Terry the actor used to say. Lewis died on his passage
homeward from Jamaica, owing to a dose of James's powders in-
judiciously administered by ' his own mere motion.' He wrote
various plays, with various success: he had an admirable notion of
dramatic construction, but the goodness of his scenes and incidents
was marred by the badness of his dialogue.

Each fire nymph his kiss from her countenance shields,
    'Twould soon set her cheekbone a frying;
He spit in the tenter ground near Spitalfields,
And the hole that it burnt, and the chalk that it yields,
    Make a capital lime-kiln for drying.

When he open'd his mouth, out there issued a blast
    (Nota bene, I do not mean swearing),
But the noise that it made, and the heat that it cast,
I've heard it from those who have seen it, surpass'd
    A shot manufactory flaring.

He blazed, and he blazed, as he gallop'd to snatch
    His bride, little dreaming of danger;
His whip was a torch, and his spur was a match,
And over the horse's left eye was a patch,
    To keep it from burning the manger.

And who is the housemaid he means to enthral
    In his cinder-producing alliance ?
'Tis Drury Lane Playhouse, so wide, and so tall,
Who, like other combustible ladies, must fall,
    If she cannot set sparks at defiance.

On his warming-pan kneepan he clattering roll'd,
    And the housemaid his hand would have taken,
But his hand, like his passion, was too hot to hold,
And she soon let it go, but her new ring of gold
    All melted, like butter or bacon !

Oh ! then she look'd sour, and indeed well she might,
    For Vinegar Yard was before her;
But, spite of her shrieks, the ignipotent knight,
Enrobing the maid in a flame of gas light,
    To the skies in a sky-rocket bore her.

Look ! look ! 'tis the Ale King, so stately and starch,
    Whose votaries scorn to be sober;
He pops from his vat, like a cedar or larch;
Brown-stout is his doublet, he hops in his march,
    And froths at the mouth in October.

His spear is a spigot, his shield is a bung;
　　He taps where the housemaid no more is,
When lo ! at his magical bidding, upsprung
A second Miss Drury, tall, tidy, and young,
　　And sported *in loco sororis.*

Back, lurid in air, for a second regale,
　　The Cinder King, hot with desire,
To Brydges Street hied; but the Monarch of Ale,
With uplifted spigot and faucet and pail,
　　Thus chided the Monarch of Fire:

' Vile tyrant, beware of the ferment I brew;
　　. I rule the roast here, dash the wig o' me !
If, spite of your marriage with Old Drury, you
Come here with your tinderbox, courting the New,
　　I'll have you indicted for bigamy !'

' " Fire and Ale," by M. G. Lewis, exhibits not only a faithful copy of the spirited, loose, and flowing versification of that singular author, but a very just representation of that mixture of extravagance and jocularity which has impressed most of his writings with the character of a sort of farcical horror.'—*Edinburgh Review.*

PLAYHOUSE MUSINGS.

BY S. T. C.[1]

Ille velut fidis arcana sodalibus olim
Credebat libris; neque si male cesserat, usquam
Decurrens alio, neque si bene.

HORACE.

My pensive Public, wherefore look you sad ?
I had a grandmother, she kept a donkey
To carry to the mart her crockery ware,
And when that donkey look'd me in the face,
His face was sad ! and you are sad, my Public !

Joy should be yours: this tenth day of October
Again assembles us in Drury Lane.

[1] SAMUEL TAYLOR COLERIDGE.

E

Long wept my eye to see the timber planks
That hid our ruins; many a day I cried,
Ah me! I fear they never will rebuild it!
Till on one eve, one joyful Monday eve,
As along Charles Street I prepared to walk,
Just at the corner, by the pastrycook's,
I heard a trowel tick against a brick.
I look'd me up, and straight a parapet
Uprose at least seven inches o'er the planks.
Joy to thee, Drury! to myself I said:
He[1] of Blackfriars' Road, who hymn'd thy downfall
In loud Hosannahs, and who prophesied
That flames, like those from prostrate Solyma,
Would scorch the hand that ventured to rebuild thee,
Has proved a lying prophet. From that hour,
As leisure offer'd, close to Mr. Spring's
Box-office door, I've stood and eyed the builders.
They had a plan to render less their labours;
Workmen in olden times would mount a ladder
With hodded heads, but these stretch'd forth a pole
From the wall's pinnacle, they placed a pulley
Athwart the pole, a rope athwart the pulley;
To this a basket dangled; mortar and bricks
Thus freighted, swung securely to the top,
And in the empty basket workmen twain
Precipitate, unhurt, accosted earth.

Oh! 'twas a goodly sound, to hear the people
Who watch'd the work, express their various thoughts!
While some believed it never would be finish'd,
Some, on the contrary, believed it would.

I've heard our front that faces Drury Lane
Much criticised; they say 'tis vulgar brick-work,
A mimic manufactory of floor-cloth.
One of the morning papers wish'd that front
Cemented like the front in Brydges Street;
As it now looks, they call it Wyatt's Mermaid,
A handsome woman with a fish's tail.

[1] 'He of Blackfriars' Road,' viz. the late Rev. Rowland Hill, who
is said to have preached a sermon congratulating his congregation
on the catastrophe.

White is the steeple of St. Bride's in Fleet Street:
The Albion (as its name denotes) is white;
Morgan and Saunders' shop for chairs and tables
Gleams like a snow-ball in the setting sun;
White is Whitehall. But not St. Bride's in Fleet Street.
The spotless Albion, Morgan, no, nor Saunders,
Nor white Whitehall, is white as Drury's face.

Oh, Mr. Whitbread![1] fie upon you, sir!
I think you should have built a colonnade;
When tender Beauty, looking for her coach,
Protrudes her gloveless hand, perceives the shower,
And draws the tippet closer round her throat,
Perchance her coach stands half a dozen off,
And, ere she mounts the step, the oozing mud
Soaks through her pale kid slipper. On the morrow,
She coughs at breakfast, and her gruff papa
Cries, ' There you go! this comes of playhouses!'
To build no portico is penny wise:
Heaven grant it prove not in the end pound foolish!

Hail to thee, Drury! Queen of Theatres!
What is the Regency in Tottenham Street,
The Royal Amphitheatre of Arts,
Astley's, Olympic, or the Sans Pareil,
Compar'd with thee? Yet when I view thee push'd
Back from the narrow street that christen'd thee,
I know not why they call thee Drury Lane.

Amid the freaks that modern fashion sanctions,
It grieves me much to see live animals
Brought on the stage. Grimaldi has his rabbit,
Laurent his cat, and Bradbury his pig;
Fie on such tricks! Johnson, the machinist
Of former Drury, imitated life
Quite to the life. The elephant in Blue Beard,
Stuff'd by his hand, wound round his lithe proboscis,

---

[1] ' Oh, Mr. Whitbread!' Sir William Grant, then Master of the Rolls, repeated this passage aloud at a Lord Mayor's dinner, to the no small astonishment of the writer, who happened to sit within ear-shot.

As spruce as he who roar'd in Padmanaba.[1]
Nought born on earth should die. On hackney stands
I reverence the coachman who cries ' Gee,'
And spares the lash. When I behold a spider
Prey on a fly, a magpie on a worm,
Or view a butcher with horn-handled knife
Slaughter a tender lamb as dead as mutton,
Indeed, indeed, I'm very, very sick !

[*Exit hastily.*

' Mr. Coleridge will not, we fear, be as much entertained as we
were with his ' Playhouse Musings,' which begin with characteristic
pathos and simplicity, and put us much in mind of the affecting
story of old Poulter's mare.'—*Quarterly Review.*

' " Playhouse Musings," ' by Mr. Coleridge, a piece which is un-
questionably Lakish, though we cannot say that we recognise in
it any of the peculiar traits of that powerful and misdirected genius
whose name it has borrowed. We rather think, however, that the
tuneful brotherhood will consider it as a respectable eclogue.'—
Edinburgh Review.

DRURY LANE HUSTINGS.

A NEW HALFPENNY BALLAD.

BY A PIC-NIC POET.

This is the very age of promise: To promise is most courtly and
fashionable. Performance is a kind of will or testament, which
argues a great sickness in his judgement that makes it.

TIMON OF ATHENS.

[*To be sung by Mr.* JOHNSTONE *in the character of*
LOONEY M'TWOLTER.]

I.

MR. JACK, your address, says the Prompter to me,
So I gave him my card—no, that a'nt it, says he;
'Tis your public address. Oh ! says I, never fear,
If address you are bother'd for, only look here.

[*Puts on hat affectedly.*

Tol de rol lol, &c.

[1] ' Padmanaba,' viz. in a pantomime called *Harlequin in Padmanaba.* This elephant, some years afterwards, was exhibited over
Exeter 'Change, where, the reader will remember, it was found
necessary to destroy the poor animal by discharges of musketry.
When he made his entrance in the pantomime above mentioned,

II.

With Drury's for sartin we'll never have done,
We've built up another, and yet there's but one;
The old one was best, yet I'd say, if I durst,
The new one is better—the last is the first.
                              Tol de rol, &c.

III.

These pillars are call'd by a Frenchified word,
A something that's jumbled of antique and verd;
The boxes may show us some verdant antiques,
Some old harridans who beplaster their cheeks.
                              Tol de rol, &c.

IV.

Only look how high Tragedy, Comedy, stick,
Lest their rivals, the horses, should give them a kick!
If you will not descend when our authors beseech ye,
You'll stop there for life, for I'm sure they can't reach ye.
                              Tol de rol, &c.

V.

Each one shilling god within reach of a nod is,
And plain are the charms of each gallery goddess—
You, Brandy-faced Moll, don't be looking askew,
When I talk'd of a goddess I didn't mean you.
                              Tol de rol, &c.

VI.

Our stage is so prettily fashion'd for viewing,
The whole house can see what the whole house is doing:
'Tis just like the Hustings, we kick up a bother;
But saying is one thing, and doing's another.
                              Tol de rol, &c.

VII.

We've many new houses, and some of them rum ones,
But the newest of all is the new House of Commons;
'Tis a rickety sort of a bantling, I'm told,
It will die of old age when it's seven years old.
                              Tol de rol, &c.

Johnson, the machinist of the rival house, exclaimed, ' I should be
very sorry if I could not make a better elephant than that !'   Johnson
was right: we go to the theatre to be pleased with the skill of the
imitator, and not to look at the reality.

VIII.

As I don't know on whom the election will fall,
I move in return for returning them all;
But for fear Mr. Speaker my meaning should miss,
The house that I wish 'em to sit in is this.

Tol de rol, &c.

IX.

Let us cheer our great Commoner, but for whose aid
We all should have gone with short commons to bed;
And since he has saved all the fat from the fire,
I move that the house be call'd Whitbread's Entire.

Tol de rol, &c.

' " A New Halfpenny Ballad," by a Pic-Nic Poet, is a good imitation of what was not worth imitating—that tremendous mixture of vulgarity, nonsense, impudence, and miserable puns, which, under the name of humorous songs, rouses our polite audiences to a far higher pitch of rapture than Garrick or Siddons ever was able to inspire.'—*Edinburgh Review.*

ARCHITECTURAL ATOMS.

TRANSLATED BY DR. B.[1]

Lege, Dick, Lege !—JOSEPH ANDREWS.

To be recited by the Translator's Son

AWAY, fond dupes ! who, smit with sacred lore,
Mosaic dreams in Genesis explore,
Doat with Copernicus, or darkling stray
With Newton, Ptolemy, or Tycho Brahe !
To you I sing not, for I sing of truth,
Primeval systems, and creation's youth;
Such as of old, with magic wisdom fraught,
Inspired LUCRETIUS to the Latians taught.

[1] DR. BUSBY. This gentleman gave living recitations of his translation of *Lucretius,* with tea and bread-and-butter. He sent in a real Address to the Drury Lane Committee, which was really rejected. The present imitation professes to be recited by the translator's son. The poet here, again, was a prophet. A few evenings after the opening of the theatre, Dr. Busby sat with his son in one of the stage-boxes. The latter, to the astonishment of the audience, at the end of the play, stepped from the box upon the stage, with

I sing how casual bricks, in airy climb,
Encounter'd casual cow-hair, casual lime;
How rafters, borne through wondering clouds elate,
Kiss'd in their slope blue elemental slate,
Clasp'd solid beams in chance-directed fury,
And gave to birth our renovated Drury.

Thee, son of Jove! whose sceptre was confess'd,
Where fair Æolia springs from Tethys' breast;
Thence on Olympus, mid celestials placed,
GOD OF THE WINDS, and Ether's boundless waste—
Thee I invoke! Oh *puff* my bold design,
Prompt the bright thought, and swell th' harmonious line;
Uphold my pinions, and my verse inspire
With Winsor's[1] patent gas, or wind of fire,
In whose pure blaze thy embryo form enroll'd,
The dark enlightens, and enchafes the cold.

But, while I court thy gifts, be mine to shun
The deprecated prize Ulysses won;
Who, sailing homeward from thy breezy shore,
The prison'd winds in skins of parchment bore.

---

his father's real rejected address in his hand, and began to recite
it as follows:—

> ' When energising objects men pursue,
> What are the miracles they cannot do ?'

Raymond, the stage-manager, accompanied by a constable, at this
moment walked upon the stage, and handed away the juvenile
dilettante performer.

The doctor's classical translation was thus noticed in one of the
newspapers of the day, in the column of births:—' Yesterday, at
his house in Queen Anne Street, Dr. Busby of a still-born *Lucretius.*'

[1] ' Winsor's patent gas '—at that time in its infancy. The first
place illumined by it was the Carlton House side of Pall Mall; the
second, Bishopsgate Street. The writer attended a lecture given
by the inventor: the charge of admittance was three shillings, but,
as the inventor was about to apply to parliament, members of both
houses were admitted gratis. The writer and a fellow-jester assumed
the parts of senators at a short notice. ' Members of parliament !'
was their important ejaculation at the door of entrance. ' What
places, gentlemen ?' ' Old Sarum and Bridgewater.' ' Walk in,
gentlemen.' Luckily, the real Simon Pures did not attend. This
Pall Mall illumination was further noticed in *Horace in London :—*

> ' And Winsor lights, with flame of gas,
> Home, to king's place, his mother.'

Speeds the fleet bark, till o'er the billowy green
The azure heights of Ithaca are seen;
But while with favouring gales her 'way she wins,
His curious comrades ope the mystic skins;
When, lo ! the rescued winds, with boisterous sweep,
Roar to the clouds and lash the rocking deep;
Heaves the smote vessel in the howling blast,
Splits the stretch'd sail, and cracks the tottering mast.
Launch'd on a plank, the buoyant hero rides,
Where ebon Afric stems the sable tides,
While his duck'd comrades o'er the ocean fly,
And sleep not in the whole skins they untie.

    So, when to raise the wind some lawyer tries,
Mysterious skins of parchment meet our èyes;
On speeds the smiling suit—' Pleas of our Lord
The King ' shine sable on the wide record;
Nods the prunella'd bar, attorneys smile,
And siren jurors flatter to beguile;
Till stript—nonsuited—he is doom'd to toss
In legal shipwreck and redeemless loss !
Lucky, if, like Ulysses, he can keep
His head above the waters of the deep.

    Æolian monarch ! Emperor of Puffs !
We modern sailors dread not thy rebuffs;
See to thy golden shorè promiscuous come
Quacks for the lame, the blind, the deaf, the dumb;
Fools are their bankers—a prolific line,
And every mortal malady's a mine.
Each sly Sangrado, with his poisonous pill,
Flies to the printer's devil with his bill,
Whose Midas touch can gild his asses' ears,
And load a knave with folly's rich arrears.
And lo ! a second miracle is thine,
For sloe-juice water stands transform'd to wine.
Where Day and Martin's patent blacking roll'd
Burst from the vase Pactolian streams of gold;
Laugh the sly wizards, glorying in their stealth
Quit the black art. and loll in lazy wealth.
See Britain's Algerines, the lottery fry,
Win annual tribute by the annual lie !

Aided by thee—but whither do I stray ?—
Court, city, borough, own thy sovereign sway;
An age of puffs an age of gold succeeds,
And windy bubbles are the spawn it breeds.

If such thy power, O hear the Muse's prayer !
Swell thy loud lungs and wave thy wings of air;
Spread, viewless giant, all thy arms of mist
Like windmill-sails to bring the poet grist;
As erst thy roaring son, with eddying gale,
Whirl'd Orithyia from her native vale—
So, while Lucretian wonders I rehearse,
Augusta's sons shall patronise my verse.

I sing of ATOMS, whose creative brain,
With eddying impulse, built new Drury Lane;
Not to the labours of subservient man,
To no young Wyatt appertains the plan—
We mortals stalk, like horses in a mill,
Impassive media of atomic will;
Ye stare ! then Truth's broad talisman discern—
'Tis Demonstration speaks—attend, and learn !

From floating elements in chaos hurl'd,
Self-form'd of atoms, sprang the infant world:
No great *First Cause* inspired the happy plot,
But all was matter—and no matter what.
Atoms, attracted by some law occult,
Settling in spheres, the globe was the result:
Pure child of *Chance*, which still directs the ball,
As rotatory atoms rise or fall.
In ether launch'd, the peopled bubble floats,
A mass of particles and confluent motes,
So nicely poised, that if one atom flings
Its weight away, aloft the planet springs,
And wings its course through realms of boundless space
Outstripping comets in eccentric race.
Add but one atom more, it sinks outright
Down to the realms of Tartarus and night.
What waters melt or scorching fires consume,
In different forms their being re-assume:
Hence can no change arise, except in name,
For weight and substance ever are the same.

Thus with the flames that from old Drury rise
Its elements primeval sought the skies;
There pendulous to wait the happy hour
When new attractions should restore their power:
So, in this procreant theatre elate,
Echoes unborn their future life await;
Here embryo sounds in ether lie conceal'd,
Like words in northern atmosphere congeal'd.
Here many a fœtus laugh and half encore
Clings to the roof, or creeps along the floor;
By puffs concipient some in ether flit,
And soar in bravos from the thundering pit;
Some forth on ticket-nights[1] from tradesmen break,
To mar the actor they design to make;
While some this mortal life abortive miss,
Crush'd by a groan, or strangled by a hiss.
So, when ' Dog's-meat ' re-echoes through the streets,
Rush sympathetic dogs from their retreats,
Beam with bright blaze their supplicating eyes,
Sink their hind-legs, ascend their joyful cries;
Each, wild with hope, and maddening to prevail.
Points the pleased ear, and wags the expectant tail.

Ye fallen bricks ! in Drury's fire calcined,
Since doom'd to slumber, couch'd upon the wind,
Sweet was the hour, when, tempted by your freaks.
Congenial trowels smooth'd your yellow cheeks.
Float dulcet serenades upon the ear,
Bends every atom from its ruddy sphere,
Twinkles each eye, and, peeping from its veil,
Marks in the adverse crowd its destined male.
The oblong beauties clap their hands of grit,
And brick-dust titterings on the breezes flit;
Then down they rush in amatory race,
Their dusty bridegrooms eager to embrace.

[1] ' Ticket-nights.' This phrase is probably unintelligible to the
untheatrical portion of the community, which may now be said to
be all the world except the actors. Ticket-nights are those whereon
the inferior actors club for a benefit: each distributes as many tickets
of admission as he is able among his friends. A motley assemblage
is the consequence; and as each actor is encouraged by his own set,
who are not in general play-going people, the applause comes (as
Chesterfield says of Pope's attempts at wit), ' generally unseasonably
and too often unsuccessfully.'

Some choose old lovers, some decide for new,
But each, when fix'd, is to her station true.
Thus various bricks are made, as tastes invite—
The red, the grey, the dingy, or the white.

Perhaps some half-baked rover, frank and free,
To alien beauty bends the lawless knee,
But of unhallow'd fascinations sick,
Soon quits his Cyprian for his married brick;
The Dido atom calls and scolds in vain,
No crisp Æneas soothes the widow's pain.

So in Cheapside, what time Aurora peeps,
A mingled noise of dustmen, milk, and sweeps,
Falls on the housemaid's ear: amazed she stands,
Then opes the door with cinder-sabled hands,
And ' Matches ' calls. The dustman, bubbled flat,
Thinks 'tis for him, and doffs his fan-tail'd hat;
The milkman, whom her second cries assail,
With sudden sink unyokes the clinking pail;
Now louder grown, by turns she screams and weeps—
Alas ! her screaming only brings the sweeps.
Sweeps but put out—she wants to raise a flame,
And calls for matches, but 'tis still the same.
Atoms and housemaids ! mark the moral true—
If once ye go astray, no *match* for you !

As atoms in one mass united mix,
So bricks attraction feel for kindred bricks;
Some in the cellar view, perchance, on high,
Fair chimney chums on beds of mortar lie;
Enamour'd of the sympathetic clod,
Leaps the red bridegroom to the labourer's hod;
And up the ladder bears the workman, taught
To think he bears the bricks—mistaken thought !
A proof behold: if near the top they find
The nymphs or broken-corner'd or unkind,
Back to the base, ' resulting with a bound,'
They bear their bleeding carriers to the ground !

So legends tell along the lofty hill
Paced the twin heroes, gallant Jack and Jill;

On trudged the Gemini to reach the rail
That shields the well's top from the expectant pail,
When, ah! Jack falls; and, rolling in the rear,
Jill feels the attraction of his kindred sphere:
Head over heels begins his toppling track,
Throws sympathetic somersets with Jack,
And at the mountain's base bobs plump against him,
    whack!

Ye living atoms, who unconscious sit,
Jumbled by chance in gallery, box, and pit,
For you no Peter opes the fabled door,
No churlish Charon plies the shadowy oar;
Breathe but a space, and Boreas' casual sweep
Shall bear your scatter'd corses o'er the deep
To gorge the greedy elements, and mix
With water, marl, and clay, and stones, and sticks;
While, charged with fancied souls, sticks, stones, and
    clay,
Shall take your seats, and hiss or clap the play.

O happy age! when convert Christians read
No sacred writings but the Pagan creed—
O happy age! when spurning Newton's dreams
Our poets' sons recite Lucretian themes,
Abjure the idle systems of their youth,
And turn again to atoms and to truth;—
O happier still! when England's dauntless dames,
Awed by no chaste alarms, no latent shames,
The bard's fourth book unblushingly peruse,
And learn the rampant lessons of the stews!

All hail, Lucretius! renovated sage!
Unfold the modest mystics of thy page;
Return no more to thy sepulchral shelf,
But live, kind bard—that I may live myself!

'In one single point the parodist has failed—there is a certain
Dr. Busby, whose supposed address is a translation called "Architectural Atoms, intended to be recited by the translator's son."
Unluckily, however, for the wag who had prepared this fun, the
genuine serious absurdity of Dr. Busby and his son has cast all his
humour into the shade. The doctor from the boxes, and the son

from the stage, have actually endeavoured, it seems, to recite addresses, which they call *monologues* and *unalogues ;* and which, for extravagant folly, tumid meanness, and vulgar affectation, set all the powers of parody at utter defiance.'—*Quarterly Review.*

' Of " Architectural Atoms," translated by Dr. Busby, we can say very little more than that they appear to us to be far more capable of combining into good poetry than the few lines we were able to read of the learned doctor's genuine address in the newspapers They might pass, indeed, for a very tolerable imitation of Darwin.'— *Edinburgh Review.*

THEATRICAL ALARM-BELL.

BY THE EDITOR OF THE M. P.[1]

Bounce, Jupiter, bounce !—O'HARA.

LADIES AND GENTLEMEN,

As it is now the universally-admitted, and indeed pretty-generally-suspected, aim of Mr. Whitbread and the infamous, bloodthirsty, and, in fact, illiberal faction to which he belongs, to burn to the ground this free and happy Protestant city, and establish himself in St. James's Palace, his fellow committee-men have thought it their duty to watch the principles of a theatre built under his auspices. The information they have received from undoubted authority—particularly from an old fruit-woman who has turned king's evidence, and whose name, for obvious reasons, we forbear to mention, though we have had it some weeks in our possession— has induced them to introduce various reforms—not such reforms as the vile faction clamour for, meaning thereby revolution, but such reforms as are necessary to preserve the glorious constitution of the only free, happy, and prosperous country now left upon the face of the earth. From the valuable and authentic source above alluded to, we have learnt that a sanguinary plot has been formed by some united Irishmen, combined with a gang of Luddites, and a special committee sent over by the Pope at the instigation of the beastly Corsican fiend, for destroying all the loyal part of the audience on the anniversary of that deeply-to-be abhorred and highly-to-be-blamed stratagem, the Gun

[1] *Morning Post.*

powder Plot, which falls this year on Thursday the 5th
of November. The whole is under the direction of a
delegated committee of O. P.'s, whose treasonable ex-
ploits at Covent Garden you all recollect, and all of
whom would have been hung from the chandeliers at
that time, but for the mistaken lenity of government.
At a given signal, a well-known O. P. was to cry out
from the gallery, 'Nosey! Music!' whereupon all the
O. P.'s were to produce from their inside-pockets a long
pair of shears, edged with felt, to prevent their making
any noise, manufactured expressly by a wretch at Bir-
mingham, one of Mr. Brougham's evidences, and now
in custody. With these they were to cut off the heads
of all the loyal N. P.'s in the house, without distinction
of sex or age. At the signal, similarly given, of 'Throw
him over!' which it now appears always alluded to the
overthrow of our never-sufficiently-enough-to-be-deeply-
and-universally-to-be-venerated constitution, all the
heads of the N. P.'s were to be thrown at the fiddlers,
to prevent their appearing in evidence, or perhaps as
a false and illiberal insinuation that they have no heads
of their own. All that we know of the further designs
of these incendiaries is, that they are by-a-great-deal-
too-much too-horrible-to-be-mentioned.

The Manager has acted with his usual promptitude
on this trying occasion. He has contracted for 300 tons
of gunpowder, which are at this moment placed in a
small barrel under the pit; and a descendant of Guy
Faux, assisted by Col. Congreve, has undertaken to
blow up the house, when necessary, in so novel and
ingenious a manner, that every O. P. shall be annihi-
lated, while not a whisker of the N. P.'s shall be singed.
This strikingly displays the advantages of loyalty and
attachment to government. Several other hints have
been taken from the theatrical regulations of the not-a-
bit-the-less-on-that-account-to-be-universally - execrated
monster Bonaparte. A park of artillery, provided with
chain-shot, is to be stationed on the stage, and play
upon the audience, in case of any indication of misplaced applause or popular discontent (which accounts
for the large space between the curtain and the lamps);
and the public will participate our satisfaction in learn-

ing that the indecorous custom of standing up with the hat on is to be abolished, as the Bow-street officers are provided with daggers, and have orders to stab all such persons to the heart, and send their bodies to Surgeons' Hall. Gentlemen who cough are only to be slightly wounded. Fruit - women bawling ' Bill of the play !' are to be forthwith shot, for which purpose soldiers will be stationed in the slips, and ball-cartridge is to be served out with the lemonade. If any of the spectators happen to sneeze or spit, they are to be transported for life; and any person who is so tall as to prevent another seeing, is to be dragged out and sent on board the tender, or, by an instrument taken out of the pocket of Procrustes, to be forthwith cut shorter, either at the head or foot, according as his own convenience may dictate.

Thus, ladies and gentlemen, have the committee, through my medium, set forth the not-in-a-hurry-to-be-paralleled plan they have adopted for preserving order and decorum within the walls of their magnificent edifice. Nor have they, while attentive to their own concerns, by any means overlooked those of the cities of London and Westminster. Finding, on enumeration, that they have with a with-two-hands-and-one-tongue-to-be-applauded liberality, contracted for more gunpowder than they want, they have parted with the surplus to the mattock-carrying and hustings-hammering high bailiff of Westminster, who has, with his own shovel, dug a large hole in the front of the parish church of St. Paul, Covent Garden, that, upon the least symptom of ill-breeding in the mob at the general election, the whole of the market may be blown into the air. This, ladies and gentlemen, may at first make provisions *rise*, but we pledge the credit of our theatre that they will soon *fall* again, and people be supplied, as usual, with vegetables, in the in-general-strewed-with-cabbage-stalks - but - on - Saturday - night - lighted-up-with-lamps market of Covent Garden.

I should expatiate more largely on the other advantages of the glorious constitution of these by-the-whole-of-Europe-envied realms, but I am called away to take an account of the ladies, and other artificial flowers, at a fashionable rout, of which a full and particular account will hereafter appear. For the present, my fashionable intelligence is scanty, on account of the opening of Drury Lane; and the ladies and gentlemen who honour me with their attention will not be surprised if they find nothing under my usual head ! !

THE THEATRE.

BY THE REV. G. C.[1]

Nil intentatum nostri liquêre poetæ,
Nec minimum meruêre decus, vestigia Græca
Ausi deserere, et celebrare domestica facta.

HORACE.

A PREFACE OF APOLOGIES.

IF the following poem should be fortunate enough to be selected for the opening address, a few words of explanation may be deemed necessary, on my part, to avert invidious misrepresentation. The animadversion I have thought it right to make on the noise created by tuning the orchestra, will, I hope, give no lasting

[1] The REV. GEORGE CRABBE. The writer's first interview with this poet, who may be designated Pope in worsted stockings, took place at William Spencer's villa at Petersham, close to what that gentleman called his gold-fish pond, though it was scarcely three feet in diameter, throwing up a *jet d'eau* like a thread. The venerable bard, seizing both the hands of his satirist, exclaimed, with a good-humoured laugh : 'Ah ! my old enemy, how do you do ?' In the course of conversation, he expressed great astonishment at his popularity in London; adding, 'In my own village they think nothing of me.' The subject happening to be the inroads of Time upon Beauty, the writer quoted the following lines:—

'Six years had pass'd, and forty ere the six,
When Time began to play his usual tricks:
My locks, once comely in a virgin's sight,
Locks of pure brown, now felt th' encroaching white;
Gradual each day I liked my horses less,
My dinner more—I learnt to play at chess.'

'That's very good !' cried the bard;—'whose is it ?' 'Your own.' 'Indeed ! hah ! well, I had quite forgotten it.' Was this affectation, or was it not ? In sooth, he seemed to push simplicity to puerility. This imitation contained in manuscript the following lines, after describing certain Sunday-newspaper critics who were

remorse to any of the gentlemen employed in the band.
It is to be desired that they would keep their instru-
ments ready tuned, and strike off at once. This would
be an accommodation to many well-meaning persons
who frequent the theatre, who, not being blest with
the ear of St. Cecilia, mistake the tuning for the over-
ture, and think the latter concluded before it is begun.

> ' One fiddle will
> Give, half-ashamed, a tiny flourish still,'

was originally written ' one hautboy will '; but, having
providentially been informed, when this poem was upon
the point of being sent off, that there is but one hautboy
in the band, I averted the storm of popular and mana-
gerial indignation from the head of its blower: as it
now stands, ' one fiddle ' among many, the faulty
individual will, I hope, escape detection. The story of
the flying play-bill is calculated to expose a practice
much too common, of pinning play-bills to the cushions
insecurely, and frequently, I fear, not pinning them at
all. If these lines save one play-bill only from the fate
I have recorded, I shall not deem my labour ill employed. The concluding episode of Patrick Jennings
glances at the boorish fashion of wearing the hat in the

---

supposed to be present at a new play, and who were rather heated in
their politics:—

> ' Hard is his task who edits—thankless job !
> A Sunday journal for the factious mob:
> With bitter paragraph and caustic jest,
> He gives to turbulence the day of rest;
> Condemn'd, this week, rash rancour to instil,
> Or thrown aside, the next, for one who will:
> Alike undone or if he praise or rail
> (For this affects his safety, that his sale),
> He sinks at last, in luckless limbo set,
> If loud for libel, and if dumb for debt.'

They were, however, never printed; being, on reflection, considered too serious for the occasion.

It is not a little extraordinary that Crabbe, who could write with
such vigour, should descend to such lines as the following:—

> ' Something had happen'd wrong about a bill
> Which was not drawn with true mercantile skill;
> So, to amend it, I was told to go
> And seek the firm of Clutterbuck and Co.'

Surely ' Emanuel Jennings,' compared with the above, rises to
sublimity.

one-shilling gallery. Had Jennings thrust his between
his feet at the commencement of the play, he might
have leaned forward with impunity, and the catastrophe
I relate would not have occurred. The line of hand-
kerchiefs formed to enable him to recover his loss, is
purposely so crossed in texture and materials as to
mislead the reader in respect to the real owner of any one
of them. For, in the satirical view of life and manners
which I occasionally present, my clerical profession has
taught me how extremely improper it would be, by any
allusion, however slight, to give any uneasiness, however trivial, to any individual, however foolish or wicked.

G. C.

The Theatre.

Interior of a Theatre described.—Pit gradually fills. — The Check-
taker.—Pit full. — The Orchestra tuned.—One Fiddle rather
dilatory.—Is reproved—and repents.—Evolutions of a Play-
bill.—Its final Settlement on the Spikes.—The Gods taken to
task—and why.— Motley Group of Play-goers. — Holywell
Street, St. Pancras.— Emanuel Jennings binds his Son apprentice—not in London—and why.—Episode of the Hat.

'Tis sweet to view, from half-past five to six,
Our long wax-candles, with short cotton wicks,
Touch'd by the lamplighter's Promethean art,
Start into light, and make the lighter start;
To see red Phœbus through the gallery-pane
Tinge with his beam the beams of Drury Lane;
While gradual parties fill our widen'd pit,
And gape, and gaze, and wonder, ere they sit.

At first, while vacant seats give choice and ease,
Distant or near, they settle where they please;
But when the multitude contracts the span,
And seats are rare, they settle where they can.

Now the full benches to late-comers doom
No room for standing, miscall'd *standing room*.

Hark ! the check-taker moody silence breaks,
And bawling ' Pit full !' gives the check he takes;
Yet onward still the gathering numbers cram,
Contending crowders shout the frequent damn,
And all is bustle, squeeze, row, jabbering, and jam.

See to their desks Apollo's sons repair—
Swift rides the rosin o'er the horse's hair !
In unison their various tones to tune,
Murmurs the hautboy, growls the hoarse bassoon;
In soft vibration sighs the whispering lute,
Tang goes the harpsichord, too-too the flute,
Brays the loud trumpet, squeaks the fiddle sharp,
Winds the French-horn, and twangs the tingling harp;
Till, like great Jove, the leader, figuring in,
Attunes to order the chaotic din.
Now all seems hush'd—but, no, one fiddle will
Give, half-ashamed, a tiny flourish still.
Foil'd in his crash, the leader of the clan
Reproves with frowns the dilatory man:
Then on his candlestick thrice taps his bow,
Nods a new signal, and away they go.

Perchance, while pit and gallery cry, ' Hats off ! '
And awed Consumption checks his chided cough,
Some giggling daughter of the Queen of Love
Drops, 'reft of pin, her play-bill from above:
Like Icarus, while laughing galleries clap,
Soars, ducks, and dives in air the printed scrap;
But, wiser far than he, combustion fears,
And, as it flies, eludes the chandeliers;
Till, sinking gradual, with repeated twirl,
It settles, curling, on a fiddler's curl;
Who from his powder'd pate the intruder strikes,
And, for mere malice, sticks it on the spikes.

Say, why these Babel strains from Babel tongues ?
Who's that calls ' Silence !' with such leathern lungs ?
He who, in quest of quiet, ' Silence !' hoots,
Is apt to make the hubbub he imputes.

What various swains our motley walls contain !—
Fashion from Moorfields, honour from Chick Lane;
Bankers from Paper Buildings here resort,
Bankrupts from Golden Square and Riches Court;
From the Haymarket canting rogues in grain,
Gulls from the Poultry, sots from Water Lane;
The lottery-cormorant, the auction-shark,
The full-price master, and the half-price clerk;

Boys who long linger at the gallery-door,
With pence twice five—they want but twopence more;
Till some Samaritan the twopence spares,
And sends them jumping up the gallery-stairs.

Critics we boast who ne'er their malice balk,
But talk their minds—we wish they'd mind their talk;
Big-worded bullies, who by quarrels live—
Who give the lie, and tell the lie they give;
Jews from St. Mary Axe, for jobs so wary,
That for old clothes they'd even axe St. Mary;
And bucks with pockets empty as their pate,
Lax in their gaiters, laxer in their gait;
Who oft, when we our house lock up, carouse
With tippling tipstaves in a lock-up house.

Yet here, as elsewhere, Chance can joy bestow,
Where scowling Fortune seem'd to threaten woe.

John Richard William Alexander Dwyer
Was footman to Justinian Stubbs, Esquire;
But when John Dwyer listed in the Blues,
Emanuel Jennings polish'd Stubbs's shoes.
Emanuel Jennings brought his youngest boy
Up as a corn-cutter—a safe employ;
In Holywell Street, St. Pancras, he was bred
(At number twenty-seven, it is said),
Facing the pump, and near the Granby's Head:
He would have bound him to some shop in town,
But with a premium he could not come down.
Pat was the urchin's name—a red-hair'd youth,
Fonder of purl and skittle-grounds than truth.

Silence, ye gods ! to keep your tongues in awe,
The Muse shall tell an accident she saw.

Pat Jennings in the upper gallery sat,
But, leaning forward, Jennings lost his hat:
Down from the gallery the beaver flew,
And· spurn'd the one to settle in the two.
How shall he act ? Pay at the gallery-door
Two shillings for what cost, when new, but four ?
Or till half-price, to save his shilling, wait,
And gain his hat again at half-past eight ?

Now, while his fears anticipate a thief,
John Mullins whispers, 'Take my handkerchief.'
'Thank you,' cries Pat; 'but one won't make a line.'
'Take mine,' cried Wilson; and cried Stokes, 'Take
    mine.'
A motley cable soon Pat Jennings ties,
Where Spitalfields with real India vies.
Like Iris' bow, down darts the painted clue,
Starr'd, striped, and spotted, yellow, red, and blue,
Old calico, torn silk, and muslin new.
George Green below, with palpitating hand,
Loops the last 'kerchief to the beaver's band—
Upsoars the prize ! The youth, with joy unfeign'd,
Regain'd the felt, and felt what he regain'd;
While to the applauding galleries grateful Pat
Made a low bow, and touch'd the ransom'd hat.

' " The Theatre," by the Rev. G. Crabbe, we rather think, is the best piece in the collection. It is an exquisite and most masterly imitation, not only of the peculiar style, but of the taste, temper, and manner of description of that most original author; and can hardly be said to be in any respect a caricature of that style or manner—except in the excessive profusion of puns and verbal jingles—which, though undoubtedly to be ranked among his characteristics, are never so thick-sown in his original works as in this admirable imitation. It does not aim, of course, at any shadow of his pathos or moral sublimity, but seems to us to be a singularly faithful copy of his passages of mere description.'—*Edinburgh Review*.

TO THE MANAGING COMMITTEE OF THE NEW DRURY-LANE THEATRE.[1]

GENTLEMEN,

    Happening to be wool-gathering at the foot of Mount Parnassus, I was suddenly seized with a violent travestie in the head. The first symptoms I felt were several triple rhymes floating about my brain, accom-

[1] ' We come next to three ludicrous parodies—of the story of *The Stranger*, of *George Barnwell*, and of the dagger-scene in *Macbeth*, under the signature of Momus Medlar. They are as good, we think, as that sort of thing can be, and remind us of the happier efforts of Colman, whose less successful fooleries are professedly copied in the last piece in the volume.'—*Edinburgh Review*.

panied by a singing in my throat, which quickly communicated itself to the ears of everybody about me. and made me a burthen to my friends and a torment to Doctor Apollo; three of whose favourite servants— that is to say, Macbeth, his butcher; Mrs. Haller, his cook; and George Barnwell, his book-keeper—I waylaid in one of my fits of insanity, and mauled after a very frightful fashion.   In this woful crisis, I accidentally heard of your invaluable New Patent Hissing Pit, which cures every disorder incident to Grub Street. I send you enclosed a more detailed specimen of my case: if you could mould it into the shape of an address, to be said or sung on the first night of your performance, I have no doubt that I should feel the immediate effects of your invaluable New Patent Hissing Pit, of which they tell me one hiss is a dose.

I am, &c.,
MOMUS MEDLAR.

CASE No. 1.

MACBETH.

[*Enter* MACBETH, *in a red nightcap.*   PAGE *following with a torch.*]

Go, boy, and thy good mistress tell
  (She knows that my purpose is cruel),
I'd thank her to tingle her bell
  As soon as she's heated my gruel.
Go, get thee to bed and repose—
  To sit up so late is a scandal;
But ere you have ta'en off your clothes,
  Be sure that you put out that candle.
      Ri fol de rol tol de rol lol.

My stars, in the air here's a knife !—
  I'm sure it can not be a hum;
I'll catch at the handle, odd's life !
  And then I shall not cut my thumb.
I've got him !—no, at him again !
  Come, come, I'm not fond of these jokes;
This must be some blade of the brain—
  Those witches are given to hoax.

I've one in my pocket, I know,
  My wife left on purpose behind her;
She bought this of Teddy-high-ho,
  The poor Caledonian grinder.
I see thee again! o'er thy middle
  Large drops of red blood now are spill'd,
Just as much as to say, diddle diddle,
  Good Duncan, pray come and be kill'd.

It leads to his chamber, I swear;
  I tremble and quake every joint—
No dog at the scent of a hare
  Ever yet made a cleverer point.
Ah, no! 'twas a dagger of straw—
  Give me blinkers, to save me from starting;
The knife that I thought that I saw
  Was naught but my eye, Betty Martin.

Now o'er this terrestrial hive
  A life paralytic is spread;
For while the one half is alive,
  The other is sleepy and dead.
King Duncan, in grand majesty,
  Has got my state-bed for a snooze;
I've lent him my slippers, so I
  May certainly stand in his shoes.

Blow softly, ye murmuring gales!
  Ye feet, rouse no echo in walking!
For though a dead man tells no tales,
  Dead walls are much given to talking.
This knife shall be in at the death—
  I'll stick him, then off safely get!
Cries the world, this could not be Macbeth,
  For he'd ne'er stick at any thing yet.

Hark, hark! 'tis the signal, by goles!
  It sounds like a funeral knell;
O, hear it not, Duncan! it tolls
  To call thee to heaven or hell.

Or if you to heaven won't fly,
  But rather prefer Pluto's ether,
Only wait a few years till I die,
  And we'll go to the devil together.
                    Ri fol de rol, &c.

CASE No. II.

THE STRANGER.

WHO has e'er been at Drury must needs know the
    Stranger,
A wailing old Methodist, gloomy and wan,
A husband suspicious—his wife acted Ranger,
She took to her heels, and left poor Hypocon.
Her martial gallant swore that truth was a libel,
That marriage was thraldom, elopement no sin;
Quoth she, I remember the words of my Bible—
My spouse is a Stranger, and I'll take him in.
  With my sentimentalibus lachrymæ roar'em,
  And pathos and bathos delightful to see;
  And chop and change ribs, à-la-mode Germanorum,
  And high diddle ho diddle, pop tweedle dee.

To keep up her dignity no longer rich enough,
Where was her plate ?—why, 'twas laid on the shelf;
Her land fuller's earth, and her great riches kitchen-stuff—
Dressing the dinner instead of herself.
No longer permitted in diamonds to sparkle,
Now plain Mrs. Haller, of servants the dread,
With a heart full of grief, and a pan full of charcoal,
She lighted the company up to their bed.

Incensed at her flight, her poor Hubby in dudgeon
Roam'd after his rib in a gig and a pout,
Till, tired with his journey, the peevish curmudgeon
Sat down and blubber'd just like a church-spout.
One day, on a bench as dejected and sad he laid,
Hearing a squash, he cried, Damn it, what's that ?
'Twas a child of the count's, in whose service lived
    Adelaide,
Soused in the river, and squall'd like a cat.

Having drawn his young excellence up to the bank, it
Appear'd that himself was all dripping, I swear;
No wonder he soon became dry as a blanket,
Exposed as he was to the count's *son* and *heir*.
Dear sir, quoth the count, in reward of your valour,
To show that my gratitude is not mere talk
You shall eat a beefsteak with my cook, Mrs. Haller,
Cut from the rump with her own knife and fork.

Behold, now the count gave the Stranger a dinner,
With gunpowder-tea, which you know brings a ball,
And, thin as he was, that he might not grow thinner,
He made of the Stranger no stranger at all.
At dinner fair Adelaide brought up a chicken—
A bird that she never had met with before;
But, seeing him, scream'd, and was carried off kicking,
And he bang'd his nob 'gainst the opposite door.

To finish my tale without roundaboutation,
Young master and missee besieged their papa;
They sung a quartetto in grand blubberation—
The Stranger cried, Oh ! Mrs. Haller cried, Ah !
Though pathos and sentiment largely are dealt in,
I have no good moral to give in exchange;
For though she, as a cook, might be given to melting,
The Stranger's behaviour was certainly strange,
 With his sentimentalibus lachrymæ roar'em,
 And pathos and bathos delightful to see,
 And chop and change ribs, à-la-mode Germanorum,
 And high diddle ho diddle, pop tweedle dee.

CASE No. III.

GEORGE BARNWELL.

GEORGE BARNWELL stood at the shop-door,
A customer hoping to find, sir;
His apron was hanging before,
But the tail of his coat was behind, sir.

A lady, so painted and smart,
Cried, Sir, I've exhausted my stock o' late;
I've got nothing left but a groat—
Could you give me four penn'orth of chocolate ?
            Rum ti, &c.

Her face was rouged up to the eyes,
Which made her look prouder and prouder;
His hair stood on end with surprise,
And hers with pomatum and powder.
The business was soon understood;
The lady, who wish'd to be more rich,
Cries, Sweet sir, my name is Milwood,
And I lodge at the Gunner's in Shoreditch.
            Rum ti, &c.

Now nightly he stole out, good lack !
And into her lodging would pop, sir;
And often forgot to come back,
Leaving master to shut up the shop, sir.
Her beauty his wits did bereave—
Determined to be quite the crack O,
He lounged at the Adam and Eve,
And call'd for his gin and tobacco.
            Rum ti, &c.

And now—for the truth must be told,
Though none of a 'prentice should speak ill—
He stole from the till all the gold,
And ate the lump-sugar and treacle.
In vain did his master exclaim,
Dear George, don't engage with that dragon;
She'll lead you to sorrow and shame,
And leave you the devil a rag on
            Your rum ti, &c.

In vain he entreats and implores
The weak and incurable ninny,
So kicks him at last out of doors,
And Georgy soon spends his last guinea.

His uncle, whose generous purse
Had often relieved him, as I know,
Now finding him grow worse and worse,
Refused to come down with the rhino.
Rum ti, &c.

Cried Milwood, whose cruel heart's core
Was so flinty that nothing could shock it,
If ye mean to come here any more,
Pray come with more cash in your pocket:
Make nunky surrender his dibs,
Rub his pate with a pair of lead towels,
Or stick a knife into his ribs—
I'll warrant he'll then show some bowels.
Rum ti, &c.

A pistol he got from his love—
'Twas loaded with powder and bullet;
He trudged off to Camberwell Grove,
But wanted the courage to pull it.
There's nunky as fat as a hog.
While I am as lean as a lizard;
Here's at you, you stingy old dog!—
And he whips a long knife in his gizzard.
Rum ti, &c.

All you who attend to my song,
A terrible end of the farce shall see,
If you join the inquisitive throng
That follow'd poor George to the Marshalsea.
If Milwood were here, dash my wigs,
Quoth he, I would pummel and lam her well;
Had I stuck to my pruins and figs,
I ne'er had stuck nunky at Camberwell.
Rum ti, &c.

Their bodies were never cut down;
For granny relates with amazement,
A witch bore 'em over the town,
And hung them on Thorowgood's casement.

The neighbours, I've heard the folks say,
The miracle noisily brag on;
And the shop is. to this very day,
The sign of the George and the Dragon.
                    Rum ti, &c.

PUNCH'S APOTHEOSIS.

BY T. H.[1]

Rhymes the rudders are of verses,
With which, like ships, they steer their courses.
                                    HUDIBRAS.

Scene draws, and discovers PUNCH *on a throne, surrounded
    by* LEAR, LADY MACBETH, MACBETH, OTHELLO,
    GEORGE BARNWELL, HAMLET, GHOST. MACHEATH,
    JULIET, FRIAR, APOTHECARY, ROMEO, *and* FAL-
    STAFF.—PUNCH *descends, and addresses them in the
    following*

RECITATIVE.

As manager of horses Mr. Merryman is,
So I with you am master of the ceremonies—
These grand rejoicings. Let me see, how name ye
    'em ?—
Oh, in Greek lingo 'tis E-pi-thalamium.
October's tenth it is: toss up each hat to-day,
And celebrate with shouts our opening Saturday!
On this great night 'tis settled by our manager,
That we, to please great Johnny Bull, should plan a
    jeer,
Dance a bang-up theatrical cotillion,
And put on tuneful Pegasus a pillion;
That every soul, whether or not a cough he has,
May kick like Harlequin, and sing like Orpheus.

---

[1] THEODORE HOOK, at that time a very young man, and the companion of the annotator in many wild frolics.   The cleverness of his
subsequent prose compositions has cast his early stage songs into
oblivion.   This parody was, in the second edition, transferred from
Colman to Hook.

So come, ye pupils of Sir John Gallini,[1]
Spin up a teetotum like Angiolini;[2]
That John and Mrs. Bull, from ale and tea-houses,
May shout huzza for Punch's Apotheosis !

They dance and sing.

Air—*' Sure such a day.'* Tom Thumb.

LEAR.

Dance, Regan ! dance, with Cordelia and Goneril—
Down the middle, up again, poussette, and cross;
Stop, Cordelia ! do not tread upon her heel,
Regan feeds on coltsfoot, and kicks like a horse.
See, she twists her mutton fists like Molyneux or Beel-
    zebub,
And t'other's clack, who pats her back, is louder far
    than hell's hubbub.
They tweak my nose, and round it goes—I fear they'll
    break the ridge of it,
Or leave it all just like Vauxhall, with only half the
    bridge of it.[3]

OMNES.

Round let us bound, for this is Punch's holiday,
Glory to Tomfoolery, huzza ! huzza !

LADY MACBETH.

I kill'd the king; my husband is a heavy dunce;
He left the grooms unmassacred, then massacred the
    stud.
One loves long gloves; for mittens, like king's evidence,
Let truth with the fingers out, and won't hide blood.

MACBETH.

When spoonys on two knees implore the aid of sorcery,
To suit their wicked purposes they quickly put the
    laws awry;

[1] Then Director of the Opera House.
[2] At that time the chief dancer at this establishment.
[3] Vauxhall Bridge then, like the Thames Tunnel at present, stood
suspended in the middle of that river.

With Adam I in wife may vie, for none could tell the
    use of her,
Except to cheapen golden pippins hawk'd about by
    Lucifer.

OMNES.

Round let us bound, for this is Punch's holiday,
Glory to Tomfoolery, huzza ! huzza !

OTHELLO.

Wife, come to life, forgive what your black lover did,
Spit the feathers from your mouth, and munch roast
    beef;
Iago he may go and be toss'd in the coverlid
That smother'd you, because you pawn'd my hand-
    kerchief.

GEORGE BARNWELL.

Why, neger, so eager about your rib immaculate ?
Milwood shows for hanging us they've got an ugly
    knack o' late;
If on beauty 'stead of duty but one peeper bent he
    sees,
Satan waits with Dolly baits to hook in us appren-
    tices.

OMNES.

Round let us bound, for this is Punch's holiday,
Glory to Tomfoolery, huzza ! huzza !

HAMLET.

I'm Hamlet in camlet, my ap and perihelia
The moon can fix, which lunatics makes sharp or flat.
I stuck by ill luck, enamour'd of Ophelia,
Old Polony like a sausage, and exclaim'd, ' Rat, rat !'

GHOST.

Let Gertrude sup the poison'd cup—no more I'll be an
    actor in
Such sorry food, but drink home-brew'd of Whitbread's
    manufacturing.

MACHEATH.

I'll Polly it, and folly it, and dance it quite the
dandy O;
But as for tunes, I have but one, and that is Drops
of Brandy O.

OMNES.

Round let us bound, for this is Punch's holiday,
Glory to Tomfoolery, huzza ! huzza !

JULIET.

I'm Juliet Capulet, who took a dose of hellebore—
A hell-of-a-bore I found it to put on a pall.

FRIAR.

And I am the friar, who so corpulent a belly bore

APOTHECARY.

And that is why poor skinny I have none at all.

ROMEO.

I'm the resurrection-man, of buried bodies amorous.

FALSTAFF.

I'm fagg'd to death, and out of breath, and am for
quiet clamorous;
For though my paunch is round and stanch, I ne'er
begin to feel it ere I
Feel that I have no stomach left for entertainment
military.

OMNES.

Round let us bound, for this is Punch's holiday,
Glory to Tomfoolery, huzza ! huzza !

[Exeunt dancing.

' " Punch's Apotheosis," by G. Colman, junior, is too purely
nonsensical to be extracted; and both gives less pleasure to the
reader, and does less justice to the ingenious author in whose name
it stands, than any other of the poetical imitations.'—*Edinburgh
Review.*

'We have no conjectures to offer as to the anonymous author of this amusing little volume. He who is such a master of disguises may easily be supposed to have been successful in concealing himself, and, with the power of assuming so many styles, is not likely to be detected by his own. We should guess, however, that he had not written a great deal in his own character—that his natural style was neither very lofty nor very grave—and that he rather indulges a partiality for puns and verbal pleasantries. We marvel why he has shut out Campbell and Rogers from his theatre of living poets, and confidently expect to have our curiosity in this and in all other particulars very speedily gratified, when the applause of the country shall induce him to take off his mask.'—*Edinburgh Review.*

THE MORNING POST.

Additional note intended for p. 61.— This journal was, at the period in question, rather remarkable for the use of the figure called by the rhetoricians *catachresis.* The Bard of Avon may be quoted in justification of its adoption, when he writes of taking arms against a sea, and seeking a bubble in the mouth of a cannon. *The Morning Post,* in the year 1812, congratulated its readers upon having stripped off Cobbett's mask and discovered his cloven foot; adding, that it was high time to give the hydra-head of Faction a rap on the knuckles !

GEORGE ELLIS.

ELEGY WRITTEN IN A COLLEGE LIBRARY.

(GRAY)

THE chapel bell, with hollow mournful sound,
  Awakes the Fellows, slumb'ring o'er their fires,
Roused by the 'customed note, each stares around,
  And sullen from th' unfinished pipe retires.

Now from the Common-Hall's restrictions free,
  The sot's full bottles in quick order move,
While gayer coxcombs sip their amorous tea,
  And Barbers' daughters soothe with tales of love.

Through the still courts a solemn silence reigns,
  Save where, the broken battlements among,
The east wind murmurs through the shattered panes,
  And hoarser ravens croak their evening song.

Where groan yon shelves beneath their learned weight,
  Heap piled on heap, and row succeeding rows,
In peaceful pomp, and undisturbed retreat,
  The labours of our ancestors repose.

No longer, sunk in ceaseless, fruitless toil,
  The half-starved student o'er their leaves shall pore;
For them no longer blaze the midnight oil,
  Their sun is set, and sinks to rise no more.

For them no more shall booksellers contend,
  Or rubric posts their matchless worth proclaim;
Beneath their weight no more the press shall bend,
  While common-sense stands wondering at their fame.

G

Oft did the Classics mourn their Critic rage,
  While still they found each meaning but the true;
Oft did they heap with notes poor Ovid's page,
  And give to Virgil words he never knew;

Yet ere the partial voice of Critic scorn
  Condemn their memory or their toils deride,
Say, have not we had equal cause to mourn
  A waste of words, and learning ill-applied ?

Can none remember ?—yes, I know all can—
  When readings against different readings jarred,
While Bentley led the stern scholastic van,
  And new editions with the old ones warred.

Nor ye, who lightly o'er each work proceed,
  Unmindful of the graver moral part,
Contemn these works, if as you run and read,
  You find no trophies of th' engraver's art.

Can Bartolozzi's all-enrapturing power
  To heavy works the stamp of merit give ?
Could Grignion's art protract Oblivion's hour,
  Or bid the epic rage of Blackmore live ?

In this lone nook, with learned dust bestrewed,
  Where frequent cobwebs kindly form a shade,
Some wondrous legend, filled with death and blood,
  Some monkish history, perhaps is laid.

With store of barbarous Latin at command,
  Though armed with puns and jingling quibble's might,
Yet could not these soothe Time's remorseless hand
  Or save their labours from eternal night.

Full many an elegy has mourned its fate,
  Beneath some pasty ' cabined, cribbed, confined ';
Full many an ode has soared in lofty state,
  Fixed to a kite, and quivering in the wind.

Here too, perhaps, neglected now, may lie
   The rude memorial of some ancient song,
Whose martial strains, and rugged minstrelsy,
   Once waked to rapture every listening throng.

To trace fair Science through each wildering course,
   With new ideas to enlarge the mind,
With useful lessons drawn from Classic source,
   At once to polish and instruct mankind,

Their times forbade; nor yet alone represt
   Their opening fancy; but alike confined
The senseless ribaldry, the scurvy jest,
   And each low triumph of the vulgar mind;

With Griffiths, Langhorne, Kenrick, and the tribe,[1]
   Whom science loathes and scorn disdains to name,
To snarl unpaid, or, softened by a bribe,
   Smear with vile praise, and deem their daubing
      fame.

Their humble science never soared so far,
   In studious trifles pleased to waste their time,
Or wage with common-sense eternal war,
   In never-ending clink of monkish rhyme.

Yet were they not averse to noisy Fame,
   Or shrank reluctant from her ruder blast,
But still aspired to raise their sinking name,
   And fondly hoped that name might ever last.

Hence each proud volume to the wondering eye,
   Rivals the gaudy glare of Tyrrel's urn,[2]
Where Ships, Wigs, Fame, and Neptune blended lie,
   And weeping cherubs for their bodies mourn.

[1] The Critical Reviewers. The others are the *London* and *Monthly*.
[2] *Vide* Admiral Tyrrel's monument in Westminster Abbey.

For who with rhymes e'er racked his weary brain,
  Or spent in search of epithets his days,
But from his lengthened labours hoped to gain
  Some present profit, or some future praise ?

Though Folly's self inspire each dead-born strain,
  Still Flattery prompts some blockhead to commend,
Perhaps e'en Kenrick hath not toiled in vain,
  Perhaps e'en Kenrick hath as dull a friend.

For thee, whose Muse with many an uncouth rhyme,
  Doth in these lines neglected worth bewail,
If chance (unknowing how to kill the time)
  Some kindred idler should inquire thy tale;

Haply some ancient Fellow may reply—
  Oft have I seen him, from the dawn of day,
E'en till the western sun went down the sky,
  Lounging his lazy, listless hours away.

Each morn he sought the cloister's cool retreat;
  At noon, at Tom's he caught the daily lie,
Or from his window looking o'er the street,
  Would gaze upon the travellers passing by.

At night, encircled with a kindred band,
  In smoke and ale rolled their dull lives away;
True as the College clock's unvarying hand,
  Each morrow was the echo of to-day.

Thus free from cares and children, noise and wife,
  Passed his smooth moments; till, by Fate's command,
A lethargy assailed his harmless life,
  And checked his course, and shook his loitering sand,

Where Merton's towers in Gothic grandeur rise,
  And shed around each soph a deeper gloom,
Beneath the centre aisle interred he lies,
  With these few lines engraved upon his tomb·

THE EPITAPH.

Of vice or virtue void, here rests a man
    By prudence taught each rude excess to shun;
Nor love nor pity marred his sober plan,
    And Dulness claimed him for her favourite son.

By no eccentric passion led astray,
    Not rash to blame, nor eager to commend,
Calmly through life he steered his quiet way,
    Nor made an enemy, nor gained a friend.

Seek not his faults—his merits—to explore,
    But quickly drop this uninstructive tale,
His works—his faults—his merits—are no more,
    Sunk in the gloom of dark oblivion's veil.

GEORGE CRABBE.

INEBRIETY.

(POPE)

THE mighty spirit, and its power, which stains
The bloodless cheek, and vivifies the brains,
I sing. Say, ye, its fiery vot'ries true,
The jovial curate, and the shrill-tongued shrew,
Ye, in the floods of limpid poison nurst,
Where bowl the second charms like bowl the first;
Say how, and why, the sparkling ill is shed,
The heart which hardens, and which rules the head. . . .
Lo ! the poor toper whose untutor'd sense,
Sees bliss in ale, and can with wine dispense;
Whose head proud fancy never taught to steer,
Beyond the muddy ecstasies of beer;
But simple nature can her longing quench,
Behind the settle's curve, or humbler bench:
Some kitchen fire diffusing warmth around,
The semi-globe by hieroglyphics crown'd;
Where canvas purse displays the brass enroll'd,
Nor waiters rave, nor landlords thirst for gold;
Ale and content his fancy's bounds confine,
He asks no limpid punch, no rosy wine;
But sees, admitted to an equal share,
Each faithful swain the heady potion bear:
Go wiser thou ! and in thy scale of taste,
Weigh gout and gravel against ale and rest;
Call vulgar palates what thou judgest so;
Say beer is heavy, windy, cold, and slow;
Laugh at poor sots with insolent pretence,
Yet cry, when tortured, where is Providence ?

CATHERINE MARIA FANSHAWE.

ODE.

(GRAY)

Lo ! where the gaily vestur'd throng,
  Fair learning's train, are seen,
Wedg'd in close ranks her walls along,
  And up her benches green.
Unfolded to their mental eye
Thy awful form, Sublimity !
  The moral teacher shows—
Sublimity of Silence born,
And Solitude 'mid caves forlorn
  And dimly-vision'd woes;
Or Stedfast Worth, that inly great
Mocks the malignity of fate.
While whisper'd pleasure's dulcet sound
Murmurs the crowded room around,
And Wisdom, borne on Fashion's pinions,
Exulting hails her new dominions.
Oh ! both on me your influence shed,
Dwell in my heart and deck my head !

Where'er a broader, browner shade
  The shaggy beaver throws,
And with the ample feather's aid
  O'er-canopies the nose;
Where'er with smooth and silken pile,
Ling'ring in solemn pause awhile,
  The crimson velvet glows;
From some high bench's giddy brink,
Clinton with me begins to think
  (As bolt upright we sit)
That dress, like dogs, should have its day,
That beavers are too hot for May,
  And velvets quite unfit.

Then taste, in maxims sweet, I draw
  From her unerring lip;
How light, how simple are the straw,
  How delicate the chip !
Hush'd is the speaker's powerful voice,
  The audience melt away,
I fly to fix my final choice
  And bless th' instructive day.

The milliner officious pours
Of hats and caps her ready stores,
  The unbought elegance of spring;
Some wide, disclose the full round face,
Some shadowy, lend a modest grace
  And stretch their sheltering wing.

Here clustering grapes appear to shed
Their luscious juices on the head,
  And cheat the longing eye;
So round the Phrygian monarch hung
Fair fruits, that from his parched tongue
  For ever seem'd to fly.

Here early blooms the summer rose;
Here ribbons wreathe fantastic bows;
Here plays gay plumage of a thousand dyes—
Visions of beauty, spare my aching eyes !
Ye cumbrous fashions, crowd not on my head !
  Mine be the chip of purest white,
  Swan-like, and as her feathers light
When on the still wave spread;
And let it wear the graceful dress
Of unadorned simpleness.

Ah ! frugal wish; ah ! pleasing thought;
  Ah ! hope indulged in vain;
Of modest fancy cheaply bought,
  A stranger yet to Payne.

With undissembled grief I tell,—
  For sorrow never comes too late,—
The simplest bonnet in Pall Mall
  Is sold for £1 8s.

To Calculation's sober view,
  That searches ev'ry plan,
Who keep the old, or buy the new,
  Shall end where they began.

Alike the shabby and the gay
Must meet the sun's meridian ray;
  The air, the dust, the damp.
This, shall the sudden shower despoil;
That, slow decay by gradual soil ;
  Those, envious boxes cramp.

Who will, their squander'd gold may pay;
  Who will, our taste deride;
We'll scorn the fashion of the day
  With philosophic pride.

Methinks we thus, in accents low,
  Might Sydney Smith address,
' Poor moralist ! and what art thou,
  Who never spoke of dress !

' Thy mental hero never hung
Suspended on a tailor's tongue,
  In agonizing doubt;
Thy tale no flutt'ring female show'd,
Who languish'd for the newest mode,
  Yet dar'd to live without.'

FRAGMENT.

(WORDSWORTH)

THERE is a river clear and fair,
  'Tis neither broad nor narrow;
It winds a little here and there—
It winds about like any hare;
And then it takes as straight a course
As on the turnpike road a horse,
  Or through the air an arrow.

The trees that grow upon the shore,
Have grown a hundred years or more;
    So long there is no knowing.
Old Daniel Dobson does not know
When first those trees began to grow;
But still they grew, and grew, and grew,
As if they'd nothing else to do,
    But ever to be growing.

The impulses of air and sky
Have reared their stately stems so high,
    And clothed their boughs with green;
Their leaves the dews of evening quaff,—
    And when the wind blows loud and keen,
I've seen the jolly timbers laugh,
    And shake their sides with merry glee—
Wagging their heads in mockery.

Fix'd are their feet in solid earth,
    Where winds can never blow;
But visitings of deeper birth
    Have reached their roots below.
For they have gained the river's brink,
And of the living waters drink.

There's little Will, a five years' child—
    He is my youngest boy;
To look on eyes so fair and wild,
    It is a very joy:—
He hath conversed with sun and shower,
And dwelt with every idle flower,
    As fresh and gay as them.
He loiters with the briar rose,—
The blue bells are his play-fellows,
    That dance upon their slender stem.

And I have said, my little Will,
Why should not he continue still
    A thing of Nature's rearing?

A thing beyond the world's control—
A living vegetable soul,—
  No human sorrow fearing.

It were a blessed sight to see
That child become a willow-tree,
  His brother trees among.
He'd be four times as tall as me,
  And live three times as long.

JOHN HOOKHAM FRERE.

A FABLE.

(DRYDEN)

A DINGY donkey, formal and unchanged,
Browsed in the lane and o'er the common ranged,
Proud of his ancient asinine possessions,
Free from the panniers of the grave professions,
He lived at ease; and chancing once to find
A lion's skin, the fancy took his mind
To personate the monarch of the wood;
And for a time the stratagem held good.
He moved with so majestical a pace
That bears and wolves and all the savage race
Gazed in admiring awe, ranging aloof,
Not over-anxious for a clearer proof—
Longer he might have triumph'd—but alas !
In an unguarded hour it came to pass
He bray'd aloud; and show'd himself an ass !

The moral of this tale I could not guess
Till Mr. Landor sent his works to press.

THE COURSE OF TIME.

(ROBERT POLLOK)

ROBERT POLLOK, A.M. ! this work of yours
Is meant, I do not doubt, extremely well,
And the design I deem most laudable,
But since I find the book laid on my table,
I shall presume (with the fair owner's leave)
To note a single slight deficiency:
I mean, in short (since it is called a poem),
That in the course of ten successive books
If something in the shape of poetry
Were to be met with, we should like it better;
But nothing of the kind is to be found,
Nothing, alas ! but words of the olden time,
Quaint and uncouth, contorted phrase and queer,
With the familiar language that befits
Tea-drinking parties most unmeetly matched.

GEORGE CANNING AND JOHN HOOKHAM FRERE.

INSCRIPTION

For the Door of the Cell in Newgate where Mrs. Brownrigg, the 'Prentice-cide, was confined previous to her Execution.

(SOUTHEY)

FOR one long term, or e'er her trial came,
Here BROWNRIGG linger'd. Often have these cells
Echoed her blasphemies, as with shrill voice
She scream'd for fresh Geneva. Not to her
Did the blithe fields of Tothill, or thy street,
St. Giles, its fair varieties expand;
Till at the last, in slow-drawn cart she went
To execution. Dost thou ask her crime?
SHE WHIPP'D TWO FEMALE 'PRENTICES TO DEATH,
AND HID THEM IN THE COAL-HOLE. For her mind
Shap'd strictest plans of discipline. Sage schemes!
Such as Lycurgus taught, when at the shrine
Of the Orthyan Goddess he bade flog
The little Spartans; such as erst chastised
Our MILTON, when at college. For this act
Did BROWNRIGG swing. Harsh laws! But time shall come
When France shall reign, and laws be all repealed!

THE SOLDIERS' FRIEND.

DACTYLICS.

(SOUTHEY)

COME, little Drummer Boy, lay down your knapsack here:
I am the soldiers' friend—here are some books for you;
Nice clever books by Tom Paine the philanthropist.

Here's half-a-crown for you—here are some handbills
    too ;
Go to the barracks and give all the soldiers some :
Tell them the sailors are all in a mutiny.

> [*Exit Drummer Boy, with Handbills and Half-Crown.*
> *—Manet Soldier's Friend.*]

Liberty's friends thus all learn to amalgamate,
Freedom's volcanic explosion prepares itself,
Despots shall bow to the fasces of liberty,
        Reason, philosophy, ' fiddledum diddledum,'
        Peace and fraternity, higgledy piggledy,
        Higgledy piggledy, ' fiddledum diddledum.'
            Et cœtera, et cœtera, et cœtera.

THE SOLDIER'S WIFE

*Being the Quintessence of all the Dactylics that ever were or ever
will be written.*

(SOUTHEY AND COLERIDGE)

WEARISOME Sonnetteer, feeble and querulous,
Painfully dragging out thy demo-cratic lays—
Moon-stricken Sonnetteer, ' ah ! for thy heavy chance !'

Sorely thy Dactylics lag on uneven feet :
Slow is the Syllable which thou would'st urge to speed,
Lame and o'erburden'd, and ' screaming its wretched-
        ness !'

    *   *   *   *   * [1]

Ne'er talk of Ears again ! look at thy Spelling-book ;
Dilworth and *Dyche* are both mad at thy quantities—
DACTYLICS, call'st thou 'em ?—' God help thee, silly
    one !'

---

[1] My worthy friend, the Bellman, had promised to supply an additional stanza, but the business of assisting the lamplighter, chimney-
sweeper, etc., with complimentary verses for their worthy masters
and mistresses, pressing on him at this season, he was obliged to
decline it.

THE FRIEND OF HUMANITY AND THE KNIFE-GRINDER.

Sapphics.

(SOUTHEY)

FRIEND OF HUMANITY.

' NEEDY Knife-grinder ! whither are you going ?
Rough is the road, your wheel is out of order—
Bleak blows the blast; your hat has got a hole in 't,
       So have your breeches !

' Weary Knife-grinder ! little think the proud ones,
Who in their coaches roll along the turnpike-
-road, what hard work 'tis crying all day "Knives and
       Scissors to grind O !"

' Tell me, Knife-grinder, how you came to grind knives ?
Did some rich man tyrannically use you ?
Was it the squire, or parson of the parish ?
       Or the attorney ?

' Was it the squire, for killing of his game ? or
Covetous parson, for his tithes distraining ?
Or roguish lawyer, made you lose your little
       All in a lawsuit ?

' (Have you not read the Rights of Man, by Tom
    Paine ?)
Drops of compassion tremble on my eyelids,
Ready to fall, as soon as you have told your
       Pitiful story.'

KNIFE-GRINDER.

' Story ! God bless you ! I have none to tell, sir,
Only last night a-drinking at the Chequers,
This poor old hat and breeches, as you see, were
       Torn in a scuffle.

' Constables came up for to take me into
Custody; they took me before the justice;
Justice Oldmixon put me in the parish-
                    -Stocks for a vagrant.

' I should be glad to drink your Honour's health in
A pot of beer, if you will give me sixpence;
But for my part, I never love to meddle
                    With politics, sir.'

FRIEND OF HUMANITY.

' *I* give thee sixpence ! I will see thee damn'd first—
Wretch ! whom no sense of wrongs can rouse to· ven-
        geance ;
Sordid, unfeeling, reprobate, degraded,
                    Spiritless outcast !"

> [*Kicks the Knife-grinder, overturns his wheel, and exit
> in a transport of Republican enthusiasm and
> universal philanthropy.*]

JOHN HOOKHAM FRERE, GEORGE CANNING, AND GEORGE ELLIS.

THE LOVES OF THE TRIANGLES.

A Mathematical and Philosophical Poem.

(ERASMUS DARWIN)

STAY your rude steps, or e'er your feet invade
The Muses' haunts, ye sons of War and Trade !
Nor you, ye legion fiends of Church and Law,
Pollute these pages with unhallow'd paw ![1]
Debased, corrupted, grovelling, and confin'd,
No DEFINITIONS touch *your* senseless mind;
To *you* no POSTULATES prefer their claim,
No ardent AXIOMS *your* dull souls inflame;
For *you* no TANGENTS touch, no ANGLES meet,
No CIRCLES join in osculation[2] sweet !

For *me*, ye CISSOIDS,[3] round my temples bend
Your wandering curves; ye CONCHOIDS extend;
Let playful PENDULES quick vibration feel,
While silent CYCLOIS rests upon her wheel;
Let HYDROSTATICS,[4] simpering as they go,
Lead the light Naiads on fantastic toe;

[1] Imitated from the introductory couplet to the ' Economy of Vegetation :'

> ' Stay your rude steps, whose throbbing breasts unfold
> The legion friends of glory and of gold.'

This sentiment is here expanded into four lines.

[2] For the *os-culation*, or kissing of circles and other curves, see *Huygens*, who has veiled this delicate and inflammatory subject in the decent obscurity of a learned language.

[3] A curve supposed to resemble the sprig of ivy, from which it has its name, and therefore peculiarly adapted to poetry.

[4] Water has been supposed, by several of our philosophers, to be capable of the passion of love. Some later experiments appear to favour this idea. Water, when pressed by a moderate degree of heat, has been observed to *simper*, or *simmer* (as it is more usually called). The same does not hold true of any other element.

H

Let shrill ACOUSTICS tune the tiny lyre;
With EUCLID sage fair ALGEBRA conspire;
The obedient pulley strong MECHANICS ply,
And wanton OPTICS roll the melting eye!

I see the fair fantastic forms appear,
The flaunting drapery and the languid leer;
Fair sylphish forms[1]—who, tall, erect, and slim,
Dart the keen glance, and stretch the length of limb;
To viewless harpings weave the meanless dance,
Wave the gay wreath, and titter as they prance.

Such rich confusion[2] charms the ravish'd sight,
When vernal Sabbaths to the Park invite.
Mounts the thick dust, the coaches crowd along,
Presses round Grosvenor Gate th' impatient throng;
White-muslin'd misses and mammas are seen,
Link'd with gay cockneys, glittering o'er the green:
The rising breeze unnumber'd charms displays,
And the tight ankle strikes th' astonish'd gaze.

But chief, thou NURSE of the DIDACTIC MUSE,
Divine NONSENSIA, all thy soul infuse;
The charms of *Secants* and of *Tangents* tell,
How LOVES and GRACES in an *Angle* dwell;
How slow progressive *Points* protract the *Line,*
As pendant spiders spin the filmy twine;
How lengthen'd *Lines,* impetuous sweeping round,
Spread the wide *Plane,* and mark its circling bound;
How *Planes,* their substance with their motion grown,
Form the huge *Cube,* the *Cylinder,* the *Cone.*

Lo! where the chimney's sooty tube ascends,
The fair TROCHAIS[3] from the corner bends!

[1] *Vide* modern prints of nymphs and shepherds dancing to nothing
at all.
[2] Imitated from the following genteel and sprightly lines in the
first canto of the ' Loves of the Plants ':
> ' So bright its folding canopy withdrawn,
> Glides the gilt landau o'er the velvet lawn,
> Of beaux and belles displays the glittering throng,
> And soft airs fan them as they glide along.'
[3] The Nymph of the Wheel, supposed to be in love with SMOKE-
JACK.

Her coal-black eyes upturn'd, incessant mark
The eddying smoke, quick flame, and volant spark;
Mark with quick ken, where flashing in between
Her much-loved *Smoke-Jack* glimmers thro' the scene;
Mark how his various parts together tend,
Point to one purpose,—in one object end:
The spiral *grooves* in smooth meanders flow,
Drags the long *chain*, the polish'd axles glow,
While slowly circumvolves the piece of beef below:
The conscious fire with bickering radiance burns,
Eyes the rich joint, and roasts it as it turns.

So youthful HORNER rolled the roguish eye,
Cull'd the dark plum from out his Christmas pie,
And cried in self-applause—' How good a boy am I.'

So, the sad victim of domestic spite,
Fair CINDERELLA, pass'd the wintry night,
In the lone chimney's darksome nook immured,
Her form disfigured, and her charms obscured.
Sudden her godmother appears in sight,
Lifts the charm'd rod, and chants the mystic rite.
The chanted rite the maid attentive hears,
And feels new ear-rings deck her listening ears;
While 'midst her towering tresses, aptly set,
Shines bright, with quivering glance, the smart aigrette;
Brocaded silks the splendid dress complete,
And the Glass Slipper grasps her fairy feet.
Six cock-tail'd mice transport her to the ball,
And liveried lizards wait upon her call.

Alas ! that partial Science should approve
The sly RECTANGLE'S[1] too licentious love !
For *three* bright nymphs the wily wizard burns;—
Three bright-ey'd nymphs requite his flame by turns.
Strange force of magic skill ! combined of yore
With PLATO'S science and MENECMUS' lore.

[1] ' A figure which has one angle, *or more*, of ninety degrees '—
Johnson's Dictionary. It here means a RIGHT-ANGLED TRIANGLE,
which is therefore incapable of having more than one angle of ninety
degrees, but which may, according to our author's *Prosopopœia.*
be supposed to be in love with THREE or any greater number of
NYMPHS.

In *Afric's* schools, amid those sultry sands
High on its base where POMPEY's pillar stands,
This learnt THE SEER; and learnt, alas! too well,
Each scribbled talisman and smoky spell:
What mutter'd charms, what soul-subduing arts,
Fell ZATANAI[1] to his sons imparts.

Gins![2]—black and huge! who in DOM-DANIEL's[3] cave
Writhe your scorch'd limbs on sulphur's azure wave,
Or, shivering, yell amidst eternal snows,
Where cloud-capp'd CAF[4] protrudes his granite toes
(Bound by *his* will, *Judæa's* fabled king,[5]
Lord of *Aladdin's* lamp and mystic ring).
Gins! YE remember! for YOUR toil convey'd
Whate'er of drugs the powerful charm could aid;
Air, earth, and sea ye search'd, and where below
Flame embryo lavas, young volcanoes glow—
GINS! ye beheld appall'd th' enchanter's hand
Wave in dark air th' *Hypothenusal* wand:
Saw him the mystic *Circle* trace, and wheel
With head erect, and far-extended heel;
Saw him, with speed that mock'd the dazzled eye,
Self-whirl'd, in quick gyrations eddying fly:
Till done the potent spell—behold him grown
Fair *Venus'* emblem—the *Phœnician Cone.*[6]

Triumphs THE SEER, and now secure observes
The kindling passions of the *rival* CURVES.

[1] Supposed to be the same with SATAN.

[2] The Eastern name for GENII.—*Vide* TALES OF DITTO.

[3] A submarine palace near Tunis, where ZATANAI usually held his Court.

[4] The Indian *Caucasus.*

[5] MR. HIGGINS does not mean to deny that SOLOMON was really King of JUDÆA. The epithet *fabled* applies to that empire over the Genii, which the retrospective generosity of the Arabian fabulists has bestowed upon this monarch.

[6] It was under this shape that *Venus* was worshipped in *Phœnicia.* MR. HIGGINS thinks it was the *Venus Urania,* or Celestial Venus; in allusion to which, he supposes that the *Phœnician* grocers first introduced the practice of preserving sugar-loaves in blue or sky-coloured paper. He also believes that the *conical* form of the original grenadiers' caps was typical of the loves of MARS and VENUS.

And first, the fair PARABOLA behold,
Her timid arms, with virgin blush, unfold!
Though, on one *focus* fix'd, her eyes betray
A heart that glows with love's resistless sway,
Though, climbing oft, she strive with bolder grace
Round his tall neck to clasp her fond embrace,
Still ere she reach it, from his polish'd side
Her trembling hands in devious *Tangents* glide.

Not thus HYPERBOLA:—with subtlest art
The blue-eyed wanton plays her changeful part;
Quick as her *conjugated axes* move
Through every posture of luxurious love,
Her sportive limbs with easiest grace expand;
Her charms unveil'd provoke the lover's hand:
Unveil'd, except in many a filmy ray,
Where light *Asymptotes* o'er her bosom play,
Nor touch her glowing skin, nor intercept the day.

Yet why, ELLIPSIS, at thy fate repine?
More lasting bliss, securer joys are thine.
Though to each Fair his treach'rous wish may stray,
Though each, in turn, may seize a transient sway,
'Tis thine with mild coercion to restrain,
Twine round his struggling heart, and bind with endless
    chain.

Thus, happy FRANCE! in thy regenerate land,
Where TASTE with RAPINE saunters hand in hand;
Where, nursed in seats of innocence and bliss,
REFORM greets TERROR with fraternal kiss;
Where mild PHILOSOPHY first taught to scan
The *wrongs* of Providence, and *rights* of MAN:
Where MEMORY broods o'er FREEDOM's earlier scene,
The *Lantern* bright, and brighter *Guillotine ;*
Three gentle swains evolve their longing arms,
And woo the young REPUBLIC's virgin charms;
And though proud BARRAS with the Fair succeed,
Though not in vain th' Attorney REWBELL plead,
Oft doth th' impartial nymph their love forgo,
To clasp thy crooked shoulders, blest LEPEAUX!

So, with dark dirge athwart the blasted heath,
Three SISTER WITCHES hail'd th' appall'd Macbeth.

So, the *Three* FATES beneath grim *Pluto's* roof,
Strain the dun warp, and weave the murky woof;
Till deadly ATROPOS with fatal shears
Slits the thin promise of th' expected years,
While midst the dungeon's gloom or battle's din,
Ambition's victims perish, as they spin.

Thus, the *Three* GRACES on the *Idalian* green
Bow with deft homage to *Cythera's* Queen;
Her polish'd arms with pearly bracelets deck,
Part her light locks, and bare her ivory neck;
Round her fair form ethereal odours throw,
And teach th' unconscious zephyrs where to blow;
Floats the thin gauze, and glittering as they play,
The bright folds flutter in phlogistic day.

So, with his daughters *Three*, th' unsceptred LEAR
Heaved the loud sigh, and pour'd the glistering tear:
His DAUGHTERS *Three*, save one alone, conspire
(Rich in *his* gifts) to spurn their generous sire;
Bid the rude storm his hoary tresses drench,
Stint the spare meal, the hundred knights retrench;
Mock his mad sorrow, and with alter'd mien
Renounce the daughter, and assert the queen.
A father's griefs his feeble frame convulse,
Rack his white head, and fire his feverous pulse;
Till kind CORDELIA soothes his soul to rest,
And folds the parent-monarch to her breast.

Thus some fair spinster grieves in wild affright,
Vex'd with dull megrim, or vertigo light;
Pleas'd round the fair *Three* dawdling doctors stand,
Wave the white wig, and stretch the asking hand,
State the grave doubt, the nauseous draught decree,
And all receive, tho' none deserve, a fee.

So down thy hill, romantic Ashbourn, glides
The DERBY *dilly*, carrying *Three* INSIDES.
One in each corner sits, and lolls at ease,
With folded arms, propt back, and outstretch'd knees;

While the press'd *Bodkin*, punch'd and squeez'd to
    death,
Sweats in the mid-most place, and pants for breath.

'Twas thine alone, O youth of giant frame,
ISOSCELES ! that rebel heart to tame !
In vain coy MATHESIS[1] thy presence flies:
Still turn her fond hallucinating eyes;
Thrills with *Galvanic* fires each tortuous nerve,
Throb her blue veins, and dies her cold reserve.
—Yet strives the Fair, till in the giant's breast
She sees the mutual passion flame confessed:
Where'er he moves, she sees his tall limbs trace
Internal Angles equal at the base;
Again she doubts him: but *produced at will,*
She sees *th' external Angles equal still.*

Say, blest Isosceles ! what favouring power,
Or love, or chance, at night's auspicious hour,
While to the *Asses'-Bridge* entranced you stray'd,
Led to the *Asses'-Bridge* th' enamour'd maid ?—
The *Asses'-Bridge*, for ages doom'd to hear
The deafening surge assault his wooden ear,
With joy repeats sweet sounds of mutual bliss,
The soft susurrant sigh, and gently-murmuring kiss.

So thy dark arches, LONDON *Bridge,* bestride
Indignant THAMES, and part his angry tide,
There oft—returning from those green retreats,
Where fair *Vauxhallia* decks her sylvan seats;—
Where each spruce nymph, from city compters free,
Sips the froth'd syllabub, or fragrant tea;
While with sliced ham, scraped beef, and burnt
    champagne,
Her 'prentice lover soothes his amorous pain;
There oft, in well-trimm'd wherry, glide along
Smart beaux and giggling belles, a glittering throng:
Smells the tarr'd rope—with undulation fine
Flaps the loose sail—the silken awnings shine;

[1] The doctrine of mathematics. Pope calls her *mad Mathesis.*—
Vide Johnson's Dictionary.

' Shoot we the bridge !' the venturous boatmen cry;
' Shoot we the bridge !' th' exulting fare reply.
—Down the steep fall the headlong waters go,
Curls the white foam, the breakers roar below.
The veering helm the dextrous steersman stops,
Shifts the thin oar, the fluttering canvas drops;
Then with closed eyes, clench'd hands, and quick-drawn
    breath,
Darts at the central arch, nor heeds the gulf beneath.
—Full 'gainst the pier the unsteady timbers knock,
The loose planks, starting, own the impetuous shock;
The shifted oar, dropp'd sail, and steadied helm,
With angry surge the closing waters whelm,
—Laughs the glad THAMES, and clasps each fair one's
    charms,
That screams and scrambles in his oozy arms.
—Drench'd each smart garb, and clogg'd each struggling
    limb,
Far o'er the stream the Cockneys sink or swim;
While each badged boatman, clinging to his oar,
Bounds o'er the buoyant wave, and climbs the applaud-
    ing shore.

So, towering ALP ! from thy majestic ridge
Young FREEDOM gazed on LODI's blood-stain'd *Bridge ;*
Saw, in thick throngs, conflicting armies rush,
Ranks close on ranks, and squadrons squadrons crush;
Burst in bright radiance through the battle's storm,
Waved her broad hands, display'd her awful form;
Bade at her feet regenerate nations bow,
And twin'd the wreath round Buonaparte's brow.
—Quick with new lights, fresh hopes, and alter'd zeal,
The slaves of despots dropp'd the blunted steel:
Exulting Victory crown'd her favourite child,
And freed LIGURIA clapp'd her hands, and smiled.

Nor long the time ere Britain's shores shall greet
The warrior-sage, with gratulation sweet:
Eager to grasp the wreath of naval fame,
The GREAT REPUBLIC plans the *Floating Frame !*
—O'er the huge frame gigantic TERROR stalks,
And counts with joy the close-compacted balks:

Of young-eyed MASSACRES the Cherub crew
Round their grim chief the mimic task pursue;
Turn the stiff screw,[1] apply the strengthening clamp,
Drive the long bolt, or fix the stubborn cramp,
Lash the reluctant beam, the cable splice,
Join the firm dove-tail with adjustment nice,
Thro' yawning fissures urge the willing wedge,
Or give the smoothing adze a sharper edge.
—Or group'd in fairy bands, with playful care,
The unconscious bullet to the furnace bear;—
Or gaily tittering, tip the match with fire,
Prime the big mortar, bid the shell aspire;
Applaud, with tiny hands, and laughing eyes,
And watch the bright destruction as it flies.

Now the fierce forges gleam with angry glare—
The windmill[2] waves his woven wings in air;
Swells the proud sail, the exulting streamers fly,
Their nimble fins unnumber'd paddles ply:
—Ye soft airs breathe, ye gentle billows waft,
And, fraught with Freedom, bear the expected RAFT!
Perch'd on her back, behold the Patriot train,
MUIR, ASHLEY, BARLOW, BUONAPARTE, PAINE!
While ROWAN's hand directs the blood-empurpled rein.

Ye IMPS of MURDER! guard her angel form,
Check the rude surge, and chase the hovering storm;
Shield from contusive rocks her timber limbs,
And guide the SWEET ENTHUSIAST[3] as she swims;

[1] The harmony and imagery of these lines are imperfectly imitated
from the following exquisite passage in the *Economy of Vegetation* :

' Gnomes, as you now dissect, with hammers fine,
The granite rock, the noduled flint calcine;
Grind with strong arm the circling Chertz betwixt,
Your pure ka—o—lins and Pe—tunt—ses mixt.'

                                        Canto 2, line 297.

[2] This line affords a striking instance of the sound conveying an
echo to the sense. I would defy the most unfeeling reader to repeat
it over without accompanying it by some corresponding gesture
imitative of the action described.

[3] A term usually applied in allegoric and technical poetry to any
person or object to which no other qualifications can be assigned.—
Chambers's Dictionary.

—And now, with web-foot oars, she gains the land,
And foreign footsteps press the yielding sand:
—The *Communes* spread, the gay *Departments* smile,
Fair *Freedom's Plant* o'ershades the laughing isle:
Fired with new hopes, the exulting peasant sees
The Gallic streamer woo the British breeze;
While, pleased to watch its undulating charms,
The smiling infant[1] spreads his little arms.

Ye Sylphs of DEATH! on demon pinions flit
Where the tall *Guillotine* is rais'd for PITT:
To the pois'd plank tie fast the monster's back,
Close the nice slider, ope the expectant sack;
Then twitch, with fairy hands, the frolic pin—
Down falls the impatient axe with deafening din;
The liberated head rolls off below,
And simpering FREEDOM hails the happy blow!

[1] Infancy is particularly interested in the diffusion of the new principles. See the 'Bloody Buoy.'   See also the following description and prediction:

> ' Here Time's huge fingers grasp his giant mace,
>   And dash proud Superstition from her base;
>   Rend her strong towers and gorgeous fanes,
>   &c.   &c.   &c.   &c.
> ' While each light moment, as it passes by,
>   With feathery foot and pleasure-twinkling eye,
>   Feeds from its baby-hand with many a kiss
>   The callow nestlings of domestic bliss.'
>   *Botanic Garden.*

GEORGE CANNING AND GEORGE ELLIS.

SONG BY ROGERO.

(GERMAN TRAGEDY)

WHENE'ER with haggard eyes I view
  This dungeon that I'm rotting in,
I think of those companions true
Who studied with me at the U-
    -niversity of Gottingen—
    -niversity of Gottingen.

> [*Weeps, and pulls out a blue 'kerchief, with which he
> wipes his eyes ; gazing tenderly at it, he proceeds.*]

Sweet 'kerchief, check'd with heavenly blue,
  Which once my love sat knotting in,
Alas, Matilda *then* was true,
At least I thought so at the U-
    -niversity of Gottingen—
    -niversity of Gottingen.

> [*At the repetition of this line* ROGERO *clanks his chains
> in cadence.*]

Barbs ! barbs ! alas ! how swift you flew,
  Her neat post-waggon trotting in !
Ye bore Matilda from my view;
Forlorn I languish'd at the U-
    -niversity of Gottingen—
    -niversity of Gottingen.

This faded form ! this pallid hue !
  This blood my veins is clotting in !
My years are many—They were few
When first I enter'd at the U-
    -niversity of Gottingen—
    -niversity of Gottingen.

There first for thee my passion grew,
  Sweet ! sweet Matilda Pottingen !

Thou wast the daughter of my tu-
-tor, Law Professor at the U-
    -niversity of Gottingen—
    -niversity of Gottingen.

Sun, moon, and thou vain world, adieu,
    That kings and priests are plotting in;
Here doom'd to starve on water gru-
-el never shall I see the U-
  ·   -niversity of Gottingen!—
    -niversity of Gottingen!

     [During the last stanza ROGERO *dashes his head re-*
      peatedly against the walls of his prison, and, finally,
      so hard as to produce a visible contusion.   He then
      throws himself on the floor in an agony.   The curtain
      drops—the music still continuing to play, till it is
      wholly fallen.]

JAMES HOGG.

WALSINGHAME'S SONG

FROM 'WAT O' THE CLEUCH.'

(SCOTT)

O HEARD ye never of Wat o' the Cleuch?
The lad that has worrying tikes enow,
Whose meat is the moss, and whose drink is the dew,
And that's the cheer of Wat o' the Cleuch!
   Wat o' the Cleuch! Wat o' the Cleuch!
   Woe's my heart for Wat o' the Cleuch!

Wat o' the Cleuch sat down to dine
With two pint stoups of good red wine;
But when he look'd they both were dry;
O poverty parts good company!
   Wat o' the Cleuch! Wat o' the Cleuch!
   O for a drink to Wat o' the Cleuch!

Wat o' the Cleuch came down the Tine
To woo a maid both gallant and fine;
But as he came o'er by Dick o' the Side
He smell'd the mutton and left the bride.
   Wat o' the Cleuch! Wat o' the Cleuch!
   What think ye now of Wat o' the Cleuch?

Wat o' the Cleuch came here to steal,
He wanted milk and he wanted veal;
But ere he wan o'er the Beetleston brow
He hough'd the calf and eated the cow!
   Wat o' the Cleuch! Wat o' the Cleuch!
   Well done, doughty Wat o' the Cleuch!

Wat o' the Cleuch came here to fight,
But his whittle was blunt and his nag took fright,
And the braggart he did what I dare not tell,
But changed his cheer at the back of the fell.
   Wat o' the Cleuch! Wat o' the Cleuch!
   O for a croudy to Wat o' the Cleuch!

Wat o' the Cleuch kneel'd down to pray,
He wist not what to do or to say;
But he pray'd for beef, and he pray'd for bree,
A two-hand spoon and a haggis to pree.
   Wat o' the Cleuch! Wat o' the Cleuch!
   That's the cheer for Wat o' the Cleuch!

But the devil is cunning as I heard say,
He knew his right, and haul'd him away;
And he's over the Border and over the heuch,
And off to hell with Wat o' the Cleuch!
   Wat o' the Cleuch! Wat o' the Cleuch!
   Lack-a-day for Wat o' the Cleuch!

But of all the wights in poor Scotland,
That ever drew bow or Border brand,
That ever drove English bullock or ewe,
There never was thief like Wat o' the Cleuch.
   Wat o' the Cleuch! Wat o' the Cleuch!
   Down for ever with Wat o' the Cleuch!

THE FLYING TAILOR.

Further Extract from 'The Recluse,' a Poem.

(WORDSWORTH)

If ever chance or choice thy footsteps lead
Into that green and flowery burial-ground
That compasseth with sweet and mournful smiles
The church of Grasmere,—by the eastern gate
Enter—and underneath a stunted yew,
Some three yards distant from the gravel-walk,
On the left-hand side, thou wilt espy a grave,
With unelaborate headstone beautified,
Conspicuous 'mid the other stoneless heaps
'Neath which the children of the valley lie.
There pause—and with no common feelings read
This short inscription—' Here lies buried
The Flying Tailor, aged twenty-nine!'

Him from his birth unto his death I knew,
And many years before he had attain'd
The fulness of his fame, I prophesied
The triumphs of that youth's agility,
And crown'd him with that name which afterwards
He nobly justified—and dying left
To fame's eternal blazon—read it here—
'The Flying Tailor !'

                    It is somewhat strange
That his mother was a cripple, and his father
Long way declined into the vale of years
When their son Hugh was born. At first the babe
Was sickly, and a smile was seen to pass
Across the midwife's cheek, when, holding up
The sickly wretch, she to the father said,
'A fine man-child !' What else could they expect ?
The mother being, as I said before,
A cripple, and the father of the child
Long way declined into the vale of years.

But mark the wondrous change—ere he was put
By his mother into breeches, Nature strung
The muscular part of his economy
To an unusual strength, and he could leap,
All unimpeded by his petticoats,
Over the stool on which his mother sat
When carding wool, or cleansing vegetables,
Or meek performing other household tasks.
Cunning he watch'd his opportunity,
And oft, as house-affairs did call her thence,
Overleapt Hugh, a perfect whirligig,
More than six inches o'er th' astonish'd stool.
What boots it to narrate, how at leap-frog
Over the breech'd and unbreech'd villagers ·
He shone conspicuous ? Leap-frog do I say ?
Vainly so named. What though in attitude
The Flying Tailor aped the croaking race
When issuing from the weed-entangled pool,
Tadpoles no more, they seek the new-mown fields,
A jocund people, bouncing to and fro
Amid the odorous clover—while amazed

The grasshopper sits idle on the stalk
With folded pinions and forgets to sing.
Frog-like, no doubt, in attitude he was;
But sure his bounds across the village green
Seem'd to my soul—(my soul for ever bright
With purest beams of sacred poesy)—
Like bounds of red-deer on the Highland hill,
When, close-environed by the tinchel's chain,
He lifts his branchy forehead to the sky,
Then o'er the many-headed multitude
Springs belling half in terror, half in rage,
And fleeter than the sunbeam or the wind
Speeds to his cloud-lair on the mountain-top.

No more of this—suffice it to narrate,
In his tenth year he was apprenticed
Unto a Master Tailor by a strong
And regular indenture of seven years,
Commencing from the date the parchment bore,
And ending on a certain day, that made
The term complete of seven solar years.
Oft have I heard him say, that at this time
Of life he was most wretched; for, constrain'd
To sit all day cross-legg'd upon a board,
The natural circulation of the blood
Thereby was oft impeded, and he felt
So numb'd at times, that when he strove to rise
Up from his work he could not, but fell back
Among the shreds and patches that bestrew'd
With various colours, brightening gorgeously,
The board all round him—patch of warlike red
With which he patched the regimental-suits
Of a recruiting military troop,
At that time stationed in a market town
At no great distance—eke of solemn black
Shreds of no little magnitude, with which
The parson's Sunday-coat was then repairing,
That in the new-roof'd church he might appear
With fitting dignity—and gravely fill
The sacred seat of pulpit eloquence,
Cheering with doctrinal point and words of faith
The poor man's heart, and from the shallow wit

Of atheist drying up each argument,
Or sharpening his own weapons only to turn
Their point against himself, and overthrow
His idols with the very enginery
Reared 'gainst the structure of our English Church.

Oft too, when striving all he could to finish
The stated daily task, the needle's point,
Slanting insidious from th' eluded stitch,
Hath pinched his finger, by the thimble's mail
In vain defended, and the crimson blood
Distain'd the lining of some wedding-suit;
A dismal omen! that to mind like his,
Apt to perceive in slightest circumstance
Mysterious meaning, yielded sore distress
And feverish perturbation, so that oft
He scarce could eat his dinner—nay, one night
He swore to run from his apprenticeship,
And go on board a first-rate man-of-war,
From Plymouth lately come to Liverpool,
Where, in the stir and tumult of a crew
Composed of many nations, 'mid the roar
Of wave and tempest, and the deadlier voice
Of battle, he might strive to mitigate
The fever that consumed his mighty heart.

But other doom was his. That very night
A troop of tumblers came into the village,
Tumbler, equestrian, mountebank,—on wire,
On rope, on horse, with cup and balls, intent
To please the gaping multitude, and win
The coin from labour's pocket—small perhaps
Each separate piece of money, but when join'd
Making a good round sum, destined ere long
All to be melted, (so these lawless folk
Name spending coin in loose debauchery)
Melted into ale—or haply stouter cheer,
Gin diuretic, or the liquid flame
Of baneful brandy, by the smuggler brought
From the French coast in shallop many-oar'd,
Skulking by night round headland and through bay,
Afraid of the King's cutter, or the barge

I

Of cruising frigate, arm'd with chosen men,
And with her sweeps across the foamy waves
Moving most beautiful with measured strokes.

It chanced that as he threw a somerset
Over three horses (each of larger size
Than our small mountain-breed) one of the troop
Put out his shoulder, and was otherwise
Considerably bruised, especially
About the loins and back. So he became
Useless unto that wandering company,
And likely to be felt a sore expense
To men just on the eve of bankruptcy,
So the master of the troop determined
To leave him in the workhouse, and proclaim'd
That if there was a man among the crowd
Willing to fill his place and able too,
Now was the time to show himself. Hugh Thwaites
Heard the proposal, as he stood apart
Striving with his own soul—and with a bound
He leapt into the circle, and agreed
To supply the place of him who had been hurt.
A shout of admiration and surprise
Then tore heaven's concave, and completely fill'd
The little field, where near a hundred people
Were standing in a circle round and fair.
Oft have I striven by meditative power,
And reason working 'mid the various forms
Of various occupations and professions,
To explain the cause of one phenomenon,
That, since the birth of science, hath remain'd
A bare enunciation, unexplain'd
By any theory, or mental light
Stream'd on it by the imaginative will,
Or spirit musing in the cloudy shrine,
The Penetralia of the immortal soul.
I now allude to that most curious fact,
That 'mid a given number, say threescore,
Of tailors, more men of agility
Will issue out, than from an equal show
From any other occupation—say
Smiths, barbers, bakers, butchers, or the like.

Let me not seem presumptuous, if I strive
This subject to illustrate; nor, while I give
My meditations to the world, will I
Conceal from it, that much I have to say
I learnt from one who knows the subject well
In theory and practice—need I name him ?
The light-heel'd author of the Isle of Palms,
Illustrious more for leaping than for song.

First, then, I would lay down this principle,
That all excessive action by the law
Of nature tends unto repose. This granted,
All action not excessive must partake
The nature of excessive action—so
That in all human beings who keep moving,
Unconscious cultivation of repose
Is going on in silence. Be it so.
Apply to men of sedentary lives
This leading principle, and we behold
That, active in their inactivity,
And unreposing in their long repose,
They are, in fact, the sole depositaries
Of all the energies by others wasted,
And come at last to teem with impulses
Of muscular motion, not to be withstood,
And either giving vent unto themselves
In numerous feats of wild agility,
Or terminating in despair and death.

Now, of all sedentary lives, none seems
So much so as the tailor's.—Weavers use
Both arms and legs, and, we may safely add,
Their bodies too, for arms and legs can't move
Without the body—as the waving branch
Of the green oak disturbs his glossy trunk.
Not so the Tailor—for he sits cross-legg'd,
Cross-legg'd for ever ! save at time of meals,
In bed, or when he takes his little walk
From shop to alehouse, picking, as he goes,
Stray patch of fustian, cloth, or cassimere,
Which, as by natural instinct, he discerns,

Though soil'd with mud, and by the passing wheel
Bruised to attenuation 'gainst the stones.

    Here then we pause—and need no farther go,
We have reach'd the sea-mark of our utmost sail.
Now let me trace the effect upon his mind
Of this despised profession. Deem not thou,
O rashly deem not, that his boyish days
Past at the shop-board, when the stripling bore
With bashful feeling of apprenticeship
The name of Tailor, deem not that his soul
Derived no genial influence from a life,
Which, although haply adverse in the main
To the growth of intellect, and the excursive power,
Yet in its ordinary forms possessed
A constant influence o'er his passing thoughts,
Moulded his appetences and his will,
And wrought out, by the work of sympathy,
Between his bodily and mental form,
Rare correspondence, wond'rous unity !
Perfect—complete—and fading not away.
While on his board cross-legg'd he used to sit,
Shaping of various garments, to his mind
An image rose of every character
For whom each special article was framed,
Coat, waistcoat, breeches. So at last his soul
Was like a storehouse, filled with images,
By musing hours of solitude supplied.
Nor did his ready fingers shape the cut
Of villager's uncouth habiliments
With greater readiness, than did his mind
Frame corresponding images of those
Whose corporal measurement the neat-mark'd paper
In many a mystic notch for ay retain'd.
Hence, more than any man I ever knew,
Did he possess the power intuitive
Of diving into character. A pair
Of breeches to his philosophic eye
Were not what unto other folks they seem,
Mere simple breeches, but in them he saw
The symbol of the soul—mysterious, high
Hieroglyphics ! such as Egypt's Priest

Adored upon the holy Pyramid,
Vainly imagined tomb of monarchs old,
But raised by wise philosophy, that sought
By darkness to illumine, and to spread
Knowledge by dim concealment—process high
Of man's imaginative, deathless soul.
Nor, haply, in th' abasement of the life
Which stern necessity had made his own,
Did he not recognise a genial power
Of soul-ennobling fortitude. He heard
Unmoved the witling's shallow contumely,
And thus, in spite of nature, by degrees
He saw a beauty and a majesty
In this despised trade, which warrior's brow
Hath rarely circled—so that when he sat
Beneath his sky-light window, he hath cast
A gaze of triumph on the godlike sun,
And felt that orb, in all his annual round,
Beheld no happier nobler character
Than him, Hugh Thwaites, a little tailor-boy.

Thus I, with no unprofitable song,
Have, in the silence of th' umbrageous wood,
Chaunted the heroic youthful attributes
Of him the Flying Tailor. Much remains
Of highest argument, to lute or lyre
Fit to be murmur'd with impassion'd voice;
And when, by timely supper and by sleep
Refresh'd, I turn me to the welcome task,
With lofty hopes,—Reader, do thou expect
The final termination of my lay.
For, mark my words,—eternally my name
Shall last on earth, conspicuous like a star
'Mid that bright galaxy of favour'd spirits,
Who, laugh'd at constantly whene'er they publish'd,
Survived the impotent scorn of base Reviews,
Monthly or Quarterly, or that accursed
Journal, the Edinburgh Review, that lives
On tears, and sighs, and groans, and brains, and blood.

THE CHERUB.

(COLERIDGE)

Was it not lovely to behold
A Cherub come down from the sky,
A beauteous thing of heavenly mould,
With ringlets of the wavy gold,
Dancing and floating curiously ?
To see it come down to the earth
This beauteous thing of heavenly birth !
Leaving the fields of balm and bliss,
To dwell in such a world as this !

   I heard a maiden sing the while,
A strain so holy, it might beguile
An angel from the radiant spheres,
That have swum in light ten thousand years;
Ten times ten thousand is too few—
Child of heaven, can this be true ?
And then I saw that beauteous thing
Slowly from the clouds descending,
Brightness, glory, beauty blending,
In the 'mid air hovering.
It had a halo round its head,
It was not of the rainbow's hue,
For in it was no shade of blue,
But a beam of amber mixed with red,
Like that which mingles in the ray
A little after the break of day.
Its raiment was the thousand dyes
Of flowers in the heavenly paradise;
Its track a beam of the sun refined,
And its chariot was the southern wind;
My heart danced in me with delight,
And my spirits mounted at the sight,
And I said within me it is well;
But where the bower, or peaceful dell,
Where this pure heavenly thing may dwell ?
Then I bethought me of the place,
To lodge the messenger of grace;

And I chose the ancient sycamore,
And the little green by Greta's shore;
It is a spot so passing fair,
That sainted thing might sojourn there.

Go tell yon stranger artisan,
Build as quickly as he can.
Heaven shield us from annoy!
What shall form this dome of joy?
The leaf of the rose would be too rude
For a thing that is not flesh and blood;
The walls must be of the sunny air,
And the roof the silvery gossamer,
And all the ceiling, round and round,
Wove half of light, and half of sound;
The sounds must be the tones that fly
From distant harp, just ere they die;
And the light the moon's soft midnight ray,
When the cloud is downy, and thin, and grey,
And such a bower of light and love,
Of beauty, and of harmonie,
In earth below, or heaven above,
No mortal thing shall ever see.

The dream is past, it is gone away!
The rose is blighted on the spray;
I look behind, I look before,
The happy vision is no more!
But in its room a darker shade
Than eye hath pierced, or darkness made;
I cannot turn, yet do not know,
What I would, or whither go;
But I have heard, to heart of sin,
A small voice whispering within,
'Tis all I know, and all I trust,—
'That man is weak, but God is just.'

ISABELLE.

(COLERIDGE)

Can there be a moon in heaven to-night,
That the hill and the grey cloud seem so light ?
The air is whiten'd by some spell,
For there is no moon, I know it well;
On this third day, the sages say,
('Tis wonderful how well they know,)
The moon is journeying far away,
Bright somewhere in a heaven below.

It is a strange and lovely night,
A greyish pale, but not white !
Is it rain, or is it dew,
That falls so thick I see its hue ?
In rays it follows, one, two, three,
Down the air so merrily,
Said Isabelle, so let it be !

Why does the Lady Isabelle
Sit in the damp and dewy dell
Counting the racks of drizzly rain,
And how often the Rail cries over again ?
For she's harping, harping in the brake,
Craik, craik—Craik, craik.
Ten times nine, and thrice eleven;—
That last call was an hundred and seven.
Craik, craik—the hour is near—
Let it come, I have no fear !
Yet it is a dreadful work, I wis,
Such doings in a night like this !

Sounds the river harsh and loud ?
The stream sounds harsh, but not loud.
There is a cloud that seems to hover,
By western hill the church-yard over,
What is it like ?—'Tis like a whale;
'Tis like a shark with half the tail,
Not half, but third and more;
Now 'tis a wolf, and now a boar;

Its face is raised—it cometh here;
Let it come—there is no fear.
There's two for heaven, and ten for hell,
Let it come—'tis well—'tis well!
Said the Lady Isabelle.

What ails that little cut-tail'd whelp,
That it continues to yelp, yelp?
Yelp, yelp, and it turns its eye
Up to the tree and half to the sky,
Half to the sky and full to the cloud,
And still it whines and barks aloud.
Why I should dread I cannot tell;
There is a spirit; I know it well!
I see it in yon falling beam—
Is it a vision, or a dream?
It is no dream, full well I know,
I have a woful deed to do!
Hush, hush, thou little murmurer;
I tell thee hush—the dead are near!

If thou knew'st all, poor tailless whelp,
Well might'st thou tremble, growl, and yelp;
But thou know'st nothing, hast no part,
(Simple and stupid as thou art)
Save gratitude and truth of heart.
But they are coming by this way
That have been dead for a year and a day;
Without challenge, without change,
They shall have their full revenge!
They have been sent to wander in woe
In the lands of flame, and the lands of snow;
But those that are dead
Shall the green sward tread,
And those that are living
Shall soon be dead!
None to pity them, none to help!
Thou may'st quake, my cut-tail'd whelp!

There are two from the grave
That I fain would save;
Full hard is the weird
For the young and the brave!

Perchance they are rapt in vision sweet,
While the passing breezes kiss their feet;
And they are dreaming of joy and love!—
Well, let them go—there's room above.

There are three times three, and three to these,
Count as you will, by twos or threes!
Three for the gallows, and three for the wave,
Three to roast behind the stone,
And three that shall never see the grave
Until the day and the hour are gone!
For retribution is mine alone!
The cloud is redder in its hue,
The hour is near, and vengeance due;
It cannot, and it will not fail,—
'Tis but a step to Borrowdale!
Why shouldst thou love and follow me,
Poor faithful thing? I pity thee!

Up rose the Lady Isabelle,
I may not of her motion tell,
Yet thou may'st look upon her frame;
Look on it with a passing eye,
But think not thou upon the same,
Turn away, and ask not why;
For if thou darest look again,
Mad of heart and seared of brain,
Thou shalt never look again!

What can ail that short-tail'd whelp?
'Tis either behind or far before,
And it hath changed its whining yelp
To a shorten'd yuff—its little core
Seems bursting with terror and dismay,
Yuff, yuff,—hear how it speeds away.
Hold thy peace, thou yemering thing,
The very night-wind's slumbering,
And thou wilt wake to woe and pain
Those that must never wake again.

Meet is its terror and its flight,
There's one on the left and two on the right!

But save the paleness of the face,
All is beauty, and all is grace !
The earth and air are tinged with blue;
There are no footsteps in the dew;
Is this to wandering spirits given,
Such stillness on the face of heaven ?
The fleecy clouds that sleep above,
Are like the wing of beauteous dove,
And the leaf of the elm-tree does not move!
Yet they are coming ! and they are three !
Jesu ! Maria ! can it be ?

THE CONCLUSION.

Sleep on, fair maiden of Borrowdale !
Sleep ! O sleep ! and do not wake !
Dream of the dance, till the foot so pale,
And the beauteous ancle shiver and shake;
Till thou shalt press, with feeling bland,
Thine own fair breast for lover's hand.
Thy heart is light as summer breeze,
Thy heart is joyous as the day;
Man never form of angel sees,
But thou art fair as they !
So lovers ween, and so they say,
So thine shall ween for many a day !
The hour's at hand, O woe is me !
For they are coming, and they are three !

THE CURSE OF THE LAUREATE.

(SOUTHEY)

CARMEN JUDICIALE.

I.

IN vale of Thirlemere, once on a time,
  When birds sung sweet and flowers were in the
    spring,
While youth and fancy wanton'd in their prime,
  I laid me down in happy slumbering;
The heavens in balmy breezes breathed deep,
My senses all were lull'd in grateful, joyous sleep.

II.

Sleep had its visions—fancy all unsway'd
  Revelled in fulness of creative power:
I ween'd that round me countless beings stray'd,
  Things of delight, illusions of an hour;
So great the number of these things divine,
Scarce could my heart believe that all the imps were
    mine.

III.

Yet mine they were, all motley as they moved;
  Careless I viewed them, yet I loved to view;
The world beheld them, and the world approved,
  And blest the train with smiles and plaudits due:
Proud of approval, to myself I said,
From out the group I'll chuse, and breed one favourite
    maid.

IV.

Joan I chose, a maid of happy mien;
  Her form and mind I polished with care;
A docile girl she proved, of moping vein,
  Slow in her motions, haughty in her air;
Some mention'd trivial blame, or slightly frown'd;
Forth to the world she went, her heavenly birth it
    own'd.

V.

The next, a son, I bred a Mussulman;
  With creeds and dogmas I was hard bested,
For which was right or wrong I could not tell,
  So I resolved my offspring should be bred
As various as their lives—the lad I loved,
A boy of wild unearthly mien he proved.

VI.

Then first I noted in my mazy dream
  A being scarcely of the human frame,
A tiny thing that from the north did seem,
  With swaggering, fuming impotence he came;
I fled not, but I shudder'd at his look;
Into his tutelage my boy he took.

VII.

Each principle of truth and purity,
  And all that merited the world's acclaim,
This fiend misled—nor could I ever free
  From his destroying grasp my darling's fame;
But yet I could not ween that heart of gall
Could be a foe to one, whose heart beat kind to all.

VIII.

My third, a Christian and a warrior true,
  A bold adventurer on foreign soil,
And next, his brother, a supreme Hindu,
  I rear'd with hope, with joy, and painful toil.
Alas! my hopes were vain! I saw them both
Reft by an emmet!—crush'd before a moth! *

IX.

Still could I not believe his vengeful spite,
  For in his guise a speciousness appear'd;
My bitterness of heart I feigned light;
  But wholly as he urged my next I reared;
He said of all the gang he was the best,
And wrung his neck before mine eyes in jest.

X.

From that time forth, an independent look,
  A bold effrontery I did essay;
But of my progeny no pains I took,
  Like lambs I rear'd them for the lion's prey;
And still as playful forth they pass'd from me,
I saw them mock'd and butcher'd wantonly.

XI.

' Just heaven !' said I, ' to thy awards I bow,
  For truth and vengeance are thine own alone;
Are these the wreaths thou deignest to bestow
  On bard, whose life and lays to virtue prone,
Have never turn'd aside on devious way ?
Is this the high reward, to be of fools the prey ?'

XII.

A laugh of scorn the welkin seem'd to rend,
   And by my side I saw a form serene;
' Thou bard of honour, virtue's firmest friend,'
   He said, ' can'st thou thus fret ? or dost thou ween
That such a thing can work thy fame's decay ?
Thou art no fading bloom—no flow'ret of a day !

XIII.

' When his o'erflowings of envenom'd spleen
   An undistinguish'd dunghill mass shall lie,
The name of SOUTHEY, like an evergreen,
   Shall spread, shall blow, and flourish to the sky;
To Milton and to Spenser next in fame,
,O'er all the world shall spread thy laurell'd name.'

XIV.

' Friend of the bard,' I said, ' behold thou hast
   The tears of one I love o'er blushes shed;
Has he not wrung the throb from parent's heart,
   And stretch'd his hand to reave my children's bread ?
For every tear that on their cheeks hath shone,
O may that Aristarch with tears of blood atone !'

XV.

' If cursing thou delight'st in,' he replied,
   ' If rage and execration is thy meed,
Mount the tribunal—Justice be thy guide,
   Before thee shall he come his rights to plead;
To thy awards his fate forthwith is given,
Only, be justice thine, the attribute of heaven.'

XVI.

Gladly I mounted, for before that time
   Merit had crown'd me with unfading bays.
Before me was brought in that man of crime,
   Who with unblushing front his face did raise;
But when my royal laurel met his sight,
He pointed with his thumb, and laughed with all his
    might.

XVII.

Maddening at impudence so thorough-bred,
　I rose from off my seat with frown severe,
I shook my regal sceptre o'er his head—
　' Hear, culprit, of thy crimes, and sentence hear !
Thou void of principle ! of rule ! of ruth !
Thou renegade from nature and from truth !

XVIII.

' Thou bane of genius !—party's sordid slave !
　Mistaken, perverse, crooked is thy mind !
No humble son of merit thou wilt save,
　Truth, virtue, ne'er from thee did friendship find;
And while of freedom thou canst fume and rave,
Of titles, party, wealth, thou art the cringing slave !

XIX.

' Thou hast renounced Nature for thy guide,
　A thousand times hast given thyself the lie,
And raised thy party-curs to wealth and pride,
　The very scavengers of poetry.
Thy quibbles are from ray of sense exempt,
Presumptuous, pitiful, below contempt !

XX.

' Answer me, viper ! here do I arraign
　Thy arrogant, self-crowned majesty !
Hast thou not prophesied of dole and pain,
　Weakening the arms of nations and of me ?
Thou foe of order !—Mercy lingers sick—
False prophet ! Canker ! Damned heretic !'

XXI.

Then pointing with my sceptre to the sky,
　With vehemence that might not be restrain'd,
I gave the awful curse of destiny !
　I was asleep, but sore with passion pain'd.
It was a dreadful curse; and to this day,
Even from my waking dreams it is not worn away.

The Curse.

May heaven and earth,
And hell underneath,
Unite to ensting thee
In horrible wrath.
May scorning surround thee,
And conscience astound thee,
High genius o'erpower,
And the devil confound thee.
The curse be upon thee
In pen and in pocket,
Thy ink turn to puddle,
And gorge in the socket;
Thy study let rats destroy,
Vermin and cats annoy,
Thy base lucubrations
To tear and to gnaw,
Thy false calculations
In Empire and Law.
The printers shall harass,
The devils shall dun thee,
The trade shall despise thee,
And C—t—e shun thee.
The judge shall not hear thee,
But frown and pass by thee,
And clients shall fear thee,
And know thee, and fly thee!
I'll hunt thee, I'll chase thee,
To scorn and deride thee,
The cloud shall not cover,
The cave shall not hide thee;
The scorching of wrath
And of shame shall abide thee,
Till the herbs of the desert
Shall wither beside thee.
Thou shalt thirst for revenge
And misrule, as for wine,
But genius shall flourish!
And royalty shine!
And thou shalt remain

While the Laureate doth reign,
With a fire in thy heart,
And a fire in thy brain,
And Fame shall disown thee
And visit thee never,
And the curse shall be on thee
For ever and ever!

THE GUDE GREYE KATT.

(JAMES HOGG)

THERE wase ane katt, and ane gude greye katt,
　　That duallit in the touir of Blain,
And mony haif hearit of that gude katt,
　　That neuir shall heare agayn.

Scho had ane brynd upon her backe,
　　And ane brent abone hir bree;
Hir culoris war the merilit heuis
　　That dappil the krene-berrye.

But scho had that withyn her ee
　　That man may neuir declaire,
For scho had that withyn hir ee
　　Quhich mortyl dochtna beare.

Sumtymis ane ladye sochte the touir,
　　Of rych and fayre beautye:
Sumtymis ane maukyn cam therin,
　　Hytchyng rycht wistfullye.

But quhan they serchit the touir of Blain,
　　And socht it sayre and lang,
They fande nocht but the gude greye katt
　　Sittyng thrummyng at hir sang;

And up scho rase and pacit hir wayis
　　Full stetlye oure the stene,
And streikit out hir braw hint-leg,
　　As nocht at all had bene.

K

Weil mocht the wyfis in that kintrye
    Rayse up ane grefous stir,
For neuir ane katt in all the lande
    Durst moop or melle wyth hir.

Quhaneuir theye lukit in hir fece
    Their fearis greue se ryfe,
Theye snirtit and theye yollit throu frychte,
    And rann for dethe and lyfe.

The lairde of Blain he had ane spouis,
    Beth cumlye, gude, and kynde;
But scho had gane to the landis of pece,
    And left him sadd behynde;

He had seuin dochteris all se fayre,
    Of mayre than yerdlye grece,
Seuin bonnyer babis neuir braithit ayre,
    Or smylit in parentis fece.

Ane daye quhan theye war all alane,
    He sayde with hevye mene ;
' Quhat will cum of ye, my deire babis,
    Now quhan your moderis gene ?

' O quha will leide your tendyr myndis,
    The pethe of ladyhoode,
To thynke as ladye ocht to thynke,
    And feele as mayden sholde ?

' Weil mot it kythe in maydenis mynde,
    And maydenis modestye,
The want of hir that weil wase fit
    For taske unmeite for me !'

But up then spak the gude greye katt
    That satt on the herthe stene,
' O hald yer tung, my deire maister,
    Nor mak se sayre ane mene;

' For I will breide your seuin dochteris,
  To winsum ladyhoode,
To thynke as ladyis ocht to thynke,
  And feile as maydenis sholde.

' I'll breide them fayre, I'll breide them free
  From every seye of syn,
Fayre as the blumyng roz withoute,
  And pure in herte withyn.'

Rychte sayre astoundit wase the lairde,
  Ane frychtenit man wase he;
But the sueite babyis war full faine,
  And chicklit joyfullye.

May Ella tooke the gude greye katt
  Rychte fondlye on hir knee,
' And hethe my pussye lernit to speike ?
  I troue scho lernit of me.'

The katt, scho thrummyt at hir sang,
  And turnit hir haffet sleike,
And drewe hir bonnye bassenyt side,
  Againste the babyis cheike.

But the lairde he was ane cunnyng lairde,
  And he saide with speechis fayre,
' I haif a feste in hall to nychte,
  Sweite pussye, be you there.'

The katt scho set ane luke on him,
  That turnit his herte til stene;
' If you haif feste in hall to nychte,
  I shall be there for ane.'

The feste wase laide, the tabil spread
  With rych and nobil store,
And there wase set the Byschope of Blain,
  With all his holy kore;

He wase ane wyce and wylie wychte
    Of wytch and warlockrye,
And mony ane wyfe had byrnit to coome,
    Or hangit on ane tre.

He kenit their merkis and molis of hell,
    And made them joifully
Ryde on the reid-het gad of ern,
    Ane pleasaunt sycht to se.

The Byschope said ane holye grace,
    Unpatiente to begyn,
But nathyng of the gude greye katt
    Wase funde the touir withyn;

But in there cam ane fayre ſadye,
    Cledd in the silken sheene,
Ane winsumer and bonnyer may
    On yerde was neuir seene;

Scho tuke her sete at tabil heide,
    With courtlye modestye,
Quhill ilken bosome byrnit with lufe
    And waulit ilken ee.

Sueite wase hir voyce to all the ryng,
    Unlesse the Lairde of Blain,
For he had hearit that very voyce,
    From off his own herthe stene.

He barrit the doris and windois fast,
    He barrit them to the jynne;
'Now in the grece of heuin,' said he,
    'Your excercyse begyn;

'There is no grece nor happynesse
    For my poor babyis soulis
Until you trye that weirdlye wytch,
    And roste hir on the colis.

'If this be scho,' the Byschope saide,
    'This beauteous cumlye may,
It is meite I try hir all alone
    To heire quhat scho will saye.'

'No,' quod the Lairde, 'I suthelye sweire
    None shall from this proceide,
Until I see that wycked wytch
    Byrnt til ane izel reide.'

The Byschope knelit doune and prayit,
    Quhill all their hayris did creipe;
And aye he hoonit and he prayit,
    Quhill all war faste asleipe;

He prayit gain syn and Sauten bothe,
    And deidis of shyft and schame;
But all the tyme his faithful handis
    Pressit the cumlye dame.

Weil saw the Lairde, but nething saide,
    He kenit, in holye zele,
He grepit for the merkis of hell,
    Whilk he did ken ful weile.

And aye he pressit hir lillye hande,
    And kyssit it ferventlye,
And prayit betweine, for och ane kynde
    And lufyng preste was he!

The Byschope stappit and sterted sore,
    Wyde gaipen with affrychte,
For och that fayre and lillye hande
    Had turned ane paw outrychte!

Ane paw with long and crukit clawis!
    That breste of heuinlye charme
Had turnit til brusket of ane katt,
    Ful hayrie and ful warme!

And there scho satt on lang-settil,
    With een of glentyng flame,
And theye war on the Byschope sett
    Lyke poynter on his game.

The Byschope turnit him runde aboute
    To se quhat he mocht se,
Scho strak ane clawe in ilken lug,
    And throu the rofe did flee.

The katt went throu withouten stop
    Lyke schado throu the daye,
But the great Byschopis fleschlye forme
    Made all the rofe gif waye;

The silyng faldit lyke ane buke,
    The serker crashit amayne,
And shredis and flenis of brokyn stenis
    Fell to the grunde lyke rayne.

The braide ful mone wase up the lyft,
    The nychte wase lyke ane daye,
As the greate Byschope tuke his jante
    Up throu the milkye-waye;

He cryit se loude and lustilye
    The hillis and skyis war riuen;
Och sicken cryis war neuir hearit
    Atwene the yerde and heuin !

They sawe him spurryng in the ayre,
    And flynging horredlye,
And than he prayit and sang ane saum,
    For ane fearit wycht was he;

But ay his waylingis fainter greue
    As the braide lyft he crossit,
Quhill sum saide that theye hearit them still,
    And sum saide all wase loste.

There was ane herd on Dollar-Lawe,
    Turnyng his flockis by nychte,
Or stealyng in ane gude haggyse
    Before the mornyng lychte.

He hearit the cryis cum yont the heuin,
    And sawe them bethe passe bye;
The katt scho skreuit up hir taile
    As sayrlye pinchit to flye.

But aye scho thrummyt at hir sang,
    Though he wase sore in thrall,
Like katt that hethe ane jollye mouse
    Gaun murryng thro' the hall.

That greye kattis sang it wase se sweete,
    As on the nychte it fell,
The Murecokis dancit ane seuinsum ryng
    Arunde the hether bell;

The Foumartis jyggit by the brukis,
    The Maukinis by the kaile,
And the Otar dancit ane minowaye
    As he gaed ouir the daile;

The Hurchanis helde ane kintrye dance
    Alang the brumye knowe,
And the gude Toop-hogg rase fra his layre
    And ualtzit with the youe.

The Greye Kattis Sang.

    Murr, my Lorde Byschope,
        I syng to you;
    Murr, my Lorde Byschope,
        Bawlillilu !
    Murr, my Lorde Byschope, &c.

That nycht ane hynde on Border syde
    Chancit at his dore to be;
He spyit ane greate clypse of the mone,
    And ben the house ran he;

He laide ane wisp upon the colis,
    And bleue full lang and sayre,
And rede the Belfaste Almanake,
    But the clypse it wase not there.

Och but that hynde wase sor aghaste,
    And haf to madnesse driuen,
For he thochte he hearit ane drounyng man
    Syching alangis the heuin.

That nychte ane greate Filossofere
    Had watchit on Etnyis height,
To merk the rysing of the sonne,
    And the blythsum mornyng lychte;

And all the lychtlyo lynis of goude,
    As on the se they fell,
And watch the fyir and the smoke,
    Cum rummilyng up fra hell.

He luket este, the daye cam on,
    Upon his gladsum pethe,
And the braid mone hang in the west,
    Her paleness wase lyke dethe;

And by her sat ane littil stern,
    Quhan all the laife war gane,
It was lyke ane wee fadyng geme
    In the wyde worild its lane.

Then the Filossofere was sadde,
    And he turnit his ee awaye,
For they mindit him of the yerdlye greate,
    In dethe or in decaye·

He turnit his face unto the north,
    The fallyng teare to drie,
And he spyit ane thyng of wonderous maike,
    Atwene the yerde and skie;

It wase lyke ane burd withoutten wyng,
    Rychte wonderous to beholde,
And it bure ane forked thyng alang,
    With swiftnesse manyfolde:

But ay it greue as neare it dreue—
    His herte bete wondir sayre !
The sonne, the mone, and sternis war gaine,
    He thocht of them ne mayre,
Quhan he behelde ane jollye preste
    Cumyng swyggyng throu the ayre.

The katt scho helde him by the luggis
    Atour the ausum hole,
And och the drede that he wase in
    Wase mayre than man colde thole;

He cryit, ' O Pussye, hald your gryp,
    O hald and dinna spaire;
O drap me in the yerde or se,
    But dinna drap me there.'

But scho wase ane doure and deidlye katt,
    And scho saide with lychtsum ayre,
' You kno heuin is ane blissit plece,
    And all the prestis gang there.'

' Och sweete, sweete Pussye, hald your gryp,
    Spaire nouther cleke nor clawe;
Is euir that lyke heuin abone,
    In quhich am lyke to fa' ?'

And aye scho hang him by the luggis
    Abone the ausum den,
Till he fande the gryp rive slowlye out,
    Sore was he quakyng then !

Doune went the Byschope, doune lyke leide
    Into the hollowe nychte,
His goune wase flapyng in the ayre,
    Quhan he wase out of sychte.

They hearit him honyng down the deep,
   Till the croone it dyit awaye,
It wase lyke the stoune of ane greate bom-be
   Gaun soundyng throu the daye.

All wase in sloomeryng quietnesse,
   Quhan he went doune to hell,
But seckn an houre wase neuir seine,
   Quhan the gude lorde Byschope fell.

Then cam the smouder and the smoke
   Up roschyng vilentlye,
And it tourackit awaye til heuin
   Ane gloryous sychte to se;

For ay it rowed its fleecye curlis
   Out to the rysing sonne,
And the estern syde was gildit goude,
   And all the westlin dunne.

Then the Filossofere wase muvit,
   And he wist not quhat til say,
For he saw nochte of the gude greye katt;
   But he saw ane ladye gay.

Hir goune wase of the gress-greene sylk,
   And hir ee wase lyke the deue,
And hir hayre wase lyke the threidis of goude
   That runde her shoulderis fleue.

Hir gairtenis war the raynbowis heme,
   That scho tyit anethe hir knee,
And ay scho kemit hir yellow hayre,
   And sang full pleasauntlye.

' I am the Queene of the Fairy Land,
   I'll do ne harme to thee,
For I am the gardian of the gude,
   Let the wycked be ware of me.

'There ar seuin pearlis in yonder touir,
    Their number sune shall wane;
There are seuin flouris in fayre Scotland,
    I'll pu them ane by ane;

' And the weeist burd in all the bouir
    Shall be the last that is taene;
The Lairde of Blain hethe seuin dochteris,
    But sune he shall haif nane.

' I'll bathe them all in the krystal streime
    Throu the Fairy Land that flouis,
I'll seike the bouris of paradyce
    For the bonnyest flouir that blouis.

' And I'll distil it in the deue
    That fallis on the hillis of heuin,
And the hues that luvelye angelis weire
    Shall to these maidis be giuen.

' And I'll trie how luvelye and how fayre
    Their formis may be to see,
And I'll trie how pure the maydenis mynde
    In this ill worild may be.'

The Lairde of Blain he walkis the wode,
    But he walkis it all alane;
The Lairde of Blain had seuin dochteris,
    But now he hethe not ane.

They neuir war on dethbed layde,
    But they elyit all awaye;
He lost his babyis ane by ane
    Atween the nychte and day.

He kend not quhat to thynk or saye,
    Or quhat did him beseime,
But he walkit throu this weirye worild
    Lyke ane that is in a dreime.

Quhan seuin lang yearis, and seuin lang daies,
    Had slowlye cumit and gane,
He walkit throu the gude grene wode,
    And he walkit all alane;

He turnit his fece unto the skie,
    And the teire stude in his ee,
For he thocht of the ladye of his lufe,
    And his lost familye:

But aye his fayth was firm and sure,
    And his trust in Heuin still,
For he hopet to meite them all agayne
    Beyond the reiche of ill:

And ay the teiris fell on the grene,
    As he knelit downe to praye,
But he wase se muvit with tendirnesse
    That ane worde he colde not saye.

He lukit oure his left shouldir
    To se quhat he mocht se:
There he behelde seuin bonnye maydis
    Cumyng tryppyng oure the le !

Sic beautye ee had neuir seine,
    Nor euir agayne shall se,
Sic luvelye formis of flesche and blude,
    On yerde can neuir be;

The joie that bemit in ilken ee
    Wase lyke the risyng sonne,
The fayriste blumis in all the wode
    Besyde their formis war dunne;

There wase ane wrethe on ilken heide,
    On ilken bosome thre,
And the brychtest flouris the worild e'er saw
    War noddyng oure the bre.

But cese yer strayne, my gude auld herpe,
    O cese and syng ne mayre !
Gin ye wolde of that meityng tell,
    O I mocht reue it sayre !

There wolde ne ee in faire Scotland,
    Nor luvelye cheike be drie;
The laveroke wolde forget hir sang,
    And drap deide fra the skie;

And the desye wolde ne mayre be quhyte,
    And the lillye wolde chainge hir heue,
For the blude-drapis wolde fal fra the mone,
    And reiden the mornyng deue.

But quhan I tell ye oute my tale,
    Ful playnlye ye will se,
That quhare there is ne syn nor schame
    Ne sorroue there can be.

SAMUEL TAYLOR COLERIDGE.

SONNETS ATTEMPTED IN THE MANNER OF CON-
TEMPORARY WRITERS.

(COLERIDGE, LAMB, AND CHARLES LLOYD)

I.

PENSIVE at eve on the *hard* world I mus'd,
And *my poor* heart was sad: so at the Moon
I gaz'd—and sigh'd, and sigh'd!—for, ah! how soon
Eve darkens into night. ' Mine eye perus'd
With tearful vacancy the *dampy* grass
Which wept and glitter'd in the *paly* ray;
And *I did pause me* on my lonely way,
And *mused me* on those *wretched ones* who pass
O'er the black heath of Sorrow.' But, alas!
Most of *Myself* I thought: when it befell
That the *sooth* Spirit of the breezy wood
Breath'd in mine ear—' All this is very well;
But much of *one* thing is for *no* thing good.'
Ah! my *poor heart's* INEXPLICABLE SWELL!

II.

To Simplicity.

O! I do love thee, meek *Simplicity!*
For of thy lays the lulling simpleness
Goes to my heart and soothes each small distress,
Distress though small, yet haply great to me!
'Tis true on Lady Fortune's gentlest pad
I amble on; yet, though I know not why,
So sad I am!—but should a friend and I
Grow cool and *miff,* O! I am *very* sad!
And then with sonnets and with sympathy
My dreamy bosom's mystic woes I pall;
Now of my false friend plaining plaintively,
Now raving at mankind in general;
But, whether sad or fierce, 'tis simple all,
All very simple, meek Simplicity!

III.

On a Ruined House in a Romantic Country.

AND this reft house is that the which he built,
Lamented Jack ! And here his malt he pil'd,
Cautious in vain ! These rats that squeak so wild,
Squeak, not unconscious of their father's guilt.
Did ye not see her gleaming thro' the glade ?
Belike, 'twas she, the maiden all forlorn.
What though she milk no cow with crumpled horn,
Yet *aye* she haunts the dale where *erst* she stray'd;
And *aye* beside her stalks her amorous knight !
Still on his thighs their wonted brogues are worn,
And thro' those brogues, still tatter'd and betorn,
His hindward charms gleam an unearthly white;
As when thro' broken clouds at night's high noon
Peeps in fair fragments forth the full-orb'd harvest
    moon !

ROBERT SOUTHEY.

THE AMATORY POEMS OF ABEL SHUFFLEBOTTOM.
(THE DELLA CRUSCANS)

SONNET I.
Delia at Play.

SHE held a *Cup and Ball* of ivory white,
Less white the ivory than her *snowy* hand!
Enrapt, I watch'd her from my secret stand,
As now, intent, in *innocent* delight,
Her *taper* fingers twirl'd the giddy ball,
Now tost it, following still with EAGLE *sight*,
Now on the pointed end *infix'd* its fall.
Marking her sport I mused, and musing sigh'd,
Methought the BALL she play'd with was my HEART;
(Alas! that sport like *that* should be her pride!)
And the *keen point* which steadfast still she eyed
Wherewith to pierce it, that was CUPID's *dart;*
Shall I not then the cruel Fair condemn
Who *on that dart* IMPALES *my* BOSOM'S GEM?

SONNET II.
To a Painter attempting Delia's Portrait.

RASH Painter! canst thou give the ORB OF DAY
In all its noontide glory? or portray
The DIAMOND, that athwart the *taper'd* hall
Flings the rich flashes of its dazzling light?
Even if thine art could boast such *magic might,*
Yet if it strove to paint *my Angel's* EYE,
Here it perforce must fail. Cease! lest I call
Heaven's vengeance on thy sin: Must thou be told
The CRIME *it is to paint* DIVINITY?
Rash Painter! should the world her charms behold,
Dim and defiled, as there they needs must be,
They to their *old idolatry* would fall,
And bend before her form the *pagan* knee,
Fairer than VENUS, DAUGHTER OF THE SEA.

SONNET III.

He proves the Existence of a Soul from his Love for Delia.

SOME have denied a soul ! THEY NEVER LOVED.
Far from my Delia now by fate removed,
At home, abroad, I view her everywhere;
Her ONLY in the FLOOD OF NOON I see,
My *Goddess-Maid*, my OMNIPRESENT FAIR,
For LOVE *annihilates the world to me !*
And when the weary SOL *around his bed
Closes the* SABLE CURTAINS *of the night,*
SUN OF MY SLUMBERS, on my dazzled sight
SHE shines confest. When *every sound is dead,*
The SPIRIT OF HER VOICE comes then to *roll*
The *surge of music* o'er my wavy brain.
Far, far from her my *Body* drags its chain,
But sure with Delia *I exist* A SOUL !

SONNET IV.

*The Poet expresses his Feelings respecting a Portrait in
Delia's Parlour.*

I WOULD I were that portly gentleman
With gold-laced hat and golden-headed cane,
Who hangs in Delia's parlour ! For whene'er
From books or needlework her looks arise,
On him *converge the* SUNBEAMS *of her eyes,*
And he *unblamed* may gaze upon MY FAIR,
And oft MY FAIR his *favour'd* form surveys.
O HAPPY PICTURE ! still on HER to gaze;
I envy him ! and jealous fear alarms,
Lest the STRONG *glance* of those *divinest* charms
WARM HIM TO LIFE, as in the ancient days,
When MARBLE MELTED in Pygmalion's arms.
I would I were that portly gentleman
With gold-laced hat and golden-headed cane.

LOVE ELEGIES.

ELEGY I.

The Poet relates how he obtained Delia's Pocket-hand-kerchief.

'TIS mine ! what accents can my joy declare ?
  Blest be the pressure of the thronging rout !
Blest be the hand so hasty of my fair,
  That left the *tempting corner* hanging out !

I envy not the joy the pilgrim feels,
  After long travel to some distant shrine,
When at the relic of his saint he kneels,
  For Delia's POCKET-HANDKERCHIEF IS MINE.

When first with *filching fingers* I drew near,
  Keen hope shot tremulous through every vein;
And when the *finish'd deed* removed my fear,
  Scarce could my bounding heart its joy contain.

What though the Eighth Commandment rose to mind,
  It only served a moment's qualm to move;
For thefts like this it could not be design'd,
  The Eighth Commandment WAS NOT MADE FOR
    LOVE !

Here when she took the macaroons from me,
  She wiped her mouth to clean the crumbs so sweet !
Dear napkin ! yes, she wiped her lips in thee !
  Lips *sweeter* than the *macaroons* she eat.

And when she took that pinch of Mocabaw,
  That made my Love so *delicately* sneeze,
Thee to her Roman nose applied I saw,
  And thou art doubly dear for things like these.

No washerwoman's filthy hand shall e'er,
  SWEET POCKET-HANDKERCHIEF ! thy worth pro-
    fane;
For thou hast touch'd the *rubies* of my fair,
  And I will kiss thee o'er and o'er again.

ELEGY II.

The Poet invokes the Spirits of the Elements to approach
Delia.—He describes Her Singing.

YE SYLPHS, who *banquet* on my Delia's blush,
　Who on her locks of FLOATING GOLD repose,
Dip in her cheek your GOSSAMERY BRUSH,
　And with its bloom of beauty *tinge* THE ROSE.

Hover around her lips on *rainbow wing*,
　Load from her honey'd breath your *viewless* feet,
Bear thence a richer fragrance for the Spring
　And make the lily and the violet sweet.

Ye GNOMES, whose toil through many a dateless year
　Its nurture to the infant gem supplies,
From central caverns bring your diamonds here,
　To *ripen in the sun* OF DELIA'S EYES.

And ye who bathe in Etna's lava springs,
　Spirits of fire ! to see my love advance;
Fly, SALAMANDERS, on ASBESTOS' wings,
　To wanton in my Delia's *fiery* glance.

She weeps, she weeps ! her eye with anguish swells,
　Some tale of sorrow melts my FEELING GIRL !
NYMPHS ! catch the tears, and in your lucid shells
　Enclose them, EMBRYOS OF THE ORIENT PEARL.

She sings ! the Nightingale with envy hears,
　The CHERUB listens from his starry throne,
And motionless are stopt the attentive SPHERES,
　To hear *more heavenly music* than their own.

Cease, Delia, cease ! for all the ANGEL THRONG,
　Hearkening to thee, let sleep their golden wires !
Cease, Delia, cease, that *too surpassing* song,
　Lest, *stung to envy*, they should break their lyres.

Cease, ere my senses are to madness driven
　By the strong joy ! Cease, Delia, lest my soul,
Enrapt, already THINK ITSELF IN HEAVEN,
　And burst the feeble Body's frail control.

ELEGY III.

The Poet Expatiates on the Beauty of Delia's Hair.

THE comb between whose ivory teeth she strains
  The straitening curls of gold so *beamy bright,*
Not spotless merely from the touch remains,
  But issues forth *more pure,* more *milky white.*

The rose-pomatum that the FRISEUR spreads
  Sometimes with honour'd fingers for my fair,
No added perfume on her tresses sheds,
  But borrows sweetness from her sweeter hair.

Happy the FRISEUR who in Delia's hair
  With licensed fingers uncontrol'd may rove !
And happy in his death the DANCING BEAR,
  Who died to make pomatum for my LOVE.

Oh could I hope that e'er my favour'd lays
  Might *curl those lovely locks* with conscious pride,
Nor Hammond, nor the Mantuan Shepherd's praise,
  I'd envy them, nor wish reward beside.

Cupid has strung from you, O tresses fine,
  The bow that in my breast impell'd his dart;
From you, sweet locks ! he wove the subtile line
  Wherewith the urchin *angled for* MY HEART.

Fine are my Delia's tresses as the threads
  That from the silk-worm, *self-interr'd,* proceed;
Fine as the GLEAMY GOSSAMER that spreads
  Its filmy web-work o'er the tangled mead.

Yet with these tresses Cupid's power elate
  My captive *heart* has *handcuff'd* in a chain,
Strong as the cables of some huge first-rate,
  THAT BEARS BRITANNIA'S THUNDERS O'ER THE MAIN.

The SYLPHS that round her radiant locks repair
  In *flowing lustre* bathe their brightening wings;
And ELFIN MINSTRELS with assiduous care
  The ringlets rob for FAERY FIDDLE-STRINGS.

ELEGY IV.

The Poet relates how he stole a Lock of Delia's Hair,
and her Anger.

OH ! be the day accurst that gave me birth !
  Ye Seas, to swallow me in kindness rise !
Fall on me, Mountains ! and thou merciful Earth,
  Open, and hide me from my Delia's eyes !

Let universal Chaos now return,
  Now let the central fires their prison burst,
AND EARTH AND HEAVEN AND AIR AND OCEAN burn . . .
  For Delia FROWNS . . . SHE FROWNS, *and I am curst !*

Oh ! I could dare the fury of the fight
  Where hostile MILLIONS sought my single life;
Would storm VOLCANO BATTERIES with delight,
  And grapple with GRIM DEATH in glorious strife.

Oh ! I could brave the bolts of angry Jove,
  When ceaseless lightnings fire the midnight skies;
What is *his wrath* to that of HER I love ?
  What is his LIGHTNING to my DELIA'S EYES ?

Go, fatal lock ! I cast thee to the wind;
  Ye *serpent* CURLS, ye *poison-tendrils,* go !
Would I could tear thy memory from my mind,
  ACCURSED LOCK, . . . thou cause of all my woe !

Seize the CURST CURLS, ye Furies, as they fly !
  Demons of Darkness, guard the infernal roll,
That thence your cruel vengeance when I die
  May *knit the* KNOTS OF TORTURE *for my* SOUL.

Last night, . . . oh, hear me, Heaven, and grant my
      prayer !
  The BOOK OF FATE before thy suppliant lay,
And let me from its ample records tear
  Only the single PAGE OF YESTERDAY.

Or let me meet OLD TIME upon his flight,
  And I will STOP HIM on his restless way:
Omnipotent in Love's resistless might,
  I'll force him back the ROAD OF YESTERDAY.

Last night, as o'er the page of Love's despair,
  My Delia bent *deliciously* to grieve,
I stood a *treacherous loiterer* by her chair,
  And drew the FATAL SCISSORS from my sleeve:

And would that at that instant o'er my thread
  The SHEARS OF ATROPOS had open'd then;
And when I reft the lock from Delia's head,
  Had cut me sudden from the sons of men!

She heard the scissors that fair lock divide,
  And whilst my heart with transport panted big,
She cast a FURY frown on me, and cried,
  'You stupid PUPPY, . . . you have spoil'd my Wig!'

CHARLES LAMB.

EPICEDIUM—GOING OR GONE.

(DRAYTON)

FINE merry franions,
Wanton companions,
My days are ev'n banyans
    With thinking upon ye;
How Death, that last stinger,
Finis-writer, end-bringer,
Has laid his chill finger,
    Or is laying on ye.

There's rich Kitty Wheatley,
With footing it featly
That took me completely,
    She sleeps in the Kirk House;
And poor Polly Perkin,
Whose Dad was still firking
The jolly ale firkin,
    She's gone to the Work-house;

Fine gard'ner, Ben Carter
(In ten counties no smarter)
Has ta'en his departure
    For Proserpine's orchards;
And Lily, postilion,
With cheeks of vermilion,
Is one of a million
    That fill up the church-yards;

And, lusty as Dido,
Fat Clemitson's widow
Flits now a small shadow
    By Stygian hid ford;
And good Master Clapton
Has thirty years nap't on
The ground he last hap't on,
    Intomb'd by fair Widford;

And gallant Tom Dockwra,
Of nature's finest crockery,
Now but thin air and mockery,
    Lurks by Avernus,
Whose honest grasp of hand
Still, while his life did stand,
At friend's or foe's command,
    Almost did burn us.

Roger de Coverley
Not more good man than he;
Yet has he equally
    Push'd for Cocytus,
With drivelling Worral,
And wicked old Dorrell,
'Gainst whom I've a quarrel,
    Whose end might affright us !—

Kindly hearts have I known;
Kindly hearts, they are flown;
Here and there if but one
    Linger yet uneffaced,
Imbecile tottering elves,
Soon to be wreck'd on shelves,
These scarce are half themselves,
    With age and care crazed.

But this day Fanny Hutton
Her last dress has put on;
Her fine lessons forgotten,
    She died, as the dunce died:
And prim Betsy Chambers,
Decay'd in her members,
No longer remembers
    Things, as she once did;

And prudent Miss Wither
Not in jest now doth *wither*,
And soon must go—whither
    Nor I well, nor you know;

And flaunting Miss Waller,
That soon must befall her,
Whence none can recall her,
 Though proud once as Juno !

HYPOCHONDRIACUS.

(ROBERT BURTON)

BY myself walking,
To myself talking,
When as I ruminate
On my untoward fate,
Scarcely seem I
Alone sufficiently,
Black thoughts continually
Crowding my privacy;
They come unbidden,
Like foes at a wedding,
Thrusting their faces
In better guests' places,
Peevish and malecontent,
Clownish, impertinent,
Dashing the merriment:
So in like fashions
Dim cogitations
Follow and haunt me,
Striving to daunt me,
In my heart festering,
In my ears whispering,
' Thy friends are treacherous,
Thy foes are dangerous,
Thy dreams ominous.'
 Fierce Anthropophagi,
Spectra, Diaboli,
What scared St. Anthony
Hobgoblins, Lemures,
Dreams of Antipodes,
Night-riding Incubi
Troubling the fantasy,

All dire illusions
Causing confusions;
Figments heretical,
Scruples fantastical,
Doubts diabolical,
Abaddon vexeth me,
Mahu perplexeth me,
Lucifer teareth me—
Jesu ! Maria ! liberate nos ab his diris tentationibus
Inimici.

NONSENSE VERSES.

(LAMB)

LAZY-BONES, lazy-bones, wake up, and peep !
The cat's in the cupboard, your mother's asleep.
There you sit snoring, forgetting her ills;
Who is to give her her bolus and pills ?
Twenty fine angels must come into town,
All for to help you to make your new gown:
Dainty Aerial Spinsters, and Singers;
Aren't you ashamed to employ such white fingers ?
Delicate hands, unaccustomed to reels,
To set 'em a working a poor body's wheels ?
Why they came down is to me all a riddle,
And left Hallelujah broke off in the middle;
Jove's Court, and the Presence angelical, cut—
To eke out the work of a lazy young slut.
Angel-duck, angel-duck, wingèd, and silly,
Pouring a watering-pot over a lily,
Gardener gratuitous, careless of pelf,
Leave her to water her lily herself,
Or to neglect it to death if she choose it:
Remember the loss is her own, if she lose it.

THOMAS MOORE.

THE NUMBERING OF THE CLERGY.

(SIR CHARLES HANBURY WILLIAMS)

We want more Churches and more Clergymen.—*Bishop of London's late Charge.*
Rectorum numerum, terris pereuntibus, augent.—CLAUDIAN *in Eutrop.*

COME, give us more Livings and Rectors,
    For richer no realm ever gave;
But why, ye unchristian objectors,
    Do ye ask us how many we crave ?

Oh, there can't be too many rich Livings
    For souls of the Pluralist kind,
Who, despising old Cocker's misgivings,
    To numbers can ne'er be confin'd.

Count the cormorants hovering about,
    At the time their fish season sets in,
When these models of keen diners-out
    Are preparing their beaks to begin.

Count the rooks that, in clerical dresses,
    Flock round when the harvest's in play,
And, not minding the farmer's distresses,
    Like devils in grain peck away.

Go, number the locusts in heaven,
    On their way to some titheable shore;
And when *so* many Parsons you've given,
    We still shall be craving for more.

Then, unless ye the Church would submerge, ye
    Must leave us in peace to augment,
For the wretch who could number the Clergy,
    With few will be ever content.

THOMAS LOVE PEACOCK.

A BORDER BALLAD.

BY AN ENCHANTER UNKNOWN.

(SCOTT)

The Scot, to rival realms a mighty bar,
Here fixed his mountain home : a wide domain,
And rich the soil, had purple heath been grain ;
But what the niggard ground of wealth denied,
From fields more blest his fearless arm supplied.
                                        LEYDEN.

THE Scotts, Kerrs, and Murrays, and Deloraines all,
The Hughies o' Hawdon, and Wills-o'-the-Wall,
The Willimondswicks, and the hard-riding Dicks,
Are staunch to the last to their old Border tricks;
Wine flows not from heath, and bread grinds not from
    stone,
They must reeve for their living, or life they'll have none.

When the Southron's strong arm with the steel and the
    law
Had tamed the moss-troopers, so bonny and braw;
Though spiders wove webs in the rusty sword-hilt,
In the niche of the hall which their forefathers built;
Yet with sly paper credit and promise to pay,
They still drove the trade which the wise call convey.

They whitewashed the front of their old Border fort;
They widened its loopholes, and opened its court;
They put in sash-windows where none were before,
And they wrote the word ' BANK ' o'er the new-painted
    door;
The cross-bow and matchlock aside they did lay,
And they shot the stout Southron with promise to pay.

They shot him from far and they shot him from near,
And they laid him as flat as their fathers laid deer:

Their fathers were heroes, though some called them
    thieves
When they ransacked their dwellings and drove off
    their beeves;
But craft undermined what force battered in vain,
And the pride of the Southron was stretched on the plain.

Now joy to the Hughies and Willies so bold !
The Southron, like Dickson, is bought and is sold;
To his goods and his chattels, his house, and his land,
Their promise to pay is as Harlequin's wand:
A touch and a word, and pass, presto, begone,
The Southron has lost, and the Willies have won.

The Hughies and Willies may lead a glad life;
They reap without sowing, they win without strife:
The Bruce and the Wallace were sturdy and fierce,
But where Scotch steel was broken Scotch paper can
    pierce;
And the true meed of conquest our minstrels shall fix,
On the promise to pay of our Willimondswicks.

THE WISE MEN OF GOTHAM.

By S. T. C., Esq., Professor of Mysticism.

(COLERIDGE)

Εκιᾶς ὄναρ.—Pindar.

In a bowl to sea went wise men three,
    On a brilliant night of June:
They carried a net, and their hearts were set
    On fishing up the moon.

The sea was calm, the air was balm,
    Not a breath stirred low or high,
And the moon, I trow, lay as bright below,
    And as round as in the sky.

The wise men with the current went,
    Nor paddle nor oar had they,
And still as the grave they went on the wave,
    That they might not disturb their prey.

Far, far at sea, were the wise men three,
  When their fishing-net they threw;
And at the throw, the moon below
  In a thousand fragments flew.

The sea was bright with the dancing light
  Of a million million gleams,
Which the broken moon shot forth as soon
  As the net disturbed her beams.

They drew in their net: it was empty and wet,
  And they had lost their pain,
Soon ceased the play of each dancing ray,
  And the image was round again.

Three times they threw, three times they drew,
  And all the while were mute;
And evermore their wonder grew,
  Till they could not but dispute.

Their silence they broke, and each one spoke
  Full long, and loud, and clear;
A man at sea their voices three
  Full three leagues off might hear.

The three wise men got home again
  To their children and their wives:
But touching their trip, and their net's vain dip,
  They disputed all their lives.

The wise men three could never agree,
  Why they missed the promised boon;
They agreed alone that their net they had thrown,
  And they had not caught the moon.

I have thought myself pale o'er this ancient tale,
  And its sense I could not ken;
But now I see that the wise men three
  Were paper-money men.

'Rub-a-dub-dub, three men in a tub,'
  Is a mystic burthen old,
Which I've pondered about till my fire went out,
  And I could not sleep for cold.

I now divine each mystic sign,
  Which robbed me oft of sleep,
Three men in a bowl, who went to troll,
  For the moon in the midnight deep.

Three men were they who science drank
  From Scottish fountains free;
The cash they sank in the Gotham bank,
  Was the moon beneath the sea.

The breaking of the imaged moon,
  At the fishing-net's first splash,
Was the breaking of the bank as soon
  As the wise men claimed their cash.

The dispute which lasted all their lives,
  Was the economic strife,
Which the son's son's son of every one
  Will maintain through all his life.

The son's son's sons will baffled be,
  As were their sires of old;
But they only agree, like the wise men three,
  That they could not get their gold.

And they'll build systems dark and deep,
  And systems broad and high;
But two of three will never agree
  About the reason why.

And he who at this day will seek
  The Economic Club,
Will find at least three sages there,
As ready as any that ever were
  To go to sea in a tub.

PROEMIUM OF AN EPIC,

WHICH WILL SHORTLY APPEAR IN QUARTO, UNDER THE TITLE OF

'FLY-BY-NIGHT.'

BY R. S., ESQ., POET LAUREATE.

(SOUTHEY)

His promises were, as he once was, mighty;
And his performance, as he is now, nothing.
SHAKESPEARE: *Henry VIII.*, Act IV., Sc. ii.

How troublesome is day !
It calls us from our sleep away;
It bids us from our pleasant dreams awake,
And sends us forth to keep or break
          Our promises to pay.
          How troublesome is day !

Now listen to my lay;
          Much have I said,
          Which few have heard or read,
And much have I to say,
Which hear ye while ye may.
Come listen to my lay,
          Come, for ye know me, as a man
          Who always praises, as he can,
All promisers to pay.
So they and I on terms agree,
And they but keep their faith with me,
Whate'er their deeds to others be,
They may to the minutest particle
Command my fingers for an ode or article.

Come listen while I strike the Epic string,
And, as a changeful song I sing,
          Before my eyes
          Bid changeful Proteus rise,
Turning his coat and skin in countless forms and dyes.

Come listen to my lay,
While I the wild and wondrous tale array,
How Fly-by-Night went down,
And set a bank up in a country town;
How like a king his head he reared;
And how the Coast of Cash he cleared;
And how one night he disappeared,
When many a scoffer jibed and jeered;
And many an old man rent his beard;
And many a young man cursed and railed;
And many a woman wept and wailed;
And many a mighty heart was quailed;
And many a wretch was caged and gaoled:
Because great Fly-by-Night had failed.
And many a miserable sinner
Went without his Sunday dinner,
Because he had not metal bright,
And waved in vain before the butcher's sight
The promises of Fly-by-Night.
And little Jackey Horner
Sat sulking in the corner,
And in default of Christmas pie
Whereon his little thumb to try,
He put his finger in his eye,
And blubbered long and lustily.

Come listen to my lay,
And ye shall say,
That never tale of errant knight,
Or captive damsel bright,
Demon, or elf, or goblin sprite,
Fierce crusade, or feudal fight,
Or cloistral phantom all in white,
Or castle or accessless height,
Upreared by necromantic might,
Was half so full of rare delight,
As this whereof I now prolong,
The memory in immortal song—
The wild and wondrous tale of Fly-by-Night.

M

YE KITE-FLYERS OF SCOTLAND.

By T. C.

(THOMAS CAMPBELL)

Quel chio vi debbo posso di parole
Pagare in parte, e d' opera d' inchiostro.
ARIOSTO.

YE kite-flyers of Scotland,
  Who live from home at ease;
Who raise the wind, from year to year,
  In a long and strong trade breeze:
Your paper kites let loose again
  On all the winds that blow;
Through the shout of the rout
  Lay the English ragmen low;
Though the shout for gold be fierce and bold,
  And the English ragmen low.

The spirits of your fathers
  Shall peep from every leaf;
For the midnight was their noon of fame,
  And their prize was living beef.
Where Deloraine on Musgrave fell,
  Your paper kites shall show,
That a way to convey
  Better far than theirs you know,
When you launch your kites upon the wind
  And raise the wind to blow.

Caledonia needs no bullion,
  No coin in iron case;
Her treasure is a bunch of rags
  And the brass upon her face;
With pellets from her paper mills
  She makes the Southrons trow,
That to pay her sole way
  Is by promising to owe,
By making promises to pay
  When she only means to owe.

The meteor ray of Scotland
  Shall float aloft like scum,
Till credit's o'erstrained line shall crack,
  And the day of reckoning come:
Then, then, ye Scottish kite-flyers,
  Your hone-a-rie must flow,
While you drink your own ink
  With your old friend Nick below,
While you burn your bills and singe your quills
  In his bonny fire below.

LOVE AND THE FLIMSIES.

By T. M., Esq.

(MOORE)

Ο δ' ῎Ερως, χιτῶνα δήσας
'Υπὲρ αὐχένος ΠΑΠΤΡΩ.
               ANACREON.

LITTLE Cupid one day on a sunbeam was floating,
  Above a green vale where a paper mill played;
And he hovered in ether, delightedly noting
  The whirl and the splash that the water-wheel made.

The air was all filled with the scent of the roses,
  Round the miller's veranda that clustered and twined;
And he thought if the sky were all made up of noses,
  This spot of the earth would be most to its mind.

And forth came the miller, a Quaker in verity,
  Rigid of limb and complacent of face,
And behind him a Scotchman was singing ' Prosperity,'
  And picking his pocket with infinite grace.

And ' Walth and prosparity,' ' Walth and prosparity,'
  His bonny Scotch burthen arose on the air,
To a song all in praise of that primitive charity,
  Which begins with sweet home and which terminates
    there.

But sudden a tumult arose from a distance,
  And in rushed a rabble with steel and with stone,
And ere the scared miller could call for assistance,
  The mill to a million of atoms was blown.

Scarce mounted the fragments in ether to hurtle,
    When the Quaker was vanished, no eye had seen
      where;
And the Scotchman thrown flat on his back, like a
    turtle,
    Was sprawling and bawling, with heels in the air.

Little Cupid continued to hover and flutter,
    Pursuing the fragments that floated on high,
As light as the fly that is christened from butter,
    Till he gathered his hands full and flew to the sky.

' Oh, mother,' he cried, as he showed them to Venus,
  ' What are these little talismans cyphered—One—
      One ?
If you think them worth having, we'll share them
    between us,
    Though their smell is like none of the sweetest, poor
      John.'

' My darling,' says Venus, ' away from you throw them,
  They're a sort of fool's gold among mortals, 'tis true;
But we want them not here, though I think you might
    know them,
    Since on earth they so often have bought and sold
      you.'

SONG BY MR. CYPRESS.

(BYRON)

THERE is a fever of the spirit,
  The brand of Cain's unresting doom,
Which in the lone dark souls that bear it
  Glows like the lamp in Tullia's tomb.

Unlike the lamp, its subtle fire
  Burns, blasts, consumes its cell, the heart.
Till, one by one, hope, joy, desire,
  Like dreams of shadowy smoke depart.

When hope, love, life itself, are only
  Dust—spectral memories—dead and cold—
The unfed fire burns bright and lonely,
  Like that undying lamp of old;
And by that drear illumination,
  Till time its clay-built home has rent,
Thought broods on feeling's desolation—
  The soul is its own monument.

HORACE TWISS.

THE PATRIOT'S PROGRESS.

(SHAKESPEARE)

ST. STEPHEN'S is a stage,
And half the opposition are but players:
For clap-traps, and deceptions, and effects,
Fill up their thoughts throughout their many parts,
Their acts being sev'n. At first the Demagogue,
Railing and mouthing at the hustings' front:
And then the cogging Candidate, with beer,
Fibs, cringes, and cockades, giving to voters
Unwillingly a pledge. And then the Member,
Crackling like furnace, with a flaming story
Made on the country's fall. Then he turns Courtier,
Full of smooth words, and secret as a midwife,
Pleas'd with all rulers, zealous for the church,
Seeking the useful fame of orthodoxy,
Ev'n from the *Canon's* mouth. And then a Secretary,
In fair white waistcoat, with boil'd chicken lin'd,
With placid smile, and speech of ready answer,
Lib'ral of promises and army contracts,
And so he rules the state. The sixth act brings him
To be a snug retired old baronet,
With ribband red on breast, and star on side:
His early zeal for change a world too hot
For his cool age: and his big eloquence,
Turning to gentler sounds, obedient pipes—
And we must pay the piper. Scene the last,
That ends this comfortable history,
Is a fat pension and a pompous peerage,
With cash, with coronet—with all but conscience.

OUR PARODIES ARE ENDED.

(SHAKESPEARE)

OUR parodies are ended. These our authors,
As we foretold you, were all Spirits, and
Are melted into air, into thin air.
And, like the baseless fabric of these verses,
The Critic's puff, the Trade's advertisement,
The Patron's promise, and the World's applause,—
Yea, all the hopes of poets,—shall dissolve,
And, like this unsubstantial fable fated,
Leave not a groat behind !

FASHION.

(MILTON)

HENCE, loath'd vulgarity,
    Of ignorance and native dullness bred,
    In low unwholesome shed,
'Mongst thieves and drabs, and street-sweeps asking
    charity:
    Find some suburban haunt,
Where the spruce 'prentice treats his flashy mate,
    And smoking cits debate:
Or at a dowdy rout, or ticket-ball,
    Giv'n at Freemasons' Hall,
With tawdry clothes and liveries ever flaunt.
    But come, thou nymph of slender waist,
Known early by the name of Taste,
    *   *   *   *   *
    Haste thee, nymph, and bring with thee
    Steed, and light-hung Tilbury,
    Undiscoverable rouge,
    Polish'd boots, and neckcloth huge,
    (Such as might deck a Dandy's cheek,
    And draw the gazers for a week.)

Mackintosh's racy phrase,
And wit, that peerless Ward might praise.
Come, and let your steps be bent
With a lively measurement,
And bring the proper airs and graces,
That make their way in certain places:
And, if I give thee honour due,
Fashion, enroll me with the few,
With Spencer, Sydney Smith, and thee
In a select society:
To ride when many a lady fair in
Her morning veil begins her airing,
And with the nurse and children stow'd
Drives down the Park, or Chelsea road:
Then to stop in spite of sorrow,
And through the window bid good-morrow
Of vis-à-vis, or barouchette,
Or half-open landaulet:
While little Burke, with lively din,
Scatters his stock of trifles thin;
And at the Bridge, or Grosvenor Gate,
Briskly bids his horses wait;
Oft listening how the Catalani
Rouses at night th' applauding many,
In some opera of Mozart,
Winning the eye, the ear, the heart.
Then in the round room not unseen,
Attending dames of noble mien,
Right to the door in Market-lane,
Where chairmen range their jostling train,
And footmen stand with torch alight,
In their thousand liveries dight,
While the doorkeeper on the stairs,
Bawls for the Marchionesses' chairs
And young dragoons enjoy the crowd,
And dowagers inveigh aloud,
And lovers write a hasty scrawl
Upon the ticket of a shawl.
Straight mine eye hath caught new pleasures,
As the circling crowd it measures;
Virgins old with tresses grey,
That in corkscrew curls do stray;

Ladies, on whose softer breast
Gallants receive a hope of rest;
Little feet with sandals tied,
Shallow heads and shoulders wide;
Necks and throats of lovely form,
Bosom'd high in tippet warm,
Where some beauty spreads her snare,
The envy of surrounding fair.
Hard by, the Op'ra being past,
To some small supper let me haste,
Where ladies, wits, and poets met,
Are at their various banquet set,
Of fifty little tempting messes,
Which the neat-handed Gunter dresses:
And there with satisfaction see
The pullet and the early pea,
Or, if the sultry dog-star reign,
The melon ice and cool champagne.
Sometimes, to a late delight
Argyll advertisements invite,
Where the wreathèd waltz goes round,
Or English tunes more briskly sound,
To twice a hundred feet or more,
Dancing on the chalky floor:
And wise mamma, well pleased to see
Her daughter paired with high degree,
Stays till the daylight glares amain:
Then in the carriage home again,
With stories told, of many a bow,
And civil speech from so and so.
She was ask'd to dance, she said,
But scarcely down the middle led,
Because his Lordship only thought
How soonest to find out a spot,
Where, seated by her side, unheard,
He whisper'd many a pretty word,
Such as no poet could excel !
Then, having paid his court so well,
Most manifestly meaning marriage,
He fetch'd the shawls and call'd the carriage,
Handed her from the crowded door
And watch'd till she was seen no more.

Thus done the tales, the flutt'ring fair
Go up to bed, and curl their hair.
Country houses please me too,
And the jocund Christmas crew,
Where chiefs of adverse politics
Awhile in social circle mix,
And tenants come, whose county franchise
Connects them with the higher branches,
Since all the great alike contend
For votes, on which they all depend.
Let Affability be there,
With cordial hand and friendly air,
And private play and glittering fête,
To make the rustic gentry prate,—
Such joys as fill young ladies' heads,
Who judge from books of masquerades.
Then will I to St. Stephen's stray,
If aught be moved by Castlereagh,
Or matchless Canning mean to roll
His thunders o'er the subject soul.
And sometimes, to divert my cares,
Give me some flirt, with joyous airs,
Married a girl, a widow now,
Such as will hear each playful vow,
Too young to lay upon the shelf:
Meaning—as little as myself:—
Still speaking, singing, walking, running,
With wanton heed and giddy cunning,
With a good mien to testify
Her converse with good company,
That Chesterfield might lift his eyes
From the dark Tartarus where he lies,
Beholding, in her air and gait,
Graces that almost compensate
The blunders of his awkward son,
And half the harm his book has done.
These delights if thou canst give,
Fashion, with thee I wish to live.

VERSES.

Supposed to be written by the Editor of the —— Newspaper, during his Solitary Abode in —— Prison.

(COWPER)

I AM tenant of nine feet by four,
　My title no lawyer denies,
From the ceiling quite down to the floor
　I am lord of the spiders and flies.

Oh, Justice ! how awkward it is
　To be gripped by thy terrible squad !
I did but indulge in a *quiz,*
　And the *Quorum* have sent me to *quod.*

Dear scandal is out of my reach,
　I must pass my dull mornings alone,
Never hear Mr. Br——m make a speech,
　Nor get audience for one of my own !

The people, provokingly quiet,
　My fate with indifference see:
They are so unaccustom'd to riot,
　Their tameness is shocking to me.

Personality, libel, and lie,
　Ye supports of our Jacobin train,
If I had but the courage to try,
　How soon I would sport you again !

My ranklings I then might assuage
　By renewing my efforts to vex,
By profaning the rev'rence of age,
　And attacking the weakness of sex.

A libel ! what treasure untold
　Resides in that dear little word,
More rich than the silver and gold
　Which the Bank is reported to hoard !

But the Bench have no bowels for pity,
    No stomach for high-season'd leaven,
And, though we be never so witty,
    They trim us when judgement is given.

O ye, who were present in Court,
    In pity convey to me here
Some well-manufactured report
    Of a lady, a prince, or a peer.

Do my writings continue to tell ?
    Does the public attend to my lines ?
O say that my Newspapers sell,
    Though the money must go for my fines !

How fleet is the growth of a fib !
    The astonishing speed of its flight
Outstrips the less mischievous squib
    Let off on a holiday night.

Then who would not vamp up a fudge,
    When he knows how it helps off his papers;
Were it not—that the thought of the judge
    Overcasts him, and gives him the vapours ?

But Cobbett has got his discharge—
    The beast is let loose from his cover:
Like him I shall yet be at large,
    When a couple of years shall be over:

For law must our liberty give,
    Though *Law* for a while may retard it:
Even I shall obtain it, who live
    By sapping the bulwarks that guard it.

GEORGE GORDON, LORD BYRON.

TO MR. MURRAY.

(COWPER)

STRAHAN, Tonson, Lintot of the times,
Patron and publisher of rhymes,
For thee the bard up Pindus climbs,
My Murray.

To thee, with hope and terror dumb,
The unfledged MS. authors come;
Thou printest all—and sellest some—
My Murray.

Upon thy table's baize so green
The last new Quarterly is seen,—
But where is thy new Magazine,
My Murray ?

Along thy sprucest bookshelves shine
The works thou deemest most divine—
The ' Art of Cookery,' and mine,
My Murray.

Tours, Travels, Essays, too, I wist,
And Sermons, to thy mill bring grist;
And then thou hast the ' Navy List,'
My Murray.

And Heaven forbid I should conclude
Without ' the Board of Longitude,'
Although this narrow paper would,
My Murray.

PARENTHETICAL ADDRESS BY DR. PLAGIARY.

(DR. BUSBY)

Half stolen, with acknowledgements ; to be spoken in an inarticulate voice by Master —— at the opening of the next new theatre. Stolen parts marked with the inverted commas of quotation—thus ' —— '.

' When energizing objects men pursue,'
Then Lord knows what is writ by Lord knows who.
'A modest monologue you here survey,'
Hiss'd from the theatre the ' other day,'
As if Sir Fretful wrote ' the slumberous ' verse,
And gave his son ' the rubbish ' to rehearse.
' Yet at the thing you'd never be amazed,'
Knew you the rumpus which the author raised :
' Nor even here your smiles would be represt.'
Knew you these lines—the badness of the best,
' Flame ! fire ! and flame !' (words borrowed from
    Lucretius,)
' Dread metaphors which open wounds ' like issues !
' And sleeping pangs awake—and—but away '
(Confound me if I know what next to say).
' Lo Hope reviving re-expands her wings,'
And Master G—— recites what Dr. Busby sings !—
' If mighty things with small we may compare,'
(Translated from the grammar for the fair !)
Dramatic ' spirit drives a conquering car,'
And burn'd poor Moscow like a tub of ' tar.'
' This spirit Wellington has shown in Spain,'
To furnish melodrames for Drury Lane.
' Another Marlborough points to Blenheim's story,'
And George and I will dramatize it for ye.

' In arts and sciences our isle hath shone '
(This deep discovery is mine alone).
' Oh British poesy, whose powers inspire '
My verse—or I'm a fool—and Fame's a liar,
' Thee we invoke, your sister arts implore '
With ' smiles,' and ' lyres,' and ' pencils,' and much
    more.

These, if we win the Graces, too, we gain
Disgraces, too ! ' inseparable train !'
' Three who have stolen their witching airs from Cupid '
(You all know what I mean, unless you're stupid) :
' Harmonious throng ' that I have kept *in petto*
Now to produce in a ' divine *sestetto* ' ! !
' While Poesy,' with these delightful doxies,
' Sustains her part ' in all the ' upper ' boxes !
' Thus lifted gloriously, you'll soar along,'
Borne in the vast balloon of Busby's song;
' Shine in your farce, masque, scenery, and play '
(For this last line George had a holiday).
' Old Drury never, never soar'd so high,'
So says the manager, and so say I.
' But hold,' you say, ' this self-complacent boast ;'
Is this the poem which the public lost ?
' True—true—that lowers at once our mounting pride ;'
But lo:—the papers print what you deride.
' 'Tis ours to look on you—you hold the prize,'
'Tis *twenty guineas*, as they advertise !
' A *double* blessing your rewards impart '—
I wish I had them, then, with all my heart.
' Our *twofold* feeling *owns* its twofold cause,'
Why son and I both beg for your applause.
' When in your fostering beams you bid us live,'
My next subscription list shall say how much you
      give !

RICHARD HARRIS BARHAM.

(' THOMAS INGOLDSBY ')

MARGATE.

(BYRON)

I've stood in Margate, on a bridge of size
   Inferior far to that described by Byron,
Where ' palaces and pris'ns on each hand rise,'
   —That 's too a stone one, this is made of iron—
   And little donkey-boys your steps environ,
Each proffering for your choice his tiny hack,
   Vaunting its excellence; and, should you hire one,
For sixpence, will he urge, with frequent thwack,
The much-enduring beast to Buenos Ayres—and back.

And then, on many a raw and gusty day,
   I've stood, and turn'd my gaze upon the pier,
And seen the crews, that did embark so gay
   That self-same morn, now disembark so queer;
   Then to myself I've sigh'd and said, ' Oh dear !
Who would believe yon sickly-looking man's a
   London Jack Tar,—a Cheapside Buccaneer !'—
But hold, my Muse !—for this terrific stanza
Is all too stiffly grand for our Extravaganza.

NOT A *SOUS* HAD HE GOT.

(CHARLES WOLFE)

Not a *sous* had he got,—not a guinea or note,
   And he look'd confoundedly flurried,
As he bolted away without paying his shot,
   And the Landlady after him hurried.

We saw him again at dead of night,
   When home from the Club returning;

We twigg'd the Doctor beneath the light
　Of the gas-lamp brilliantly burning.

All bare, and exposed to the midnight dews,
　Reclined in the gutter we found him;
And he look'd like a gentleman taking a snooze,
　With his *Marshall* cloak around him.

' The Doctor's as drunk as the d——,' we said,
　And we managed a shutter to borrow;
We raised him, and sigh'd at the thought that his head
　Would ' consumedly ache ' on the morrow.

We bore him home, and we put him to bed,
　And we told his wife and his daughter
To give him, next morning, a couple of red
　Herrings, with soda-water.

Loudly they talk'd of his money that's gone,
　And his Lady began to upbraid him;
But little he reck'd, so they let him snore on
　'Neath the counterpane just as we laid him.

We tuck'd him in, and had hardly done
　When, beneath the window calling,
We heard the rough voice of a son of a gun
　Of a watchman ' One o'clock !' bawling.

Slowly and sadly we all walk'd down
　From his room in the uppermost story;
A rushlight we placed on the cold hearth-stone,
　And we left him alone in his glory.

THE DEMOLISHED FARCE; OR, 'WHO IS THE AUTHOR ?'

BY A NEWSPAPER CRITIC.

[Lines suggested by the failure of Mr. Thomas Haines Bayly's
farce ' Decorum.']

(T. H. BAYLY)

OH no ! we'll never mention him;
    We won't, upon our word !
' Decorum ' now forbids to name
    An unsuccessful bard.
From Drury Lane we'll toddle to
    Our ' office ' with regret,
And if they ask us, ' *Who's* been dished ?'
    We'll say that ' we forget !'

We'll bid him now forsake ' the Scene,'
    And try his ancient strain;
He'd better ' be a butterfly '
    Than write a farce again.
'Tis true that he can troll a song,
    Or tender Canzonette;
But if you ask us, ' What beside ?'
    Why, really, ' we forget.'

And, oh, there are so many now,
    Who write good come-dy,—
There's Mister Planché, Mister Peake,
    And Poole, who wrote *Paul Pry,*
Moncrieff and Mister Buckstone join
    To make a funny set,
With some half-dozen jokers more,
    Whose names we quite forget.

They tell us he has got, behind,
    A bran-new five-act play;
They say that it is devilish droll,
    But heed not what they say;
Perchance, indeed, 'twill struggle on
    A night or two, but yet
If 'tis no better than his farce,
    The pair you'll soon forget !

PERCY BYSSHE SHELLEY.

PETER BELL THE THIRD.

BY MICHING MALLECHO, ESQ.

(WORDSWORTH)

Is it a party in a parlour,
Crammed just as they on earth were crammed,
Some sipping punch—some sipping tea;
But, as you by their faces see,
All silent, and all——damned !

Peter Bell, by W. WORDSWORTH.

OPHELIA. What means this, my lord ?
HAMLET. Marry, this is Miching Mallecho; it means mischief.

SHAKESPEARE.

PROLOGUE.

PETER BELLS, one, two and three,
O'er the wide world wandering be.—
First, the antenatal Peter,
Wrapped in weeds of the same metre,
The so-long-predestined raiment
Clothed in which to walk his way meant
The second Peter; whose ambition
Is to link the proposition,
As the mean of two extremes—
(This was learned from Aldric's themes)
Shielding from the guilt of schism
The orthodoxal syllogism;
The First Peter—he who was
Like the shadow in the glass
Of the second, yet unripe,
His substantial antitype.—
Then came Peter Bell the Second,
Who henceforward must be reckoned
The body of a double soul,
And that portion of the whole
Without which the rest would seem
Ends of a disjointed dream.—
And the Third is he who has
O'er the grave been forced to pass
To the other side, which is,—

Go and try else,—just like this.
Peter Bell the First was Peter
Smugger, milder, softer, neater,
Like the soul before it is
Born from *that* world into *this*.
The next Peter Bell was he,
Predevote, like you and me,
To good or evil as may come;
His was the severer doom,—
For he was an evil Cotter,
And a polygamic Potter.[1]
And the last is Peter Bell,
Damned since our first parents fell,
Damned eternally to Hell—
Surely he deserves it well!

PART THE FIRST.

Death.

I.

And Peter Bell, when he had been
  With fresh-imported Hell-fire warmed,
Grew serious—from his dress and mien
'Twas very plainly to be seen
  Peter was quite reformed.

II.

His eyes turned up, his mouth turned down;
  His accent caught a nasal twang;
He oiled his hair[2]; there might be heard
The grace of God in every word
  Which Peter said or sang.

---

[1] The oldest scholiasts read—

A *dodecagamic* Potter.

This is at once more descriptive and more megalophonous,—but the alliteration of the text had captivated the vulgar ear of the herd of later commentators.

[2] To those who have not duly appreciated the distinction between *Whale* and *Russia* oil, this attribute might rather seem to belong to the Dandy than the Evangelic. The effect, when to the windward, is indeed so similar, that it requires a subtle naturalist to discriminate the animals. They belong, however, to distinct genera.

III.

But Peter now grew old, and had
  An ill no doctor could unravel;
His torments almost drove him mad;—
Some said it was a fever bad—
  Some swore it was the gravel.

IV.

His holy friends then came about,
  And with long preaching and persuasion
Convinced the patient that, without
The smallest shadow of a doubt,
  He was predestined to damnation.

V.

They said—' Thy name is Peter Bell;
  Thy skin is of a brimstone hue;
Alive or dead—ay, sick or well—
The one God made to rhyme with hell;
  The other, I think, rhymes with you.'

VI.

Then Peter set up such a yell!—
  The nurse, who with some water gruel
Was climbing up the stairs, as well
As her old legs could climb them—fell,
  And broke them both—the fall was cruel.

VII.

The parson from the casement leapt
  Into the lake of Windermere—
And many an eel—though no adept
In God's right reason for it—kept
  Gnawing his kidneys half a year.

VIII.

And all the rest rushed through the door,
  And tumbled over one another,
And broke their skulls.—Upon the floor
Meanwhile sat Peter Bell, and swore,
  And cursed his father and his mother;

IX.

And raved of God, and sin, and death,
  Blaspheming like an infidel;
And said, that with his clenchèd teeth
He'd seize the earth from underneath,
  And drag it with him down to hell.

X.

As he was speaking came a spasm,
  And wrenched his gnashing teeth asunder;
Like one who sees a strange phantasm
He lay,—there was a silent chasm
  Between his upper jaw and under.

XI.

And yellow death lay on his face;
  And a fixed smile that was not human
Told, as I understand the case,
That he was gone to the wrong place:—
  I heard all this from the old woman.

XII.

Then there came down from Langdale Pike
  A cloud, with lightning, wind and hail;
It swept over the mountains like
An ocean,—and I heard it strike
  The woods and crags of Grasmere vale.

XIII.

And I saw the black storm come
  Nearer, minute after minute;
Its thunder made the cataracts dumb;
With hiss, and clash, and hollow hum,
  It neared as if the Devil was in it.

XIV.

The Devil *was* in it:—he had bought
  Peter for half-a-crown; and when
The storm which bore him vanished, nought
That in the house that storm had caught
  Was ever seen again.

XV.

The gaping neighbours came next day—
 They found all vanished from the shore:
The Bible, whence he used to pray,
Half scorched under a hen-coop lay;
 Smashed glass—and nothing more !

PART THE SECOND.

The Devil.

I.

The Devil, I safely can aver,
 Has neither hoof, nor tail, nor sting;
Nor is he, as some sages swear,
A spirit, neither here nor there,
 In nothing—yet in everything.

II.

He is—what we are; for sometimes
 The Devil is a gentleman;
At others a bard bartering rhymes
For sack; a statesman spinning crimes;
 A swindler, living as he can;

III.

A thief, who cometh in the night,
 With whole boots and net pantaloons,
Like some one whom it were not right
To mention;—or the luckless wight
 From whom he steals nine silver spoons.

IV.

But in this case he did appear
 Like a slop-merchant from Wapping,
And with smug face, and eye severe,
On every side did perk and peer
 Till he saw Peter dead or napping.

v.

He had on an upper Benjamin
  (For he was of the driving schism)
In the which he wrapped his skin
From the storm he travelled in,
  For fear of rheumatism.

vi.

He called the ghost out of the corse;—
  It was exceedingly like Peter,—
Only its voice was hollow and hoarse—
It had a queerish look of course—
  Its dress too was a little neater.

vii.

The Devil knew not his name and lot;
  Peter knew not that he was Bell:
Each had an upper stream of thought,
Which made all seem as it was not;
  Fitting itself to all things well.

viii.

Peter thought he had parents dear,
  Brothers, sisters, cousins, cronies,
In the fens of Lincolnshire;
He perhaps had found them there
  Had he gone and boldly shown his

ix.

Solemn phiz in his own village;
  Where he thought oft when a boy
He'd clomb the orchard walls to pillage
The produce of his neighbour's tillage,
  With marvellous pride and joy.

x.

And the Devil thought he had,
  'Mid the misery and confusion
Of an unjust war, just made
A fortune by the gainful trade
Of giving soldiers rations bad--
  The world is full of strange delusion—

XI.

That he had a mansion planned
  In a square like Grosvenor Square,
That he was aping fashion, and
That he now came to Westmoreland
  To see what was romantic there.

XII.

And all this, though quite ideal,—
  Ready at a breath to vanish,—
Was a state not more unreal
Than the peace he could not feel,
  Or the care he could not banish.

XIII.

After a little conversation,
  The Devil told Peter, if he chose,
He'd bring him to the world of fashion
By giving him a situation
  In his own service—and new clothes.

XIV.

And Peter bowed, quite pleased and proud,
  And after waiting some few days
For a new livery—dirty yellow
Turned up with black—the wretched fellow
  Was bowled to Hell in the Devil's chaise.

PART THE THIRD.

Hell.

I.

HELL is a city much like London—
  A populous and a smoky city;
There are all sorts of people undone,
And there is little or no fun done;
  Small justice shown, and still less pity.

II.

There is a Castles, and a Canning,
   A Cobbett, and a Castlereagh;
All sorts of caitiff corpses planning
All sorts of cozening for trepanning
   Corpses less corrupt than they.

III.

There is a * * *, who has lost
   His wits, or sold them, none knows which;
He walks about a double ghost,
And though as thin as Fraud almost—
   Ever grows more grim and rich.

IV.

There is a Chancery Court; a King;
   A manufacturing mob; a set
Of thieves who by themselves are sent
Similar thieves to represent;
   An army; and a public debt.

V.

Which last is a scheme of paper money,
   And means—being interpreted—
' Bees, keep your wax—give us the honey,
And we will plant, while skies are sunny,
   Flowers, which in winter serve instead.'

VI.

There is a great talk of revolution—
   And a great chance of despotism—
German soldiers—camps—confusion—
Tumults—lotteries—rage—delusion—
   Gin—suicide—and methodism;

VII.

Taxes too, on wine and bread,
   And meat, and beer, and tea, and cheese,
From which those patriots pure are fed,
Who gorge before they reel to bed
   The tenfold essence of all these.

VIII.

There are mincing women, mewing,
 (Like cats, who *amant miserè*[1],)
Of their own virtue, and pursuing
Their gentler sisters to that ruin,
 Without which—what were chastity ?

IX.

Lawyers—judges—old hobnobbers
 Are there—bailiffs—chancellors—
Bishops—great and little robbers—
Rhymesters—pamphleteers—stock-jobbers—
 Men of glory in the wars,—

X.

Things whose trade is, over ladies
 To lean, and flirt, and stare, and simper,
Till all that is divine in woman
Grows cruel, courteous, smooth, inhuman,
 Crucified 'twixt a smile and whimper.

XI.

Thrusting, toiling, wailing, moiling,
 Frowning, preaching—such a riot !
Each with never-ceasing labour,
Whilst he thinks he cheats his neighbour,
 Cheating his own heart of quiet.

XII.

And all these meet at levees;—
 Dinners convivial and political;—
Suppers of epic poets;—teas,
Where small talk dies in agonies;—
 Breakfasts professional and critical;

[1] One of the attributes in Linnæus's description of the Cat. To a similar cause the caterwauling of more than one species of this genus is to be referred;—except, indeed, that the poor quadruped is compelled to quarrel with its own pleasures, whilst the biped is supposed only to quarrel with those of others.

XIII.

Lunches and snacks so aldermanic
　That one would furnish forth ten dinners,
Where reigns a Cretan-tonguèd panic,
Lest news Russ, Dutch, or Alemannic
　Should make some losers, and some winners;—

XIV.

At conversazioni—balls—
　Conventicles—and drawing-rooms—
Courts of law—committees—calls
Of a morning—clubs—book-stalls—
　Churches—masquerades—and tombs.

XV.

And this is Hell—and in this smother
　All are damnable and damned;
Each one damning, damns the other;
They are damned by one another,
　By none other are they damned.

XVI.

'Tis a lie to say, ' God damns[1] !'
　Where was Heaven's Attorney General
When they first gave out such flams ?
Let there be an end of shams,
　They are mines of poisonous mineral.

XVII.

Statesmen damn themselves to be
　Cursed; and lawyers damn their souls
To the auction of a fee;
Churchmen damn themselves to see
　God's sweet love in burning coals.

---

[1] This libel on our national oath, and this accusation of all our
countrymen of being in the daily practice of solemnly asseverating
the most enormous falsehood, I fear deserves the notice of a more
active Attorney General than that here alluded to.

XVIII.

The rich are damned, beyond all cure,
  To taunt, and starve, and trample on
The weak and wretched; and the poor
Damn their broken hearts to endure
  Stripe on stripe, with groan on groan.

XIX.

Sometimes the poor are damned indeed
  To take,—not means for being blessed,—
But Cobbett's snuff, revenge; that weed
From which the worms that it doth feed
  Squeeze less than they before possessed.

XX.

And some few, like we know who,
  Damned—but God alone knows why—
To believe their minds are given
To make this ugly Hell a Heaven;
  In which faith they live and die.

XXI.

Thus, as in a town, plague-stricken,
  Each man be he sound or no
Must indifferently sicken;
As when day begins to thicken,
  None knows a pigeon from a crow,—

XXII.

So good and bad, sane and mad,
  The oppressor and the oppressed;
Those who weep to see what others
Smile to inflict upon their brothers;
  Lovers, haters, worst and best;

XXIII.

All are damned—they breathe an air,
  Thick, infected, joy-dispelling:
Each pursues what seems most fair,
Mining like moles, through mind, and there
Scoop palace-caverns vast, where Care
  In thronèd state is ever dwelling.

PART THE FOURTH.

Sin.

I.

Lo, Peter in Hell's Grosvenor Square,
　A footman in the Devil's service !
And the misjudging world would swear
That every man in service there
　To virtue would prefer vice.

II.

But Peter, though now damned, was not
　What Peter was before damnation.
Men oftentimes prepare a lot
Which ere it finds them, is not what
　Suits with their genuine station.

III.

All things that Peter saw and felt
　Had a peculiar aspect to him;
And when they came within the belt
Of his own nature, seemed to melt,
　Like cloud to cloud, into him.

IV.

And so the outward world uniting
　To that within him, he became
Considerably uninviting
To those who, meditation slighting,
　Were moulded in a different frame.

V.

And he scorned them, and they scorned him;
　And he scorned all they did; and they
Did all that men of their own trim
Are wont to do to please their whim,
　Drinking, lying, swearing, play.

VI.

Such were his fellow-servants; thus
  His virtue,· like our own, was built
Too much on that indignant fuss
Hypocrite Pride stirs up in us
  To bully one another's guilt.

VII.

He had a mind which was somehow
  At once circumference and centre
Of all he might or feel or know;
Nothing went ever out, although
  Something did ever enter.

VIII.

He had as much imagination
  As a pint-pot;—he never could
Fancy another situation,
From which to dart his contemplation,
  Than that wherein he stood.

IX.

Yet his was individual mind,
  And new created all he saw
In a new manner, and refined
Those new creations, and combined
  Them, by a master-spirit's law.

X.

Thus—though unimaginative—
  An apprehension clear, intense,
Of his mind's work, had made alive
The things it wrought on; I believe
  Wakening a sort of thought in sense.

XI.

But from the first 'twas Peter's drift
· To be a kind of moral eunuch,
He touched the hem of Nature's shift,
Felt faint—and never dared uplift
  The closest, all-concealing tunic.

XII.

She laughed the while, with an arch smile,
    And kissed him with a sister's kiss.
And said:—' My best Diogenes,
I love you well—but, if you please,
    Tempt not again my deepest bliss.

XIII.

' 'Tis you are cold—for I, not coy,
    Yield love for love, frank, warm, and true;
And Burns, a Scottish peasant boy—
His errors prove it—knew my joy
    More, learnèd friend, than you.

XIV.

' Bocca bacciata non perde ventura,
    Anzi rinnuova come fa la luna :—
So thought Boccaccio, whose sweet words might
        cure a
Male prude, like you, from what you now endure, a
    Low-tide in soul, like a stagnant laguna.'

XV.

Then Peter rubbed his eyes severe,
    And smoothed his spacious forehead down
With his broad palm;—'twixt love and fear,
He looked, as he no doubt felt, queer,
    And in his dream sate down.

XVI.

The Devil was no uncommon creature;
    A leaden-witted thief—just huddled
Out of the dross and scum of nature;
A toad-like lump of limb and feature,
    With mind, and heart, and fancy muddled.

XVII.

He was that heavy, dull, cold thing,
    The spirit of evil well may be:
A drone too base to have a sting;
Who gluts, and grimes his lazy wing,
    And calls lust, luxury.

XVIII.

Now he was quite the kind of wight
  Round whom collect, at a fixed aera,
Venison, turtle, hock, and claret,—
Good cheer,—and those who come to share it—
  And best East Indian madeira !

XIX.

It was his fancy to invite
  Men of science, wit, and learning,
Who came to lend each other light;
He proudly thought that his gold's might
  Had set those spirits burning.

XX.

And men of learning, science, wit,
  Considered him as you and I
Think of some rotten tree, and sit
Lounging and dining under it,
  Exposed to the wide sky.

XXI.

And all the while, with loose fat smile,
  The willing wretch sat winking there,
Believing 'twas his power that made
That jovial scene—and that all paid
  Homage to his unnoticed chair.

XXII.

Though to be sure this place was Hell;
  He was the Devil—and all they—
What though the claret circled well,
And wit, like ocean, rose and fell ?—
  Were damned eternally.

PART THE FIFTH.

Grace.

I.

AMONG the guests who often stayed
  Till the Devil's petits-soupers

o

A man there came, fair as a maid,
And Peter noted what he said,
 Standing behind his master's chair.

II.

He was a mighty poet—and
 A subtle-souled psychologist;
All things he seemed to understand,
Of old or new—of sea or land—
 But his own mind—which was a mist.

III.

This was a man who might have turned
 Hell into Heaven—and so in gladness
A Heaven unto himself have earned;
But he in shadows undiscerned
 Trusted,—and damned himself to madness.

IV.

He spoke of poetry, and how
 ' Divine it was—a light—a love—
A spirit which like wind doth blow
As it listeth, to and fro;
 A dew rained down from God above ;

V.

' A power which comes and goes like dream,
 And which none can ever trace—
Heaven's light on earth—Truth's brightest beam.'
And when he ceased there lay the gleam
 Of those words upon his face.

VI.

Now Peter, when he heard such talk,.
 Would, heedless of a broken pate,
Stand like a man asleep, or balk
Some wishing guest of knife or fork,
 Or drop and break his master's plate.

VII.

At night he oft would start and wake
  Like a lover, and began
In a wild measure songs to make
On moor, and glen, and rocky lake,
  And on the heart of man—

VIII.

And on the universal sky—
  And the wide earth's bosom green,—
And the sweet, strange mystery
Of what beyond these things may lie,
  And yet remain unseen.

IX.

For in his thought he visited
  The spots in which, ere dead and damned,
He his wayward life had led;
Yet knew not whence the thoughts were fed
  Which thus his fancy crammed.

X.

And these obscure remembrances
  Stirred such harmony in Peter,
That, whensoever he should please,
He could speak of rocks and trees
  In poetic metre.

XI.

For though it was without a sense
  Of memory, yet he remembered well
Many a ditch and quick-set fence;
Of lakes he had intelligence,
  He knew something of heath and fell.

XII.

He had also dim recollections
  Of pedlars tramping on their rounds;
Milk-pans and pails; and odd collections
Of saws, and proverbs; and reflections
  Old parsons make in burying-grounds.

XIII.

But Peter's verse was clear, and came
   Announcing from the frozen hearth
Of a cold age, that none might tame
The soul of that diviner flame
   It augured to the Earth:

XIV.

Like gentle rains, on the dry plains,
   Making that green which late was gray,
Or like the sudden moon, that stains
Some gloomy chamber's window-panes
   With a broad light like day.

XV.

For language was in Peter's hand
   Like clay while he was yet a potter,
And he made songs for all the land,
Sweet both to feel and understand,
   As pipkins late to mountain Cotter.

XVI.

And Mr. ——, the bookseller,
   Gave twenty pounds for some;—then scorning
A footman's yellow coat to wear,
Peter, too proud of heart, I fear,
   Instantly gave the Devil warning.

XVII.

Whereat the Devil took offence,
   And swore in his soul a great oath then,
'That for his damned impertinence
He'd bring him to a proper sense
   Of what was due to gentlemen !'

PART THE SIXTH.

Damnation.

I.

'O THAT mine enemy had written
   A book !'—cried Job :—a fearful curse,

If to the Arab, as the Briton,
'Twas galling to be critic-bitten:—
 The Devil to Peter wished no worse.

II.

When Peter's next new book found vent,
 The Devil to all the first Reviews
A copy of it slyly sent,
With five-pound note as compliment,
 And this short notice—' Pray abuse.'

III.

Then *seriatim*, month and quarter,
 Appeared such mad tirades.—One said—
' Peter seduced Mrs. Foy's daughter,
Then drowned the mother in Ullswater,
 The last thing as he went to bed.'

IV.

Another—' Let him shave his head !
 Where's Dr. Willis ?—Or is he joking ?
What does the rascal mean or hope,
No longer imitating Pope,
 In that barbarian Shakespeare poking ?'

V.

One more, ' Is incest not enough ?
 And must there be adultery too ?
Grace after meat ? Miscreant and Liar !
Thief ! Blackguard ! Scoundrel ! Fool ! Hell-
  fire
 Is twenty times too good for you.

VI.

' By that last book of yours WE think
 You've double damned yourself to scorn;
We warned you whilst yet on the brink
You stood. From your black name will shrink
 The babe that is unborn.'

VII.

All these Reviews the Devil made
  Up in a parcel, which he had
Safely to Peter's house conveyed.
For carriage, tenpence Peter paid—
  Untied them—read them—went half mad.

VIII.

' What !' cried he, ' this is my reward
  For nights of thought, and days of toil ?
Do poets, but to be abhorred
By men of whom they never heard,
  Consume their spirits' oil ?

IX.

'What have I done to them ?—and who
  Is Mrs. Foy ? 'Tis very cruel
To speak of me and Betty so !
Adultery ! God defend me ! Oh !
  I've half a mind to fight a duel.

X.

' Or,' cried he, a grave look collecting,
  ' Is it my genius, like the moon,
Sets those who stand her face inspecting,
That face within their brain reflecting,
  Like a crazed bell-chime, out of tune ?'

XI.

For Peter did not know the town,
  But thought, as country readers do,
For half a guinea or a crown,
He bought oblivion or renown
  From God's own voice[1] in a review.

XII.

All Peter did on this occasion
  Was writing some sad stuff in prose.
It is a dangerous invasion

---

[1] *Vox populi, vox dei.* As Mr. Godwin truly observes of a more famous saying, *of some merit as a popular maxim, but totally destitute of philosophical accuracy.*

When poets criticize; their station
  Is to delight, not pose.

XIII.

The Devil then sent to Leipsic fair
  For Born's translation of Kant's book;
A world of words, tail foremost, where
Right—wrong—false—true—and foul—and fair
  As in a lottery-wheel are shook.

XIV.

Five thousand crammed octavo pages
  Of German psychologics,—he
Who his *furor verborum* assuages
Thereon, deserves just seven months' wages
  More than will e'er be due to me.

XV.

I looked on them nine several days,
  And then I saw that they were bad;
A friend, too, spoke in their dispraise,—
He never read them;—with amaze
  I found Sir William Drummond had.

XVI.

When the book came, the Devil sent
  It to P. Verbovale[1], Esquire,
With a brief note of compliment,
By that night's Carlisle mail. It went,
  And set his soul on fire.

XVII.

Fire, which *ex luce praebens fumum*,
  Made him beyond the bottom see
Of truth's clear well—when I and you, Ma'am,
Go, as we shall do, *subter humum*,
  We may know more than he.

[1] Quasi, *Qui valet verba*—*i.e.*, all the words which have been, are, or may be expended by, for, against, with, or on him. A sufficient proof of the utility of this history. Peter's progenitor who selected this name seems to have possessed *a pure anticipated cognition* of the nature and modesty of this ornament of his posterity.

XVIII.

Now Peter ran to seed in soul
  Into a walking paradox;
For he was neither part nor whole,
Nor good, nor bad—nor knave nor fool;
  —Among the woods and rocks

XIX.

Furious he rode, where late he ran,
  Lashing and spurring his tame hobby;
Turned to a formal puritan,—
A solemn and unsexual man,—
  He half believed *White Obi*.

XX.

This steed in vision he would ride,
  High trotting over nine-inch bridges,
With Flibbertigibbet, imp of pride,
Mocking and mowing by his side—
A mad-brained goblin for a guide—
  Over corn-fields, gates,' and hedges.

XXI.

After these ghastly rides, he came
  Home to his heart, and found from thence
Much stolen of its accustomed flame;
His thoughts grew weak, drowsy, and lame
  Of their intelligence.

XXII.

To Peter's view, all seemed one hue;
  He was no Whig, he was no Tory;
No Deist and no Christian he;—
He got so subtle, that to be
  Nothing, was all his glory.

XXIII.

One single point in his belief
  From his organization sprung,
The heart-enrooted faith, the chief
Ear in his doctrines' blighted sheaf,
  That ' Happiness is wrong ';

XXIV.

So thought Calvin and Dominic;
 So think their fierce successors, who
Even now would neither stint nor stick
Our flesh from off our bones to pick,
 If they might ' do their do.'

XXV.

His morals thus were undermined:—
 The old Peter—the hard, old Potter—
Was born anew within his mind;
He grew dull, harsh, sly, unrefined,
 As when he tramped beside the Otter.[1]

XXVI.

In the death hues of agony
 Lambently flashing from a fish,
Now Peter felt amused to see
Shades like a rainbow's rise and flee,
 Mixed with a certain hungry wish.[2]

XXVII.

So in his Country's dying face
 He looked—and, lovely as she lay,
Seeking in vain his last embrace,
Wailing her own abandoned case,
 With hardened sneer he turned away:

XXVIII.

And coolly to his own soul said;—
 ' Do you not think that we might make
A poem on her when she's dead:—
Or, no—a thought is in my head—
 Her shroud for a new sheet I'll take:

[1] A famous river in the new Atlantis of the Dynastophylic Pantisocratists.
[2] See the description of the beautiful colours produced during the agonizing death of a number of trout, in the fourth part of a long poem in blank verse, published within a few years. That poem contains curious evidence of the gradual hardening of a strong but circumscribed sensibility, of the perversion of a penetrating but panic-stricken understanding.

XXIX.

' My wife wants one.—Let who will bury
   This mangled corpse ! And I and you,
My dearest Soul, will then make merry,
As the Prince Regent did with Sherry,—'
   ' Ay—and at last desert me too.'

XXX.

And so his Soul would not be gay,
   But moaned within him; like a fawn
Moaning within a cave, it lay
Wounded and wasting, day by day,
   Till all its life of life was gone.

XXXI.

As troubled skies stain waters clear,
   The storm in Peter's heart and mind
Now made his verses dark and queer:
They were the ghosts of what they were,
   Shaking dim grave-clothes in the wind.

XXXII.

For he now raved enormous folly,
   Of Baptisms, Sunday-schools, and Graves,
'Twould make George Colman melancholy
To have heard him, like a male Molly,
   Chanting those stupid staves.

XXXIII.

Yet the Reviews, who heaped abuse
   On Peter while he wrote for freedom,
So soon as in his song they spy
The folly which soothes tyranny,
   Praise him, for those who feed 'em.

XXXIV.

' He was a man, too great to scan;—
   A planet lost in truth's keen rays:—
His virtue, awful and prodigious;—
He was the most sublime, religious,
   Pure-minded Poet of these days.'

XXXV.

As soon as he read that, cried Peter,
  ' Eureka ! I have found the way
To make a better thing of metre
Than e'er was made by living creature
  Up to this blessèd day.'

XXXVI.

Then Peter wrote odes to the Devil;—
  In one of which he meekly said:
' May Carnage and Slaughter,
Thy niece and thy daughter,
May Rapine and Famine,
Thy gorge ever cramming,
  Glut thee with living and dead !

XXXVII.

' May Death and Damnation,
  And Consternation,
Flit up from Hell with pure intent !
  Slash them at Manchester,
  Glasgow, Leeds, and Chester;
Drench all with blood from Avon to Trent.

XXXVIII.

' Let thy body-guard yeomen
  Hew down babes and women,
And laugh with bold triumph till Heaven be rent !
  When Moloch in Jewry
  Munched children with fury,
It was thou, Devil, dining with pure intent.'[1]

---

[1] It is curious to observe how often extremes meet. Cobbett and Peter use the same language for a different purpose: Peter is indeed a sort of metrical Cobbett. Cobbett is, however, more mischievous than Peter, because he pollutes a holy and now unconquerable cause with the principles of legitimate murder; whilst the other only makes a bad one ridiculous and odious. If either Peter or Cobbett should see this note, each will feel more indignation at being compared to the other than at any censure implied in the moral perversion laid to their charge.

Part the Seventh.

Double Damnation.

I.

THE Devil now knew his proper cue.—
 Soon as he read the ode, he drove
To his friend Lord MacMurderchouse's,
A man of interest in both houses,
 And said:—' For money or for love,

II.

' Pray find some cure or sinecure;
 To feed from the superfluous taxes
A friend of ours—a poet—fewer
Have fluttered tamer to the lure
 Than he.' His lordship stands and racks his

III.

Stupid brains, while one might count
 As many beads as he had boroughs,—
At length replies; from his mean front,
Like one who rubs out an account,
 Smoothing away the unmeaning furrows:

IV.

' It happens fortunately, dear Sir,
 I can. I hope I need require
No pledge from you, that he will stir
In our affairs;—like Oliver,
 That he'll be worthy of his hire.'

V.

These words exchanged, the news sent off
 To Peter, home the Devil hied,—
Took to his bed; he had no cough,
No doctor,—meat and drink enough,—
 Yet that same night he died.

VI.

The Devil's corpse was leaded down;
 His decent heirs enjoyed his pelf,
Mourning-coaches, many a one,

Followed his hearse along the town:—
Where was the Devil himself ?

VII.

When Peter heard of his promotion,
  His eyes grew like two stars for bliss:
There was a bow of sleek devotion
Engendering in his back; each motion
  Seemed a Lord's shoe to kiss.

VIII.

He hired a house, bought plate, and made
  A genteel drive up to his door,
With sifted gravel neatly laid,—
As if defying all who said,
  Peter was ever poor.

IX.

But a disease soon struck into
  The very life and soul of Peter—
He walked about—slept—had the hue
Of health upon his cheeks—and few
  Dug better—none a heartier eater.

X.

And yet a strange and horrid curse
  Clung upon Peter, night and day;
Month after month the thing grew worse,
And deadlier than in this my verse
  I can find strength to say.

XI.

Peter was dull—he was at first
  Dull—oh, so dull—so very dull !
Whether he talked, wrote, or rehearsed—
Still with this dullness was he cursed—
  Dull—beyond all conception—dull.

XII.

No one could read his books—no mortal,
  But a few natural friends, would hear him;
The parson came not near his portal;
His state was like that of the immortal
  Described by Swift—no man could bear him.

XIII.

His sister, wife, and children yawned,
  With a long, slow, and drear ennui,
All human patience far beyond;
Their hopes of Heaven each would have pawned,
  Anywhere else to be.

XIV.

But in his verse, and in his prose,
  The essence of his dullness was
Concentred and compressed so close,
'Twould have made Guatimozin doze
  On his red gridiron of brass.

XV.

A printer's boy, folding those pages,
  Fell slumbrously upon one side;
Like those famed Seven who slept three ages,
To wakeful frenzy's vigil-rages,
  As opiates, were the same applied.

XVI.

Even the Reviewers who were hired
  To do the work of his reviewing,
With adamantine nerves, grew tired;—
Gaping and torpid they retired,
  To dream of what they should be doing.

XVII.

And worse and worse, the drowsy curse
  Yawned in him, till it grew a pest—
A wide contagious atmosphere,
Creeping like cold through all things near;
  A power to infect and to infest.

XVIII.

His servant-maids and dogs grew dull;
  His kitten, late a sportive elf;
The woods and lakes so beautiful,
Of dim stupidity were full.
  All grew dull as Peter's self.

XIX.

The earth under his feet—the springs,
  Which lived within it a quick life,
The air, the winds of many wings,
That fan it with new murmurings,
  Were dead to their harmonious strife.

XX.

The birds and beasts within the wood,
  The insects, and each creeping thing,
Were now a silent multitude;
Love's work was left unwrought—no brood
  Near Peter's house took wing.

XXI.

And every neighbouring cottager
  Stupidly yawned upon the other:
No jackass brayed; no little cur
Cocked up his ears:—no man would stir
  To save a dying mother.

XXII.

Yet all from that charmed district went
  But some half-idiot and half-knave,
Who rather than pay any rent,
Would live with marvellous content,
  Over his father's grave.

XXIII.

No bailiff dared within that space,
  For fear of the dull charm, to enter;
A man would bear upon his face,
For fifteen months in any case,
  The yawn of such a venture.

XXIV.

Seven miles above—below—around—
  This pest of dullness holds its sway;
A ghastly life without a sound;
To Peter's soul the spell is bound—
  How should it ever pass away?

WILLIAM MAGINN.

THE RIME OF THE AUNCIENT WAGGONERE.

(COLERIDGE)

PART FIRST.

An auncient wag-gonere stoppeth ane tailore going to a wedding, whereat he hath been ap-pointed to be best manne, and to take a hand in the casting of the slippere.

It is an auncient Waggonere,
  And hee stoppeth one of nine :—
' Now wherefore dost thou grip me soe
  With that horny fist of thine ?

' The bridegroom's doors are opened wide,
  And thither I must walke;
Soe, by youre leave, I must be gone,
  I have noe time for talke !'

The waggonere in mood for chat, and admits of no excuse.

The tailore seized with the ague.

Hee holds him with his horny fist—
  ' There was a wain,' quothe hee,
' Hold offe, thou raggamouffine tykke.'
  Eftsoones his fist dropped hee.

He listeneth like a three years and a half child.

Hee satte him downe upon a stone,
  With ruefulle looks of feare;
And thus began this tippsye manne,
  The red-nosed waggonere.

The appetite of the tailore whetted by the smell of cabbage.

' The waine is fulle, the horses pulle,
  Merrilye did we trotte
Alonge the bridge, alonge the road,
  A jolly crewe, I wotte;'—
And here the tailore smotte his breaste,
  He smelte the cabbage potte !

The waggonere in talking anent Boreas, maketh bad orthographye.

' The night was darke, like Noe's arke,
  Oure waggone moved alonge;
The hail pour'd faste, loude roared the blaste,
  Yet stille we moved alonge;
And sung in chorus, " Cease, loud Borus,"
  A very charminge songe.

' " Bravoe, bravissimoe," I cried,
  The sounde was quite elatinge;
But, in a trice, upon the ice,   Their mirth in-
  We hearde the horses skaitinge.   terrupted.

' The ice was here, the ice was there,   And the passengers
  It was a dismale mattere,   exercise themselves
To see the cargoe, one by one,   in the pleasant art
  Flounderinge in the wattere !   of swimminge, as
                                                   doeth also their
                                                   prog, to witte, great
' With rout and roare, we reached the shore,   store of colde roas-
  And never a soul did sinke;   ted beef; item, ane
But in the rivere, gone for evere,   beef - s t a k e pye :
  Swum our meate and drinke.   item, viii choppines
                                                   of usquebaugh.

' At lengthe we spied a goode grey goose,   The   waggonere
  Thorough the snow it came;   hailethe ane goose
And with the butte ende of my whippe,   with   ane   novel
  I hailed it in Goddhis name.   salutatione

' It staggered as it had been drunke,
  So dexterous was it hitte;
Of brokene boughs we made a fire,
  Thomme Loncheone roasted itte.'—

' Be done, thou tipsye waggonere,   The   tailore   im-
  To the feaste I must awaye.'—   patient to be gone,
The waggonere seized him bye the coatte,   but is forcibly per-
  And forced him there to staye,   suaded to remain.
Begginge, in gentlemanlie style,
  Butte halfe ane hour's delaye.

PART SECOND.

' The crimson sunne was rising o'ere   The   waggonere's
  The verge of the horizon;   bowels   yearn to-
Upon my worde, as faire a sunne   wards the sunne.
  As ever I clapped eyes onne.

P

The passengers
throwe the blame
of the goose mass-
acre on the inno-
cent waggonere.

' " 'Twill bee ane comfortable thinge,"
    The mutinous crewe 'gan crye;
" 'Twill be ane comfortable thinge,
    Within the jaile to lye;
Ah ! execrable wretche," saide they,
    " Thatte caused the goose to die !' "

The sunne suf-
feres ane artificial
eclipse, and horror
follows, the same
not being mentioned
in the Belfaste Al-
manacke.

' The day was drawing near itte's close,
    The sunne was well nighe settinge;
When lo ! it seemed as iffe his face
    Was veiled with fringe-warke-nettinge.

Various hypo-
theses on the sub-
ject, frome which
the passengeres draw
wronge conclusions.

' Somme saide itte was ane apple tree,
    Laden with goodlye fruite,
Somme swore itte was ane foreigne birde,
    Some said it was ane brute;
Alas ! it was ane bumbailiffe
    Riding in pursuite !

Ane lovelye sound
ariseth; ittes ef-
fects described.

    hue and crye sterte uppe behind,
    Whilke smote our ears like thunder.
Within the waggone there was drede,
    Astonishmente and wonder.

The passengers
throw somersets.

' One after one, the rascalls rann,
    And from the carre did jump;
One after one, one after one,
    They felle with heavy thump.

' Six miles ane houre theye offe did scoure,
    Like shippes on ane stormye ocean,
Theire garments flappinge in the winde,
    With ane shorte uneasy motion.

The waggonere
complimenteth the
bumbailiffe with ane
Mendoza.

' Their bodies with their legs did flye,
    Theye fled with feare and glyffe;
Why star'st thoue soe ?—With one goode
      blow,
    I felled the bumbailiffe !'

PART THIRD.

'I feare thee, auncient waggonere,
　I feare thy hornye fiste,
For itte is stained with goose's gore,
　And bailiffe's blood, I wist.

The tailore meet-
eth Corporal Feare.

'I fear to gette ane fisticuffe
　From thy leathern knuckles brown';
With that the tailore strove to ryse—
　The waggonere thrusts him down.

'Thou craven, if thou mov'st a limbe,
　I'll give thee cause for feare;'
And thus went on that tipsye man,
　The red-billed waggonere.

'The bumbailiffe so beautiful
　Declared itte was no joke,
For, to his knowledge, both his legs
　And fifteen ribbes were broke.

The bailiffe com-
plaineth of con-
siderable derange-
ment of his animal
economye.

'The lighte was gone, the nighte came on,
　Ane hundrede lantherns' sheen
Glimmerred upon the kinge's highwaye—
　Ane lovelye sighte, I ween.

Policemen with
their lanthornes
pursue the wag-
gonere.

'"Is it he," quoth one, "is this the manne?
　I'll laye the rascalle stiffe;"—
With cruel stroke the beak he broke
　Of the harmless bumbailiffe.

'The threatening of the saucye rogue
　No more I coulde abide;
Advancing forthe my goode right legge
　Three paces and a stride,
I sent my lefte foot dexterously
　Seven inches thro' his side.

Steppeth twenty
feete in imitatione
of the Admirable
Crichtovn.

'Up came the seconde from the vanne;
　We had scarcely fought a round,
When someone smote me from behinde,
　And I fell down in a swound:

Complaineth of
foul play and falleth
down in ane trance.

One acteth the
parte of Job's com-
fortere.

' And when my head began to clear,
    I heard the yemering crew—
Quoth one, " this man hath penance done,
    And penance more shall do." '

Part Fourth.

The waggonere
maketh ane shrewd
observation.

' O Freedom is a glorious thing !—
    And, tailore, by the by,
I'd rather in a halter swing,
    Than in a dungeon lie.

The waggonere
tickleth the spleen
of the jailer, who
daunces ane Fan-
dango.

' The jailere came to bring me foode,
    Forget it will I never,
How he turned up the white o' his eye
    When I stuck him in the liver.

Rejoicethe in the
fragrance of the aire.

' His threade of life was snapt: once more
    I reached the open streete;
The people sung out " Gardyloo "
    As I ran down the streete.
Methought the blessed air of heaven
    Never smelte so sweete.

Dreadeth Shoan
Dhu, the corporal
of the guarde.

' Once more upon the broad highwaye,
    I walked with feare and drede;
And every fifteen steppes I tooke
    I turned about my heade,
For feare the corporal of the guarde
    Might close behind me trede !

' Behold, upon the western wave
    Setteth the broad bright sunne;
So I must onward, as I have
    Full fifteen miles to runne;—

The waggonere
taketh leave of the
tailore,

' And should the bailiffes hither come
    To aske whilke way I've gone,
Tell them I took the othere road,'
    Said hee, and trotted onne.

The tailore rushed into the roome,
    O'erturning three or foure;
Fractured his skulle against the walle,
    And worde spake never more ! !

MORALE.

Such is the fate of foolish men,
    The danger all may see,
Of those, who list to waggonere,
    And keepe bad companye.

to whome ane small accidente happeneth. Whereupon followeth the morale very proper to be had in minde by all members of the Dilettanti Society when they come over the bridge at these houres. Wherefore let them take heed and not lay blame where it lyeth nott.

TO A BOTTLE OF OLD PORT.

(MOORE)

WHEN he who adores thee has left but the dregs
    Of such famous old stingo behind,
Oh ! say will he bluster and weep ? No, 'ifegs !
    He'll seek for some more of the kind.
He'll laugh and though doctors perhaps may condemn—
    Thy tide shall efface the decree,
For many can witness, though subject to phlegm,
    He has always been faithful to thee !

With thee were the dreams of his earliest love,
    Every rap in his pocket was thine,
And his very last prayer, every morning, by Jove !
    Was to finish the evening in wine.
How blest are the tipplers whose heads can outlive
    The effects of four bottles of thee,
But the next dearest blessing that heaven can give,
    Is to stagger home muzzy from three !

THE LAST LAMP OF THE ALLEY.

(MOORE)

THE last lamp of the alley
  Is burning alone !
All its brilliant companions
  Are shivered and gone.
No lamp of her kindred,
  No burner is nigh,
To rival her glimmer,
  Or light to supply.

I'll not leave thee, thou lone one !
  To vanish in smoke;
As the bright ones are shattered,
  Thou too shalt be broke:
Thus kindly I scatter
  Thy globe o'er the street;
Where the watch in his rambles
  Thy fragments shall meet.

Then home will I stagger,
  As well as I may;
By the light of my nose sure
  I'll find out the way.
When thy blaze is extinguished,
  Thy brilliancy gone,
Oh ! my beak shall illumine
  The alley alone.

THE GALIONGEE.

A FRAGMENT OF A TURKISH TALE.

(BYRON)

THE Pacha sat in his divan,
With silver-sheathed ataghan;
And called to him a Galiongee,
Come lately from the Euxine Sea

To Stamboul; chains were on his feet,
  And fetters on his hands were seen,
  Because he was a Nazarene:
When, duly making reverence meet,
With haughty glance on that divan,
And curling lip, he thus began:

  ' By broad Phingari's silver light,
When sailing at the noon of night,
Bismillah ! whom did we descry
  But dark corsairs, who, bent on spoil,
  Athwart the deep sea ever toil !
We knew their blood-red flags on high:
The Capitan he called, belike,
With gesture proud, to bid us strike,
And told his Sonbachis to spare
Of not one scalp a single hair,
Though garbs of green showed Emirs there !
It boots not, Pacha, to relate
  What souls were sent to Eblis throne,
How Azrael's arrows scattered fate,
  How wild, wet, wearied, and alone,
When all my crew were drench'd in blood,
Or floated lifeless on the flood,
I fought unawed, nor e'er thought I
To shout " Amaun !" the craven's cry—
  I took my handkerchief to wipe
  My burning brow, and then I took,
With placid hand, my long chibouque,
That is to say, my Turkish pipe,
And having clapp'd it in my cheek
Disdaining e'er a word to speak,
I shouted to the pirate, " Now,
You've fairly beat me, I allow," ' &c.

JOHN KEATS.

STANZAS ON CHARLES ARMITAGE BROWN.

(SPENSER)

HE is to weet a melancholy carle:
Thin in the waist, with bushy head of hair,
As hath the seeded thistle when in parle
It holds the Zephyr, ere it sendeth fair
Its light balloons into the summer air;
Therto his beard had not begun to bloom,
No brush had touch'd his chin, or razor sheer;
No care had touch'd his cheek with mortàl doom,
But new he was and bright as scarf from Persian loom.

Ne cared he for wine, or half and half,
Ne cared he for fish or flesh or fowl,
And sauces held he worthless as the chaff;
He 'sdeigned the swine-head at the wassail-bowl;
Ne with lewd ribbalds sat he cheek by jowl;
Ne with sly Lemans in the scorner's chair;
But after water-brooks this Pilgrim's soul
Panted, and all his food was woodland air
Though he would oft-times feast on gilliflowers rare.

The slang of cities in no wise he knew,
Tipping the wink to him was heathen Greek;
He sipp'd no olden Tom or ruin blue,
Or nantz or cherry-brandy drank full meek
By many a damsel hoarse and rouge of cheek;
Nor did he know each aged watchman's beat,
Nor in obscured purlieus would he seek
For curlèd Jewesses, with ankles neat,
Who as they walk abroad make tinkling with their feet.

ON OXFORD.

(WORDSWORTH)

THE Gothic looks solemn,
The plain Doric column
Supports an old Bishop and Crosier;
The mouldering arch,
Shaded o'er by a larch
Stands next door to Wilson the Hosier.

Vicè—that is, by turns,—
O'er pale faces mourns
The black tassell'd trencher and common hat;
The Chantry boy sings,
The Steeple-bell rings,
And as for the Chancellor—*dominat.*

There are plenty of trees,
And plenty of ease,
And plenty of fat deer for Parsons;
And when it is venison,
Short is the benison,—
Then each on a leg or thigh fastens.

HARTLEY COLERIDGE.

HE LIVED AMIDST TH' UNTRODDEN WAYS.

(WORDSWORTH)

HE lived amidst th' untrodden ways
　　To Rydal Lake that lead;
A bard whom there were none to praise,
　　And very few to read.

Behind a cloud his mystic sense,
　　Deep hidden, who can spy?
Bright as the night when not a star
　　Is shining in the sky.

Unread his works—his ' Milk White Doe '
　　With dust is dark and dim;
It's still in Longman's shop, and oh!
　　The difference to him!

JOHN HAMILTON REYNOLDS.

PETER BELL: A LYRICAL BALLAD.

(WORDSWORTH)

I do affirm that I am the REAL SIMON PURE.—*Bold Stroke for a Wife.*

I.

IT is the thirty-first of March,
A gusty evening—half-past seven;
The moon is shining o'er the larch,
A simple shape—a cock'd-up arch,
Rising bigger than a star,
Though the stars are thick in Heaven.

II.

Gentle moon ! how canst thou shine
Over graves and over trees,
With as innocent a look
As my own grey eyeball sees,
When I gaze upon a brook ?

III.

Od's me ! how the moon doth shine:
It doth make a pretty glitter,
Playing in the waterfall;
As when Lucy Gray doth litter
Her baby-house with bugles small.

IV.

Beneath the ever blessed moon
An old man o'er an old grave stares,
You never look'd upon his fellow;
His brow is covered with grey hairs,
As though they were an umbrella

V.

He hath a noticeable look,[1]
'This old man hath—this grey old man;
He gazes at the graves, and seems,
With over waiting, over wan,
Like Susan Harvey's[2] pan of creams.

VI.

'T is Peter Bell—'t is Peter Bell,
Who never stirreth in the day;
His hand is wither'd—he is old !
On Sundays he is us'd to pray,
In winter he is very cold.[3]

VII.

I've seen him in the month of August,
At the wheatfield, hour by hour,
Picking ear,—by ear,—by ear,—
Through wind,—and rain,—and sun,—and shower,
From year,—to year,—to year,—to year.

VIII.

You never saw a wiser man,
He knows his Numeration Table;
He counts the sheep of Harry Gill,[4]
Every night that he is able,
When the sheep are on the hill.

IX.

Betty Foy—*My* Betty Foy,—
Is the aunt of Peter Bell;

[1] ' A noticeable man with large grey eyes.'—*Lyrical Ballads.*

[2] Dairy-maid to Mr. Gill.

[3] Peter Bell resembleth Harry Gill in this particular:

      ' His teeth they chatter, chatter, chatter.'

I should have introduced this fact in the text, but that Harry Gill
would not rhyme.   I reserve this for my blank verse.

[4] Harry Gill was the original proprietor of Barbara Lewthwaite's
pet lamb; and he also bred Betty Foy's celebrated pony, got originally out of a Nightmare, by a descendant of the great Trojan horse.

And credit me, as I would have you,
Simon Lee was once his nephew,
And his niece is Alice Fell.[1]

X.

He is rurally related;
Peter Bell hath country cousins,
(He had once a worthy mother)
Bells and Peters by the dozens,
But Peter Bell he hath no brother.

XI.

Not a brother owneth he,
Peter Bell he hath no brother,
His mother had no other son,
No other son e'er call'd her mother;
Peter Bell hath brother none.

XII.

Hark ! the churchyard brook is singing
Its evening song amid the leaves;
And the peering moon doth look
Sweetly on that singing brook,
Round[2] and sad as though it grieves.

XIII.

Peter Bell doth lift his hand,
That thin hand, which in the light
Looketh like to oiled paper;
Paper oiled,—oily bright,—
And held up to a waxen taper.

XIV.

The hand of Peter Bell is busy,
Under the pent-house of his hairs;

[1] Mr. Sheridan, in his sweet poem of the *Critic*, supplies one of his heroes with as singularly clustering a relationship.

[2] I have here changed the shape of the moon, not from any poetical heedlessness, or human perversity, but because man is fond of change, and in this I have studied the metaphysical varieties of our being.

His eye is like a solemn sermon;
The little flea severely fares,
'Tis a sad day for the vermin.

XV.

He is thinking of the Bible—
Peter Bell is old and blest;
He doth pray and scratch away,
He doth scratch, and bitten, pray
To *flee* away, and be at rest.

XVI.

At home his foster child is cradled—
Four brown bugs are feeding there[1];
Catch as many, sister Ann,
Catch as many as you can[2]
And yet the little insects spare.

XVII.

Why should blessed insects die ?
The flea doth skip o'er Betty Foy,
Like a little living thing:
Though it hath not fin or wing,
Hath it not a moral joy ?

XVIII.

I the poet of the mountain,
Of the waterfall and fell,
I the mighty mental medlar,
I the lonely lyric pedlar,
I the Jove of Alice Fell,

XIX.

I the Recluse—a gentle man,[3]
A gentle man—a simple creature,

[1] I have a similar idea in my Poem on finding a Bird's Nest:
'Look ! *five* blue eggs are gleaming there.'
But the numbers are different, so I trust no one will differ with the numbers.

[2] I have also given these lines before; but in thus printing them again, I neither tarnish their value, nor injure their novelty.

[3] See my Sonnet to Sleep:—
'I surely not a man ungently made.'

Who would not hurt—God shield the thing,—
The merest, meanest May-bug's wing,
Am tender in my tender nature.

XX.

I do doat on my dear wife,
On the linnet, on the worm,
I can see sweet written salads
Growing in the Lyric Ballads,
And always find them green and firm.

XXI.

Peter Bell is laughing now,
Like a dead man making faces;
Never saw I smile so old,
On face so wrinkled and so cold,
Since the Idiot Boy's grimaces.

XXII.

He is thinking of the moors,
Where I saw him in his breeches;
Ragged though they were, a pair
Fit for a grey old man to wear;
Saw him poking,—gathering leeches.[1]

XXIII.

And gather'd leeches are to him,
To Peter Bell, like gather'd flowers;
They do yield him such delight,
As roses poach'd from porch at night,
Or pluck'd from oratoric[2] bowers.

XXIV.

How that busy smile doth hurry
O'er the cheek of Peter Bell;

[1] See my story of the Leech-gatherer, the finest poem in the world,—except this.

[2] ' Ah !' said the Briar, ' blame me not.'
Waterfall and Eglantine.

Also,—
' The Oak, a Giant and a Sage,
His neighbour thus address'd.'

He is surely in a flurry,
Hurry skurry—hurry skurry,
Such delight I may not tell.

XXV.

His stick is made of wilding wood,
His hat was formerly of felt,
His duffel cloak of wool is made,
His stockings are from stock in trade,
His belly's belted with a belt.

XXVI.

His father was a bellman once,
His mother was a beldame old;
They kept a shop at Keswick Town,
Close by the Bell, (beyond the Crown,)
And pins and peppermint they sold.

XXVII.

He is stooping now about
O'er the gravestones one and two;
The clock is now a striking eight,
Four more hours and 't will be late,
And Peter Bell hath much to do.

XXVIII.

O'er the gravestones three and four.
Peter stoopeth old and wise;
He counteth with a wizard glee
The graves of all his family,
While the hooting owlet cries.

XXIX.

Peter Bell, he readeth ably,
All his letters he can tell;
Roman W,— Roman S,
In a minute he can guess,
Without the aid of Dr. Bell.

XXX.

Peter keeps a gentle pony,
But the pony is not here;

Susan who is very tall,[1]
And very sick and sad withal,
Rides it slowly far and near.

XXXI.

Hark ! the voice of Peter Bell,
And the belfry bell is knelling;
It soundeth drowsily and dead,
As though a corse th' ' Excursion ' read;
Or Martha Ray her tale was telling

XXXII.

Do listen unto Peter Bell,
While your eyes with tears do glisten:
Silence ! his old eyes do read
All, on which the boys do tread
When holidays do come—Do listen !

XXXIII.

The ancient Marinere lieth here,
Never to rise, although he pray'd,—
But all men, all, must have their fallings;
And, like the Fear of Mr. Collins,[2]
He died ' of sounds himself had made.'

XXXIV.

Dead mad mother,—Martha Ray,
Old Matthew too, and Betty Foy,
Lack-a-daisy ! here's a rout full;
Simon Lee whose age was doubtful,[3]
Simon even the Fates destroy.

---

[1] ' *Long Susan* lay deep lost in thought.'—*The Idiot Boy.*

[2] See what I have said of this man in my excellent supplementary *Preface.*

[3] I cannot resist quoting the following lines, to show how I preserve my system from youth to age. As Simon was, so he is. And one and twenty years have scarcely altered (except by death) that cheerful and cherry-cheeked Old Huntsman. This is the truth of Poetry.

> In the sweet shire of Cardigan,
>   Not far from pleasant Ivor-hall;
> An old man dwells—a little man—
>   I've heard he once was tall;

XXXV.

Harry Gill is gone to rest,
Goody Blake is food for maggot;
They lie sweetly side by side,
Beautiful as when they died;
Never more shall she pick faggot.

XXXVI.

Still he reads, and still the moon
On the churchyard's mounds doth shine;
The brook is still demurely singing,
Again the belfry bell is ringing,
'T is nine o'clock, six, seven, eight, nine!

XXXVII.

Patient Peter pores and proses
On, from simple grave to grave;
Here marks the children snatch'd to heaven,
None left to blunder ' we are seven ';—
Even Andrew Jones[1] no power could save.

XXXVIII.

What a Sexton's work[2] is here,
Lord! the Idiot Boy is gone;
And Barbara Lewthwaite's fate the same,
And cold as mutton is her lamb;
And Alice Fell is bone by bone.

XXXIX.

And tears are thick with Peter Bell,
Yet still he sees one blessed tomb;
Tow'rds it he creeps with spectacles,
And bending on his leather knees,
He reads the *Lake*iest Poet's doom.

Of years he has upon his back,
No doubt, a burthen weighty;
He says he is threescore and ten,
But others say he's eighty.'
These lines were written in the summer of 1798, and I bestowed
great labour upon them.

[1] Andrew Jones was a very singular old man. See my Poem,
' I hate that Andrew Jones—he'll breed,' etc.

[2] ' Let thy wheelbarrow alone,' etc. See my Poem to a Sexton.

XL.

The letters printed are by fate,
The death they say was suicide;
He reads—' Here lieth W. W.
Who never more will trouble you, trouble you ':
The old man smokes who 't is that died.

XLI.

Go home, go home—old Man, go home;
Peter, lay thee down at night,
Thou art happy, Peter Bell,
Say thy prayers for Alice Fell,
Thou hast seen a blessed sight.

XLII.

He quits that moonlight yard of skulls,
And still he feels right glad, and smiles
With moral joy at that old tomb;
Peter's cheek recalls its bloom,
And as he creepeth by the tiles,
He mutters ever —' W. W.
Never more will trouble you, trouble you.'

Here endeth the ballad of Peter Bell.

ROBERT GILFILLAN.

BLUE BONNETS OVER THE BORDER.

(SCOTT)

READ, read, *Woodstock* and *Waverley*,
  Turn every page and read forward in order;
Read, read, every tale cleverly,
  All the old novels are over the border.
        Many a book lies dead,
        Dusty and never read,
Many a chiel wants a thread to his story;
        While Walter, that king o' men,
        Just with his single pen,
Like a giant, well *grogged*, marches on in his glory!

Come from your tales full of murders amazing,
  Come from romaunts gone to bed long ago;
Come from the scribblers whom pye-men are praising,
  Come to *Redgauntlet* and brave *Ivanhoe!*
        Scott's fame is sounding,
        Readers abounding,
May laurels long circle his locks thin and hoary!
        Scotland shall many a day
        Speak of her bard, and say,
He lived for his country, and wrote for her glory!

THOMAS HOOD.

THE IRISH SCHOOLMASTER.

(SPENSER)

I.

ALACK ! 'tis melancholy theme to think
How Learning doth in rugged states abide,
And, like her bashful owl, obscurely blink,
In pensive glooms and corners, scarcely spied;
Not, as in Founders' Halls and domes of pride,
Served with grave homage, like a tragic queen,
But with one lonely priest compell'd to hide,
In midst of foggy moors and mosses green,
In that clay cabin hight the College of Kilreen !

II.

This College looketh South and West alsoe,
Because it hath a cast in windows twain;
Crazy and crack'd they be, and wind doth blow
Thorough transparent holes in every pane,
Which Dan, with many paines, makes whole again
With nether garments, which his thrift doth teach
To stand for glass, like pronouns, and when rain
Stormeth, he puts, ' once more unto the breach,'
Outside and in, tho' broke, yet so he mendeth each.

III.

And in the midst a little door there is,
Whereon a board that doth congratulate
With painted letters, red as blood I wis,
Thus written,
            ' CHILDREN TAKEN IN TO BATE.'
And oft, indeed, the inward of that gate,
Most ventriloque, doth utter tender squeak,
And moans of infants that bemoan their fate,
In midst of sounds of Latin, French, and Greek,
Which, all i' the Irish tongue, he teacheth them to
    speak.

IV.

For some are meant to right illegal wrongs,
And some for Doctors of Divinitie,
Whom he doth teach to murder the dead tongues,
And so win academical degree;
But some are bred for service of the sea,
Howbeit, their store of learning is but small.
For mickle waste he counteth it would be
To stock a head with bookish wares at all,
Only to be knocked off by ruthless cannon ball.

V.

Six babes he sways,—some little and some big,
Divided into classes six;—alsoe,
He keeps a parlour boarder of a pig,
That in the College fareth to and fro,
And picketh up the urchins' crumbs below,—
And eke the learned rudiments they scan,
And thus his A, B, C, doth wisely know,—
Hereafter to be shown in caravan,
And raise the wonderment of many a learned man.

VI.

Alsoe, he schools some tame familiar fowls,
Whereof, above his head, some two or three
Sit darkly squatting, like Minerva's owls,
But on the branches of no living tree,
And overlook the learned family;
While, sometimes, Partlet, from her gloomy perch,
Drops feather on the nose of Dominie,
Meanwhile, with serious eye, he makes research
In leaves of that sour tree of knowledge—now a birch.

VII.

No chair he hath, the awful Pedagogue,
Such as would magisterial hams imbed,
But sitteth lowly on a beechen log,
Secure in high authority and dread:
Large, as a dome for learning, seems his head,
And like Apollo's, all beset with rays,

Because his locks are so unkempt and red,
   And stand abroad in many several ways:—
No laurel crown he wears, howbeit his cap is baize.

VIII.

And, underneath, a pair of shaggy brows
O'erhang as many eyes of gizzard hue,
That inward giblet of a fowl, which shows
A mongrel tint, that is ne brown ne blue;
His nose,—it is a coral to the view;
Well nourished with Pierian Potheen,—
For much he loves his native mountain dew;—
But to depict the dye would lack, I ween,
A bottle-red, in terms, as well as bottle-green.

IX.

As for his coat, 'tis such a jerkin short
As Spencer had, ere he composed his Tales;
But underneath he hath no vest, nor aught,
So that the wind his airy breast assails;
Below, he wears the nether garb of males,
Of crimson plush, but non-plushed at the knee;—
Thence further down the native red prevails,
Of his own naked fleecy hosiery:—
Two sandals, without soles, complete his cap-a-pee.

X.

Nathless, for dignity, he now doth lap
His function in a magisterial gown,
That shows more countries in it than a map,—
Blue tinct, and red, and green, and russet brown,
Besides some blots, standing for country-town;
And eke some rents, for streams and rivers wide;
But, sometimes, bashful when he looks adown,
He turns the garment of the other side,
Hopeful that so the holes may never be espied !

XI.

And soe he sits, amidst the little pack,
That look for shady or for sunny noon,

Within his visage, like an almanack,—
His quiet smile foretelling gracious boon:
But when his mouth droops down, like rainy moon,
With horrid chill each little heart unwarms,
Knowing that infant show'rs will follow soon,
And with forebodings of near wrath and storms
They sit, like timid hares, all trembling on their forms.

XII.

Ah ! luckless wight, who cannot then repeat
' Corduroy Colloquy,'—or ' Ki, Kæ, Kod,'—
Full soon his tears shall make his turfy seat
More sodden, tho' already made of sod,
For Dan shall whip him with the word of God,—
Severe by rule, and not by nature mild,
He never spoils the child and spares the rod,
But spoils the rod and never spares the child,
And soe with holy rule deems he is reconcil'd.

XIII.

But, surely, the just sky will never wink
At men who take delight in childish throe,
And stripe the nether-urchin like a pink
Or tender hyacinth, inscribed with woe;
Such bloody Pedagogues, when they shall know,
By useless birches, that forlorn recess,
Which is no holiday, in Pit below,
Will hell not seem designed for their distress,—
A melancholy place, that is all bottomlesse ?

XIV.

Yet would the Muse not chide the wholesome use
Of needful discipline, in due degree.
Devoid of sway, what wrongs will time produce,
Whene'er the twig untrained grows up a tree.
This shall a Carder, that a Whiteboy be,
Ferocious leaders of atrocious bands,
And Learning's help be used for infamie,
By lawless clerks, that, with their bloody hands,
In murder'd English write Rock's murderous com-
mands.

XV.

But ah ! what shrilly cry doth now alarm
The sooty fowls that dozed upon the beam,
All sudden fluttering from the brandish'd arm,
And cackling chorus with the human scream;
Meanwhile, the scourge plies that unkindly seam,
In Phelim's brogues, which bares his naked skin,
Like traitor gap in warlike fort, I deem,
That falsely lets the fierce besieger in,
Nor seeks the pedagogue by other course to win.

XVI.

No parent dear he hath to heed his cries;—
Alas ! his parent dear is far aloof,
And deep in Seven-Dial cellar lies,
Killed by kind cudgel-play, or gin of proof;
Or climbeth, catwise, on some London roof,
Singing, perchance, a lay of Erin's Isle,
Or, whilst he labours, weaves a fancy-woof,
Dreaming he sees his home,—his Phelim smile;
Ah me ! that luckless imp, who weepeth all the while !

XVII.

Ah ! who can paint that hard and heavy time,
When first the scholar lists in learning's train,
And mounts her rugged steep, enforc'd to climb,
Like sooty imp, by sharp posterior pain,
From bloody twig, and eke that Indian cane,
Wherein, alas ! no sugar'd juices dwell,
For this the while one stripling's sluices drain
Another weepeth over chilblains fell,
Always upon the heel, yet never to be well !

XVIII.

Anon a third, for his delicious root,
Late ravish'd from his tooth by elder chit,
So soon is human violence afoot,
So hardly is the harmless biter bit !
Meanwhile, the tyrant, with untimely wit
And mouthing face, derides the small one's moan,

Who, all lamenting for his loss, doth sit,
Alack,—mischance comes seldomtimes alone,
But aye the worried dog must rue more curs than one.

XIX.

For lo ! the Pedagogue, with sudden drub,
Smites his scald head, that is already sore,—
Superfluous wound,—such is Misfortune's rub !
Who straight makes answer with redoubled roar,
And sheds salt tears twice faster than before,
That still, with backward fist he strives to dry;
Washing, with brackish moisture, o'er and o'er,
His muddy cheek, that grows more foul thereby,
Till all his rainy face looks grim as rainy sky.

XX.

So Dan, by dint of noise, obtains a peace,
And with his natural untender knack,
By new distress, bids former grievance cease,
Like tears dried up with rugged huckaback,
That sets the mournful visage all awrack;
Yet soon the childish countenance will shine
Even as thorough storms the soonest slack,
For grief and beef in adverse ways incline,
This keeps, and that decays, when duly soak'd in brine.

XXI.

Now all is hushed, and, with a look profound,
The Dominie lays ope the learned page
(So be it called); although he doth expound
Without a book, both Greek and Latin sage;
Now telleth he of Rome's rude infant age,
How Romulus was bred in savage wood,
By wet-nurse wolf, devoid of wolfish rage;
And laid foundation-stone of walls of mud,
But watered it, alas ! with warm fraternal blood.

XXII.

Anon, he turns to that Homeric war,
How Troy was sieged like Londonderry town;

And stout Achilles, at his jaunting-car,
Dragged mighty Hector with a bloody crown:
And eke the bard, that sung of their renown,
In garb of Greece most beggar-like and torn,
He paints, with collie, wand'ring up and down:
Because, at once, in seven cities born;
And so, of parish rights, was, all his days, forlorn.

XXIII.

Anon, through old Mythology he goes,
Of gods defunct, and all their pedigrees,
But shuns their scandalous amours, and shows
How Plato wise, and clear-ey'd Socrates,
Confess'd not to those heathen hes and shes;
But thro' the clouds of the Olympic cope
Beheld St. Peter, with his holy keys,
And own'd their love was naught, and bow'd to Pope,
Whilst all their purblind race in Pagan mist did grope.

XXIV.

From such quaint themes he turns, at last, aside,
To new philosophies, that still are green,
And shows what rail-roads have been track'd to guide
The wheels of great political machine;
If English corn should grow abroad, I ween,
And gold be made of gold, or paper sheet;
How many pigs be born to each spalpeen;
And, ah ! how man shall thrive beyond his meat,—
With twenty souls alive, to one square sod of peat !

XXV.

Here, he makes end; and all the fry of youth,
That stood around with serious look intense,
Close up again their gaping eyes and mouth,
Which they had opened to his eloquence,
As if their hearing were a threefold sense;
But now the current of his words is done,
And whether any fruits shall spring from thence,
In future time, with any mother's son,
It is a thing, God wot ! that can be told by none.

XXVI.

Now by the creeping shadows of the noon,
The hour is come to lay aside their lore;
The cheerful pedagogue perceives it soon,
And cries, ' Begone !' unto the imps,—and four
Snatch their two hats, and struggle for the door,
Like ardent spirits vented from a cask,
All blythe and boisterous,—but leave two more,
With Reading made Uneasy for a task,
To weep, whilst all their mates in merry sunshine bask,

XXVII.

Like sportive Elfins, on the verdant sod,
With tender moss so sleekly overgrown,
That doth not hurt, but kiss, the sole unshod,
So soothly kind is Erin to her own !
And one, at Hare and Hound, plays all alone,—
For Phelim's gone to tend his step-dame's cow;
Ah ! Phelim's step-dame is a canker'd crone !
Whilst other twain play at an Irish row,
And, with shillelagh small, break one another's brow !

XXVIII.

But careful Dominie, with ceaseless thrift,
Now changeth ferula for rural hoe;
But, first of all, with tender hand doth shift
His college gown, because of solar glow,
And hangs it on a bush, to scare the crow:
Meanwhile, he plants in earth the dappled bean,
Or trains the young potatoes all a-row,
Or plucks the fragrant leek for pottage green,
With that crisp curly herb, call'd Kale in Aberdeen.

XXIX.

And so he wisely spends the fruitful hours,
Linked each to each by labour, like a bee;
Or rules in Learning's hall, or trims her bow'rs;—
Would there were many more such wights as he,
To sway each capital academie
Of Cam and Isis, for, alack ! at each
There dwells, I wot, some dronish Dominie,
That does no garden work, nor yet doth teach.
But wears a floury head, and talks in flow'ry speech !

HUGGINS AND DUGGINS.

A Pastoral after Pope.

Two swains or clowns—but call them swains—
While keeping flocks on Salisbury Plains,
For all that tend on sheep as drovers,
Are turned to songsters, or to lovers,
Each of the lass he call'd his dear
Began to carol loud and clear.
First Huggins sang, and Duggins then,
In the way of ancient shepherd men;
Who thus alternate hitch'd in song,
' All things by turns, and nothing long.'

Huggins.

Of all the girls about our place,
There's one beats all in form and face;
Search through all Great and Little Bumpstead
You'll only find one Peggy Plumstead.

Duggins.

To groves and streams I tell my flame;
I make the cliffs repeat her name:
When I'm inspired by gills and noggins,
The rocks re-echo Sally Hoggins !

Huggins.

When I am walking in the grove,
I think of Peggy as I rove.
I'd carve her name on every tree,
But I don't know my A, B, C.

Duggins.

Whether I walk in hill or valley,
I think of nothing else but Sally.
I'd sing her praise, but I can sing
No song, except ' God save the King.'

Huggins.

My Peggy does all nymphs excel,
And all confess she bears the bell,—
Where'er she goes swains flock together,
Like sheep that follow the bellwether.

Duggins.

Sally is tall and not too straight,—
Those very poplar shapes I hate;
But something twisted like an S,—
A crook becomes a shepherdess.

Huggins.

When Peggy's dog her arms emprison,
I often wish my lot was hisn;
How often I should stand and turn,
To get a pat from hands like hern.

Duggins.

I tell Sall's lambs how blest they be,
To stand about and stare at she;
But when I look, she turns and shies,
And won't bear none but their sheep's-eyes!

Huggins.

Love goes with Peggy where she goes,—
Beneath her smile the garden grows;
Potatoes spring, and cabbage starts,
'Tatoes have eyes, and cabbage hearts!

Duggins.

Where Sally goes it's always Spring,
Her presence brightens everything;
The sun smiles bright, but where her grin is,
It makes brass farthings look like guineas.

Huggins.

For Peggy I can have no joy,
She's sometimes kind, and sometimes coy,
And keeps me, by her wayward tricks,
As comfortless as sheep with ticks.

Duggins.

Sally is ripe as June or May,
And yet as cold as Christmas day;
For when she's asked to change her lot,
Lamb's wool,—but Sally, she wool not.

Huggins.

Only with Peggy and with health,
I'd never wish for state or wealth;
Talking of having health and more pence,
I'd drink her health if I had fourpence.

Duggins.

Oh, how that day would seem to shine,
If Sally's banns were read with mine;
She cries, when such a wish I carry,
'Marry come up!' but will not marry.

SEA SONG.

(DIBDIN)

PURE water it plays a good part in
The swabbing the decks and all that—
And it finds its own level for sartin—
For it sartinly drinks very flat:—
For my part a drop of the creatur
I never could think was a fault,
For if Tars should swig water by natur,
The sea would have never been salt!—
Then off with it into a jorum
And make it strong, sharpish, or sweet,
For if I've any sense of decorum,
It never was meant to be neat!—

One day when I was but half sober,—
Half measures I always disdain—
I walk'd into a shop that sold Soda,
And ax'd for some Water Champagne:—

Well, the lubber he drew and he drew, boys,
Till I'd shipped my six bottles or more,
And blow off my last limb but it's true, boys,
Why, I warn't half so drunk as afore!—
Then off with it into a jorum,
And make it strong, sharpish, or sweet,
For if I've any sense of decorum,
It never was meant to be neat.

'WE MET—'TWAS IN A CROWD.'

(T. H. BAYLY)

WE met—'twas in a mob—and I thought he had done
    me—
I felt—I could not feel—for no watch was upon me;
He ran—the night was cold—and his pace was un-
    alter'd,
I too longed much to pelt—but my small-boned legs
    falter'd.
I wore my bran new boots—and unrivall'd their
    brightness;
They fit me to a hair—how I hated their tightness!
I call'd, but no one came, and my stride had a tether,
Oh *thou* hast been the cause of this anguish, my
    leather!

And once again we met—and an old pal was near him,
He swore, a something low—but 'twas no use to fear
    him;
I seized upon his arm, he was mine and mine only,
And stept—as he deserv'd—to cells wretched and
    lonely:
And there he will be tried—but I shall ne'er receive
    her,
The watch that went too sure for an artful deceiver;
The world may think me gay,—heart and feet ache
    together,
Oh *thou* hast been the cause of this anguish, my
    leather!

THOSE EVENING BELLS.

(MOORE)

THOSE Evening Bells, those Evening Bells,
How many a tale their music tells,
Of Yorkshire cakes and crumpets prime,
And letters only just in time !—

The Muffin-boy has pass'd away,
The Postman gone—and I must pay,
For down below Deaf Mary dwells,
And does not hear those Evening Bells.

And so 'twill be when she is gone,
That tuneful peal will still ring on,
And other maids with timely yells
Forget to stay those Evening Bells.

THE WATER PERI'S SONG.

(MOORE)

FAREWELL, farewell, to my mother's own daughter,
The child that she wet-nursed is lapp'd in the wave ;
The *Mussul*-man coming to fish in this water
Adds a tear to the flood that weeps over her grave.

This sack is her coffin, this water's her bier,
This greyish *bath* cloak is her funeral pall;
And, stranger, O stranger ! this song that you hear
Is her epitaph, elegy, dirges, and all !

Farewell, farewell, to the child of Al Hassan,
My mother's own daughter—the last of her race—
She's a corpse, the poor body ! and lies in this basin,
And sleeps in the water that washes her face.

R

WILLIAM MAKEPEACE THACKERAY.

CABBAGES.

(LETITIA ELIZABETH LANDON)

CABBAGES ! bright green cabbages !
April's loveliest gifts, I guess.
There is not a plant in the garden laid,
Raised by the dung, dug by the spade,
None by the gardener watered, I ween,
So sweet as the cabbage, the cabbage green.

I do remember how sweet a smell
Came with the cabbage I loved so well,
Served up with the beef that beautiful looked,
The beef that the dark-eyed Ellen cooked.
I have seen beef served with radish of horse,
I have seen beef served with lettuce of Cos,
But it is far nicer, far nicer, I guess,
As bubble and squeak, beef and cabbages.

And when the dinner-bell sounds for me—
I care not how soon that time may be—
Carrots shall never be served on my cloth;
They are far too sweet for a boy of my broth;
But let me have there a mighty mess
Of smoking hot beef and cabbages.

LARRY O'TOOLE.

(LEVER)

YOU'VE all heard of Larry O'Toole,
Of the beautiful town of Drumgoole;
　　He had but one eye,
　　To ogle ye by—
Oh, murther, but that was a jew'l !
　　A fool
He made of de girls, dis O'Toole.

'Twas he was the boy didn't fail,
That tuck down pataties and mail;
    He never would shrink
    From any sthrong dthrink,
Was it whisky or Drogheda ale;
    I'm bail
That Larry would swallow a pail.

Oh, many a night, at the bowl,
With Larry I've sot cheek by jowl;
    He's gone to his rest,
    Where there's dthrink of the best,
And so let us give his old sowl
    A howl,
For 'twas he made the noggin to rowl.

THE WILLOW TREE.

(THACKERAY)

LONG by the willow-trees
  Vainly they sought her,
Wild rang the mother's screams
  O'er the grey water:
' Where is my lovely one ?
  Where is my daughter ?

' Rouse thee, sir constable—
  Rouse thee and look;
Fisherman, bring your net,
  Boatman, your hook.
Beat in the lily-beds,
  Dive in the brook !'

Vainly the constable
  Shouted and called her;
Vainly the fisherman
  Beat the green alder,
Vainly he flung the net,
  Never it hauled her !

Mother, beside the fire
  Sat, her nightcap in;
Father, in easy-chair,
  Gloomily napping,
When at the window-sill
  Came a light tapping !

And a pale countenance
  Looked through the casement.
Loud beat the mother's heart,
  Sick with amazement,
And at the vision, which
  Came to surprise her,
Shrieked in an agony—
  ' Lor' ! it's Elizar !'

Yes, 'twas Elizabeth—
  Yes, 'twas their girl;
Pale was her cheek, and her
  Hair out of curl.
' Mother !' the loving one,
  Blushing, exclaimed,
' Let not your innocent
  Lizzy be blamed.

' Yesterday, going to Aunt
  Jones's to tea,
Mother, dear mother, I
  Forgot the door-key !
And as the night was cold,
  And the way steep,
Mrs. Jones kept me to
  Breakfast and sleep.'

Whether her pa and ma
  Fully believed her,
That we shall never know:
  Stern they received her;
And for the work of that
  Cruel, though short, night,
Sent her to bed without
  Tea for a fortnight.

Moral.

Hey diddle diddlety,
Cat and the Fiddlety !
Maidens of England, take caution by she !
Let love and suicide
Never tempt you aside,
And always remember to take the door-key !

DEAR JACK.

(FRANCIS FAWKES)

DEAR Jack, this white mug that with Guinness I fill,
And drink to the health of sweet Nan of the Hill,
Was once Tommy Tosspot's, as jovial a sot,
As e'er drew a spigot, or drain'd a full pot—
In drinking, all round 'twas his joy to surpass,
And with all merry tipplers he swigg'd off his glass.

One morning in summer, while seated so snug,
In the porch of his garden, discussing his jug,
Stern Death, on a sudden, to Tom did appear,
And said, ' Honest Thomas, come take your last bier ;'
We kneaded his clay in the shape of this can,
From which let us drink to the health of my Nan.

THE GHAZUL, OR ORIENTAL LOVE-SONG.

I. *The Rocks.*

I WAS a timid little antelope;
My home was in the rocks, the lonely rocks.

I saw the hunters scouring on the plain;
I lived among the rocks, the lonely rocks.

I was a-thirsty in the summer-heat;
I ventured to the tents beneath the rocks.

Zuleikah brought me water from the well;
Since then I have been faithless to the rocks.

I saw her face reflected in the well;
Her camels since have marched into the rocks.

I look to see her image in the well;
I only see my eyes, my own sad eyes.
My mother is alone among the rocks.

II. *The Merry Bard.*

Zuleikah! The young Agas in the bazaar are slim-waisted and wear yellow slippers. I am old and hideous. One of my eyes is out, and the hairs of my beard are mostly grey. Praise be to Allah! I am a merry bard.

There is a bird upon the terrace of the Emir's chief wife. Praise be to Allah! He has emeralds on his neck, and a ruby tail. I am a merry bard. He deafens me with his diabolical screaming.

There is a little brown bird in the basket-maker's cage. Praise be to Allah! He ravishes my soul in the moonlight. I am a merry bard.

The peacock is an Aga, but the little bird is a Bulbul.

I am a little brown Bulbul. Come and listen in the moonlight. Praise be to Allah! I am a merry bard.

III. *The Caïque.*

Yonder to the kiosk, beside the creek,
Paddle the swift caïque.
Thou brawny oarsman with the sunburnt cheek,
Quick! for it soothes my heart to hear the Bulbul
  speak!

Ferry me quickly to the Asian shores,
Swift bending to your oars.
Beneath the melancholy sycamores,
Hark! what a ravishing note the lovelorn Bulbul pours.

Behold, the boughs seem quivering with delight,
The stars themselves more bright,
As 'mid the waving branches out of sight
The Lover of the Rose sits singing through the night.

Under the boughs I sat and listened still,
I could not have my fill.
'How comes,' I said, 'such music to his bill?
Tell me for whom he sings so beautiful a trill.'

'Once I was dumb,' then did the Bird disclose,
'But looked upon the Rose;
And in the garden where the loved one grows,
I straightway did begin sweet music to compose.'

'O bird of song, there's one in this caïque
The Rose would also seek,
So he might learn like you to love and speak.'
Then answered me the bird of dusky beak,
'The Rose, the Rose of Love blushes on Leilah's cheek.'

THE ALMACK'S ADIEU.

('WAPPING OLD STAIRS')

Your Fanny was never false-hearted,
  And this she protests and she vows,
From the *triste moment* when we parted
  On the staircase at Devonshire House!
I blushed when you asked me to marry,
  I vowed I would never forget;
And at parting I gave my dear Harry
  A beautiful *vinegarette!*

We spent *en province* all December,
  And I ne'er condescended to look
At Sir Charles, or the rich county member,
  Or even at that darling old Duke.
You were busy with dogs and with horses,
  Alone in my chamber I sat,
And made you the nicest of purses,
  And the smartest black satin cravat!

At night with that vile Lady Frances
  (*Je faisais moi tapisserie*)
You danced every one of the dances,
  And never once thought of poor me !
Mon pauvre petit cœur ! what a shiver
  I felt as she danced the last set,
And you gave, *ô mon Dieu !* to revive her,
  My beautiful *vinegarette !*

Return, love ! away with coquetting;
  This flirting disgraces a man !
And ah ! all the while you're forgetting
  The heart of your poor little Fan !
Reviens ! break away from these Circes,
  Reviens for a nice little chat;
And I've made you the sweetest of purses,
  And a lovely black satin cravat !

THE KNIGHTLY GUERDON.

(' WAPPING OLD STAIRS ')

UNTRUE to my Ulric I never could be,
I vow by the saints and the blessed Marie.
Since the desolate hour when we stood by the shore,
And your dark galley waited to carry you o'er,
My faith then I plighted, my love I confessed,
As I gave you the BATTLE-AXE marked with your
  Crest.

When the bold barons met in my father's old hall,
Was not Edith the flower of the banquet and ball ?
In the festival hour, on the lips of your bride,
Was there ever a smile save with THEE at my side ?
Alone in my turret I loved to sit best,
To blazon your BANNER and broider your crest.

The knights were assembled, the tourney was gay !
Sir Ulric rode first in the warrior-*mêlée*.
In the dire battle-hour, when the tourney was done,

And you gave to another the wreath you had won !
Though I never reproached thee, cold, cold was my
   breast,
As I thought of that BATTLE-AXE, ah ! and that crest !

But away with remembrance, no more will I pine
That others usurped for a time what was mine !
There's a FESTIVAL HOUR for my Ulric and me;
Once more, as of old, shall he bend at my knee;
Once more by the side of the knight I love best
Shall I blazon his BANNER and broider his CREST.

WILLIAM EDMONDSTOUNE AYTOUN.

THE MASSACRE OF THE MACPHERSON.

('FROM THE GAELIC')

FHAIRSHON swore a feud
  Against the clan M'Tavish;
Marched into their land
  To murder and to rafish;
For he did resolve
  To extirpate the vipers,
With four-and-twenty men
  And five-and-thirty pipers.

But when he had gone
  Half-way down Strath Canaan,
Of his fighting tail
  Just three were remainin'.
They were all he had,
  To back him in ta battle;
All the rest had gone
  Off, to drive ta cattle.

'Fery coot!' cried Fhairshon,
  'So my clan disgraced is;
Lads, we'll need to fight
  Pefore we touch the peasties.
Here's Mhic-Mac-Methusaleh
  Coming wi' his fassals,
Gillies seventy-three
  And sixty Dhuinéwassails!'

'Coot tay to you, sir;
  Are you not ta Fhairshon?
Was you coming here
  To fisit any person?
You are a plackguard, sir!
  It is now six hundred
Coot long years, and more,
  Since my glen was plunder'd.'

' Fat is tat you say ?
  Dare you cock your peaver ?
I will teach you, sir,
  Fat is coot pehaviour !
You shall not exist
  For another day more;
I will shoot you, sir,
  Or stap you with my claymore !'

' I am fery glad
  To learn what you mention,
Since I can prevent
  Any such intention.'
So Mhic-Mac-Methusaleh
  Gave some warlike howls,
Trew his skhian-dhu,
  An' stuck it in his powels.

In this fery way
  Tied ta faliant Fhairshon,
Who was always thought
  A superior person.
Fhairshon had a son,
  Who married Noah's daughter,
And nearly spoil'd ta Flood,
  By trinking up ta water:

Which he would have done,
  I at least believe it,
Had ta mixture peen
  Only half Glenlivet.
This is all my tale:
  Sirs, I hope 'tis new t'ye !
Here's your fery good healths,
  And tamn ta whusky duty !

A MIDNIGHT MEDITATION

(BULWER LYTTON)

FILL me once more the foaming pewter up!
   Another board of oysters, ladye mine!
To-night Lucullus with himself shall sup.
   These mute inglorious Miltons are divine!
   And as I here in slipper'd ease recline,
Quaffing of Perkins's Entire my fill,
I sigh not for the lymph of Aganippe's rill.

A nobler inspiration fires my brain,
   Caught from Old England's fine time-hallow'd drink;
I snatch the pot again, and yet again,
   And as the foaming fluids shrink and shrink,
   Fill me once more, I say, up to the brink!
This makes strong hearts—strong heads attest its
    charm—
This nerves the might that sleeps in Britain's brawny
    arm!

But these remarks are neither here nor there.
   Where was I? Oh, I see—old Southey's dead!
They'll want some bard to fill the vacant chair,
   And drain the annual butt—and oh, what head
   More fit with laurel to be garlanded
Than this, which, curled in many a fragrant coil,
Breathes of Castalia's streams, and best Macassar oil?

I know a grace is seated on my brow,
   Like young Apollo's with his golden beams
There should Apollo's bays be budding now:—
   And in my flashing eyes the radiance beams
   That marks the poet in his waking dreams,
When, as his fancies cluster thick and thicker,
He feels the trance divine of poesy and liquor.

They throng around me now, those things of air,
   That from my fancy took their being's stamp:

There Pelham sits and twirls his glossy hair,
   There Clifford leads his pals upon the tramp;
   There pale Zanoni, bending o'er his lamp,
Roams through the starry wilderness of thought,
Where all is everything, and everything is nought.

Yes, I am he who sang how Aram won
   The gentle ear of pensive Madeline !
How love and murder hand in hand may run,
   Cemented by philosophy serene,
   And kisses bless the spot where gore has been !
Who breathed the melting sentiment of crime,
And for the assassin waked a sympathy sublime !

Yes, I am he, who on the novel shed
   Obscure philosophy's enchanting light !
Until the public, 'wildered as they read,
   Believed they saw that which was not in sight—
   Of course 'twas not for me to set them right;
For in my nether heart convinced I am,
Philosophy's as good as any other bam.

Novels three-volumed I shall write no more—
   Somehow or other now they will not sell;
And to invent new passions is a bore—
   I find the Magazines pay quite as well.
   Translating's simple, too, as I can tell,
Who've hawked at Schiller on his lyric throne,
And given the astonish'd bard a meaning all my own.

Moore, Campbell, Wordsworth, their best days are
     grass'd :
   Batter'd and broken are their early lyres.
Rogers, a pleasant memory of the past,
   Warm'd his young hands at Smithfield's martyr fires,
   And, worth a plum, nor bays nor butt desires.
But these are things would suit me to the letter,
For though this Stout is good, old Sherry's greatly
     better.

A fico for your small poetic ravers,
   Your Hunts, your Tennysons, your Milnes, and
     these !

Shall they compete with him who wrote ' Maltravers,'
  Prologue to ' Alice or the Mysteries ' ?
  No ! Even now my glance prophetic sees
My own high brow girt with the bays about.
What ho ! within there, ho ! another pint of STOUT !

THE HUSBAND'S PETITION.

(AYTOUN)

COME hither, my heart's darling,
  Come, sit upon my knee,
And listen, while I whisper
  A boon I ask of thee.
You need not pull my whiskers
  So amorously, my dove;
'Tis something quite apart from
  The gentle cares of love.

I feel a bitter craving—
  A dark and deep desire,
That glows beneath my bosom
  Like coals of kindled fire.
The passion of the nightingale,
  When singing to the rose,
Is feebler than the agony
  That murders my repose !

Nay, dearest ! do not doubt me,
  Though madly thus I speak—
I feel thy arms about me,
  Thy tresses on my cheek:
I know the sweet devotion
  That links thy heart with mine,—
I know my soul's emotion
  Is doubly felt by thine:

And deem not that a shadow
  Hath fallen across my love:
No, sweet, my love is shadowless,
  As yonder heaven above.

These little taper fingers—
    Ah, Jane ! how white they be !—
Can well supply the cruel want
    That almost maddens me.

Thou wilt not sure deny me
    My first and fond request;
I pray thee, by the memory
    Of all we cherish best—
By all the dear remembrance
    Of those delicious days
When, hand in hand, we wander'd
    Along the summer braes;

By all we felt, unspoken,
    When 'neath the early moon,
We sat beside the rivulet,
    In the leafy month of June;
And by the broken whisper
    That fell upon my ear,
More sweet than angel music,
    When first I woo'd thee, dear !

By that great vow which bound thee
    For ever to my side,
And by the ring that made thee
    My darling and my bride !
Thou wilt not fail nor falter,
    But bend thee to the task—
A BOILED SHEEP'S HEAD ON SUNDAY
    Is all the boon I ask !

CHARLES WILLIAM SHIRLEY BROOKS.

SONNET CCCI.

To My Five New Kittens.

(TUPPER)

SOFT little beasts, how pleasantly ye lie
  Snuggling and snoozling by your purring sire,
  Mother I mean (but sonnet-rhymes require
A shorter word, and boldly I defy
Those who would tie the bard by pedant rule).
  O kittens, you're not thinking, I'll be bound,
  How three of you had yesterday been drowned
But that my little boy came home from school,
And begged your lives, though Cook remonstrance
      made,
  Declaring we were overrun with cats,
  That licked her cream-dish and her butter-pats,
But childhood's pleadings won me, and I said—
' O Cook, we'll keep the innocents alive;
They're five, consider, and you've fingers five.'

FOR A' THAT AND A' THAT.

A New Version, respectfully recommended to sundry whom it concerns.

(BURNS)

MORE luck to honest poverty,
    It claims respect, and a' that;
But honest wealth's a better thing,
    We dare be rich for a' that.
    For a' that, and a' that,
        And spooney cant and a' that,
    A man may have a ten-pun note,
        And be a brick for a' that.

What though on soup and fish we dine,
  Wear evening togs and a' that,
A man may like good meat and wine,
  Nor be a knave for a' that.
    For a' that, and a' that,
      Their fustian talk and a' that,
    A gentleman, however clean,
      May have a heart for a' that.

You see yon prater called a Beales,
  Who bawls and brays and a' that,
Tho' hundreds cheer his blatant bosh,
  He's but a goose for a' that.
    For a' that, and a' that,
      His Bubblyjocks, and a' that,
    A man with twenty grains of sense,
      He looks and laughs at a' that.

A prince can make a belted knight,
  A marquis, duke, and a' that,
And if the title's earned, all right,
  Old England's fond of a' that.
    For a' that, and a' that,
      Beales' balderdash, and a' that,
    A name that tells of service done
      Is worth the wear, for a' that.

Then let us pray that come it may
  And come it will for a' that,
That common sense may take the place
  Of common cant and a' that.
    For a' that, and a' that,
      Who cackles trash and a' that,
    Or be he lord, or be he low,
      The man's an ass for a' that.

SIR THEODORE MARTIN.

THE LAY OF THE LOVELORN.

(TENNYSON)

COMRADES, you may pass the rosy. With permission
   of the chair,
I shall leave you for a little, for I'd like to take the air.

Whether 'twas the sauce at dinner, or that glass of
   ginger-beer,
Or these strong cheroots, I know not, but I feel a
   little queer.

Let me go. Nay, Chuckster, blow me, 'pon my soul,
   this is too bad!
When you want me, ask the waiter; he knows where
   I'm to be had.

Whew! This is a great relief now! Let me but
   undo my stock;
Resting here beneath the porch, my nerves will steady
   like a rock.

In my ears I hear the singing of a lot of favourite
   tunes—
Bless my heart, how very odd! Why, surely there's
   a brace of moons!

See! the stars! how bright they twinkle, winking with
   a frosty glare,
Like my faithless cousin Amy when she drove me to
   despair.

Oh, my cousin, spider-hearted ! Oh, my Amy ! No,
  confound it !
I must wear the mournful willow—all around my heart
  I've bound it.[1]

Falser than the bank of fancy, frailer than a shilling
  glove,
Puppet to a father's anger, minion to a nabob's love !

Is it well to wish thee happy ? Having known me,
  could you ever
Stoop to marry half a heart, and little more than half
  a liver ?

Happy ! Damme ! Thou shalt lower to his level day
  by day,
Changing from the best of china to the commonest of
  clay.

[1] The reference here and in a subsequent verse is to a song very
popular at the time:

  ' All round my hat I vears a green villow,
    All round my hat for a twelvemonth and a day,
    And if any van should arsk you the reason vy I vears it,
    Say, all for my true love that's far, far away.

  ' 'Twas agoin of my rounds on the streets I first did meet her,
    'Twas agoin of my rounds that first she met my heye,
    And I never heard a voice more louder nor more sweeter,
    As she cried, " Who'll buy my cabbages, my cabbages who'll
      buy ?" '

There were several more verses, and being set to a very taking air,
it was a reigning favourite with the ' Social Chucksters ' of the day.
Even scholars thought it worth turning into Latin verse. I remember reading in some short-lived journal a very clever version of it,
the first verse of which ran thus:

  ' Omne circa petusum sertum gero viridem
    Per annum circa petasum et unum diem plus.
    Si quis te rogaret, cur tale sertum gererem,
    Dic, " Omne propter corculum qui est inpartibus." '

Allusions to the willow, as an emblem of grief, are of a very old
date. ' Sing all, a green willow must be my garland,' is the refrain
of the song which haunted Desdemona on the eve of her death
(*Othello*, Act IV., Scene 3).   That exquisite scene, and the beautiful
air to which some contemporary of Shakespeare wedded it, will
make ' The Willow Song ' immortal.

As the husband is, the wife is,—he is stomach-plagued
and old;
And his curry soups will make thy cheek the colour
of his gold.

When his feeble love is sated, he will hold thee surely
then
Something lower than his hookah,—something less
than his cayenne.

What is this ?   His eyes are pinky.   Was't the claret ?
Oh, no, no,—
Bless your soul ! it was the salmon,—salmon always
makes him so.

Take him to thy dainty chamber—soothe him with
thy lightest fancies;
He will understand thee, won't he ?—pay thee with a
lover's glances ?

Louder than the loudest trumpet, harsh as harshest
ophicleide,
Nasal respirations answer the endearments of his bride.

Sweet response, delightful music ! Gaze upon thy
noble charge,
Till the spirit fill thy bosom that inspired the meek
Laffarge.[1]

Better thou wert dead before me,—better, better that
I stood,
Looking on thy murdered body, like the injured Daniel
Good ![1]

[1] Madame Laffarge and Daniel Good were the two most talked
about criminals of the time when these lines were written.   Madame
Laffarge was convicted of poisoning her husband under extenuating
circumstances, and was imprisoned for life, but many believed in
her protestations of innocence—this, of course, she being a woman
and unhappily married.   Daniel Good died on the scaffold on the
23rd of May, 1842, protesting his innocence to the last, and asserting
that his victim, Jane Sparks, had killed herself, an assertion which
a judge and jury naturally could not reconcile with the fact that her
head, arms, and legs had been cut off and hidden with her body in
a stable.   He, too, found people to maintain that his sentence was
unjust.

Better thou and I were lying, cold and timber-stiff and
   dead,
With a pan of burning charcoal underneath our nuptial
   bed !

Cursed be the Bank of England's notes, that tempt the
   soul to sin !
Cursed be the want of acres,—doubly cursed the want
   of tin !

Cursed be the marriage-contract, that enslaved thy
   soul to greed !
Cursed be the sallow lawyer, that prepared and drew
   the deed !

Cursed be his foul apprentice, who the loathsome fees
   did earn !
Cursed be the clerk and parson,—cursed be the whole
   concern !

   *   *   *   *   *

Oh, 'tis well that I should bluster,—much I'm like to
   make of that;
Better comfort have I found in singing ' All Around
   my Hat.'

But that song, so wildly plaintive, palls upon my
   British ears.
'Twill not do to pine for ever,—I am getting up in
   years.

Can I turn the honest penny, scribbling for the weekly
   press,
And in writing Sunday libels drown my private wretchedness ?[1]

Oh, to feel the wild pulsation that in manhood's dawn
   I knew,
When my days were all before me, and my years were
   twenty-two !

[1] The two papers here glanced at were *The Age* and *The Satirist*,
long since dead.

When I smoked my independent pipe along the Quad-
rant wide,
With the many larks of London flaring up on every
side;

When I went the pace so wildly, caring little what
might come;
Coffee-milling care and sorrow, with a nose-adapted
thumb;[1]

Felt the exquisite enjoyment, tossing nightly off, oh
heavens!
Brandies at the Cider Cellars, kidneys smoking-hot at
Evans'![2]

Or in the Adelphi sitting, half in rapture, half in tears,
Saw the glorious melodrama conjure up the shades of
years!

Saw Jack Sheppard, noble stripling, act his wondrous
feats again,
Snapping Newgate's bars of iron, like an infant's daisy
chain.

Might was right, and all the terrors, which had held
the world in awe,
Were despised, and prigging prospered, spite of Laurie,
spite of law.[3]

In such scenes as these I triumphed, ere my passion's
edge was rusted,
And my cousin's cold refusal left me very much dis-
gusted!

[1] The expression of contemptuous defiance, signified by the application of the thumb of one hand to the nose, spreading out the fingers,
and attaching to the little finger the stretched-out fingers of the
other hand, and working them in a circle. Among the graffiti in
Pompeii are examples of the same subtle symbolism.

[2] Well known to readers of Thackeray's *Newcomes* as 'The Cave
of Harmony.'

[3] Sir Peter Laurie, Lord Mayor; afterwards Alderman, and
notable for his sagacity and severity as a magistrate in dealing with
evil-doers.

Since, my heart is sere and withered, and I do not
  care a curse,
Whether worse shall be the better, or the better be
  · the worse.

Hark ! my merry comrades call me, bawling for another
  jorum;
They would mock me in derision, should I thus appear
  before 'em.

Womankind no more shall vex me, such at least as go
  arrayed
In the most expensive satins and the newest silk
  brocade.

I'll to Afric, lion-haunted, where the giant forest yields
Rarer robes and finer tissue than are sold at Spitalfields.

Or to burst all chains of habit, flinging habit's self
  aside,
I shall walk the tangled jungle in mankind's primeval
  pride;

Feeding on the luscious berries and the rich cassava
  root,
Lots of dates and lots of guavas, clusters of forbidden
  fruit.

Never comes the trader thither, never o'er the purple
  main
Sounds the oath of British commerce, or the accent of
  Cockaigne.

There, methinks, would be enjoyment, where no envious
  rule prevents;
Sink the steamboats ! cuss the railways ! rot, O rot the
  Three per Cents !

There the passions, cramped no longer, shall have
  space to breathe, my cousin !
I will wed some savage woman—nay, I'll wed at least
  a dozen.

There I'll rear my young mulattoes, as no Bond Street
brats are reared :
They shall dive for alligators, catch the wild goats by
the beard—

Whistle to the cockatoos, and mock the hairy-faced
baboon,
Worship mighty Mumbo Jumbo in the Mountains of
the Moon.

I myself, in far Timbuctoo, leopard's blood will daily
quaff,
Ride a-tiger-hunting, mounted on a thoroughbred
giraffe.

Fiercely shall I shout the war-whoop, as some sullen
stream he crosses,
Startling from their noonday slumbers iron-bound
rhinoceroses.

Fool ! again the dream, the fancy ! But I know my
words are mad,
For I hold the grey barbarian lower than the Christian
cad.

I the swell—the city dandy ! I to seek such horrid
places,—
I to haunt with squalid negroes, blubber-lips, and
monkey-faces !

I to wed with Coromantees ! I, who managed—very
near—
To secure the heart and fortune of the widow Shilli-
beer !

Stuff and nonsense ! let me never fling a single chance
away;
Maids ere now, I know, have loved me, and another
maiden may.

Morning Post (*The Times* won't trust me), help me, as
    I know you can;
I will pen an advertisement,—that's a never-failing
    plan.

' Wanted—By a bard, in wedlock, some young inter-
    esting woman:
Looks are not so much an object, if the shiners be
    forthcoming !

' Hymen's chains the advertiser vows shall be but
    silken fetters;
Please address to A. T., Chelsea. N.B.—You must
    pay the letters.'

That's the sort of thing to do it. Now I'll go and
    taste the balmy,—
Rest thee with thy yellow nabob, spider-hearted
    Cousin Amy !

TOM TAYLOR.

THE LAUREATE'S BUST AT TRINITY.

A Fragment of an Idyll.

(TENNYSON)

    —So the stately bust abode
For many a month, unseen, among the Dons.
Nor in the lodge, nor in the library,
Upon its pedestal appeared, to be
A mark for reverence of green gownsman-hood,
Of grief to ancient fogies, and reproof
To those who knew not Alfred, being hard
And narrowed in their honour to old names
Of poets, who had vogue when *they* were young,
And not admitting later bards; but now,
Last week, a rumour widely blown about,
Walking the windy circle of the Press,
Came, that stern Whewell, with the Seniors,
Who rule the destinies of Trinity,
Had of the sanctuary barred access
Unto the bust of Alfred Tennyson,
By Woolner carved, subscribed for by the youth
Who loved the Poet, hoped to see him set
Within the Library of Trinity,
One great man more o' the house, among the great,
Who grace that still Valhalla, ranged in row,
Along the chequered marbles of the floor,
Two stately ranks—to where the fragrant limes
Look thro' the far end window, cool and green.
A band it is, of high companionship,—
Chief, Newton, and the broad-browed Verulam,
And others only less than these in arts
Or science: names that England holds on high.
Among whom, hoped the youth, would soon be set,
The living likeness of a living Bard,—
Great Alfred Tennyson, the Laureate,
Whom Trinity most loves of living sons.
But other thought had Whewell and the Dons,

Deeming such honour only due to those
Upon whose greatness Death had set his seal.
So fixed their faces hard, and shut the doors
Upon the living Poet: for, said one,
' It is too soon,' and when they heard the phrase,
Others caught up the cue, and chorussed it,
Until, the Poet echoing ' Soon ? too soon ?'
As if in wrath, Whewell looked up, and said:—
' O Laureate, if indeed you list to try,
Try, and unfix our purpose in this thing.'
Whereat full shrilly sang th' excluded bard :

   ' Soon, soon, so soon ! Whewell looks stern and chill,
   Soon, soon, so soon ! but I can enter still.'
      ' Too soon, too soon ! You cannot enter now.'

   ' I am not dead: of that I do repent.
   But to my living prayer, oh now relent:'
      ' Too soon, too soon ! You cannot enter now.'

   ' Honour in life is sweet: my fame is wide,
   Let me to stand at Dryden's, Byron's side.'
      ' Too soon, too soon ! You cannot enter now !'

   ' Honour that comes in life is rare as sweet;
   I cannot taste it long: for life is fleet.'
      ' No, no, too soon ! You cannot enter now !'

So sang the Laureate, while all stonily,
Their chins upon their hands, as men that had
No entrails to be moved, sat the stern Dons.

FREDERICK LOCKER-LAMPSON

UNFORTUNATE MISS BAILEY.

An Experiment.

(TENNYSON)

WHEN he whispers, ' O Miss Bailey,
　Thou art brightest of the throng '—
She makes murmur, softly-gaily—
　' Alfred, I have loved thee long.'

Then he drops upon his knees, a
　Proof his heart is soft as wax:
She's—I don't know who, but he's a
　Captain bold from Halifax.

Though so loving, such another
　Artless bride was never seen;
Coachee thinks that she's his mother
　—Till they get to Gretna Green.

There they stand, by him attended,
　Hear the sable smith rehearse
That which links them, when 'tis ended,
　Tight for better—or for worse.

Now her heart rejoices—ugly
　Troubles need disturb her less—
Now the Happy Pair are snugly
　Seated in the night express.

So they go with fond emotion,
　So they journey through the night—
London is their land of Goshen—
　See, its suburbs are in sight !

Hark ! the sound of life is swelling,
　Pacing up, and racing down,
Soon they reach her simple dwelling—
　Burley Street, by Somers Town.

What is there to so astound them ?
  She cries ' Oh !' for he cries ' Hah !'
When five brats emerge, confound them !
  Shouting out, ' Mamma !—Papa !'

While at this he wonders blindly,
  Nor their meaning can divine,
Proud she turns them round, and kindly,
  ' All of these are mine and thine !'

    .   .   .   .   .

Here he pines, and grows dyspeptic,
  Losing heart he loses pith—
Hints that Bishop Tait's a sceptic—
  Swears that Moses was a myth.

Sees no evidence in Paley—
  Takes to drinking ratafia :
Shies the muffins at Miss Bailey
  While she's pouring out the tea.

One day, knocking up his quarters,
  Poor Miss Bailey found him dead,
Hanging in his knotted garters,
  Which she knitted ere they wed.

PHOEBE CARY.

' THE DAY IS DONE.'

(LONGFELLOW)

THE day is done, and darkness
  From the wing of night is loosed,
As a feather is wafted downward
  From a chicken going to roost.

I see the lights of the baker
  Gleam through the rain and mist,
And a feeling of sadness comes o'er me
  That I cannot well resist.

A feeling of sadness and *longing*,
  That is not like being sick,
And resembles sorrow only
  As a brickbat resembles a brick.

Come, get for me some supper,—
  A good and regular meal,
That shall soothe this restless feeling,
  And banish the pain I feel.

Not from the pastry baker's,
  Not from the shops for cake,
I wouldn't give a farthing
  For all that they can make.

For, like the soup at dinner,
  Such things would but suggest
Some dishes more substantial,
  And to-night I want the best.

Go to some honest butcher,
  Whose beef is fresh and nice
As any they have in the city,
  And get a liberal slice.

Such things through days of labour,
  And nights devoid of ease,
For sad and desperate feelings
  Are wonderful remedies.

They have an astonishing power
  To aid and reinforce,
And come like the ' Finally, brethren,'
  That follows a long discourse.

Then get me a tender sirloin
  From off the bench or hook,
And lend to its sterling goodness
  The science of the cook.

And the night shall be filled with comfort,
  And the cares with which it begun
Shall fold up their blankets like Indians,
  And silently cut and run.

(SHAKESPEARE)

THAT very time I saw, (but thou couldst not,)
Walking between the garden and the barn,
Reuben, all armed; a certain aim he took
At a young chicken, standing by a post,
And loosed his bullet smartly from his gun,
As he would kill a hundred thousand hens.
But I might see young Reuben's fiery shot
Lodged in the chaste board of the garden fence,
And the domesticated fowl passed on,
In henly meditation, bullet free.

' WHEN LOVELY WOMAN.'

(GOLDSMITH)

WHEN lovely woman wants a favour,
  And finds, too late, that man won't bend,
What earthly circumstance can save her
  From disappointment in the end ?

The only way to bring him over,
  The last experiment to try,
Whether a husband or a lover,
  If he have feeling, is, to cry !

EDWARD BRADLEY ('CUTHBERT BEDE').

ON A TOASTED MUFFIN.

(BY SIR E. L. B. L. B. L. B. LITTLE, BART., AUTHOR OF ' THE NEW SIMON,' ETC.)

(LYTTON)

OBJECT belov'd ! when day to eve gives place,
  And Life's best nectar thy fond vot'ry sips,
How sweet to gaze upon thy shining face,
  And press thy tender form unto my lips !

Fair as the Naiad of the Grecian stream,
  And beautiful as Oread of the lawn ;
Bright-beaming as the iv'ry-palac'd dream,
  And melting as the dewy Urns of Dawn.

For thee I strike the sounding Lyre of Song,
  And hymn the Beautiful, the Good, the True;
The dying notes of thankfulness prolong,
  And light the Beacon-fires of Praise for you.

Butter'd Ideal of Life's coarser food !
  Thou calm Egeria in a world of strife !
Antigone of crumpets ! mild as good,
  Decent in death, and beautiful in life !

Fairest where all is *fare !* shine on me still,
  And gild the dark To-Morrow of my days;
In public Marts and crowded Senates thrill,
  My soul, with Tea-time thoughts and Muffin lays.

IN IMMEMORIAM.

[Ascribed to the author of ' In Memoriam,' but not believed to be his.]

(TENNYSON)

WE seek to know, and, knowing, seek;
  We seek, we know, and every sense
  Is trembling with the great intense,
And vibrating to what we speak.

We ask too much, we seek too oft;
  We know enough, and should no more;
  And yet we skim through Fancy's lore,
And look to earth, and not aloft.

A something comes from out the gloom—
  I know it not, nor seek to know—
  I only see it swell and grow,
And more than this would not presume.

Meseems, a circling void I fill,
  And I unchanged where all is change;
  It seems unreal—I own it strange—
Yet nurse the thoughts I cannot kill.

I hear the ocean's surging tide
  Raise, quiring on, its carol-tune;
  I watch the golden-sickled moon,
And clearer voices call beside.

O sea ! whose ancient ripples lie
  On red-ribbed sands where seaweeds shone;
  O moon ! whose golden sickle's gone,
O voices all ! like you, I die !   (*Dies.*)

T

BAYARD TAYLOR.

ODE ON A JAR OF PICKLES.

(KEATS)

I.

A SWEET, acidulous, down-reaching thrill
   Pervades my sense: I seem to see or hear
The lushy garden-grounds of Greenwich Hill
   In autumn, when the crispy leaves are sere:
And odours haunt me of remotest spice
   From the Levant or musky-aired Cathay,
Or from the saffron-fields of Jericho,
          Where everything is nice:
   The more I sniff, the more I swoon away,
And what else mortal palate craves, forgo.

II.

Odours unsmelled are keen, but those I smell
   Are keener; wherefore let me sniff again!
Enticing walnuts, I have known ye well
   In youth, when pickles were a passing pain;
Unwitting youth, that craves the candy stem,
   And sugar-plums to olives doth prefer,
And even licks the pots of marmalade
          When sweetness clings to them:
   But now I dream of ambergris and myrrh,
Tasting these walnuts in the poplar shade.

III.

Lo! hoarded coolness in the heart of noon,
   Plucked with its dew, the cucumber is here,
As to the Dryad's parching lips a boon,
   And crescent bean-pods, unto Bacchus dear;

And, last of all, the pepper's pungent globe,
The scarlet dwelling of the sylph of fire,
Provoking purple draughts; and, surfeited,
    I cast my trailing robe
O'er my pale feet, touch up my tuneless lyre,
And twist the Delphic wreath to suit my head.

IV.

Here shall my tongue in other wise be soured
  Than fretful men's in parched and palsied days;
And, by the mid-May's dusky leaves embowered,
  Forget the fruitful blame, the scanty praise.
No sweets to them who sweet themselves were born,
  Whose natures ooze with lucent saccharine;
Who, with sad repetition soothly cloyed,
    The lemon-tinted morn
Enjoy, and find acetic twilight fine:
Wake I, or sleep? The pickle-jar is void.

GWENDOLINE.

(E. B. BROWNING)

Twas not the brown of chestnut boughs
  That shadowed her so finely;
It was the hair that swept her brows
  And framed her face divinely;
Her tawny hair, her purple eyes,
  The spirit was ensphered in,
That took you with such swift surprise,
  Provided you had peered in.

Her velvet foot amid the moss
  And on the daisies patted,
As, querulous with sense of loss,
  It tore the herbage matted:
' And come he early, come he late,'
  She saith, ' it will undo me;
The sharp fore-speeded shaft of fate
  Already quivers through me.

' When I beheld his red-roan steed,
　I knew what aim impelled it;
And that dim scarf of silver brede,
　·I guessed for whom he held it;
I recked not, while he flaunted by,
　Of Love's relentless vi'lence,
Yet o'er me crashed the summer sky,
　In thunders of blue silence.

' His hoof-prints crumbled down the vale,
　But left behind their lava;
What should have been my woman's mail,
　Grew jellied as guava:
I looked him proud, but 'neath my pride
　I felt a boneless tremor;
He was the Beër, I descried,
　And I was but the Seemer !

' Ah, how to be what then I seemed,
　And bid him seem that is so !
We always tangle threads we dreamed,
　And contravene our bliss so.
I see the red-roan steed again !
　He looks, as something sought he:
Why, hoity toity !—*he* is fain,
　So *I*'ll be cold and haughty !'

ANGELO ORDERS HIS DINNER.

(R. BROWNING)

I, ANGELO, obese, black-garmented,
Respectable, much in demand, well fed
With mine own larder's dainties,—where, indeed,
Such cakes of myrrh or fine alyssum seed,
Thin as a mallow-leaf, embrowned o' the top,
Which, cracking, lets the ropy, trickling drop
Of sweetness touch your tongue, or potted nests
Which my recondite recipe invests
With cold conglomerate tidbits—ah, the bill !
(You say,) but given it were mine to fill

My chests, the case so put were yours, we'll say,
(This counter, here, your post, as mine to-day,)
And you've an eye to luxuries, what harm
In smoothing down your palate with the charm
Yourself concocted ? There we issue take;
And see ! as thus across the rim I break
This puffy paunch of glazed embroidered cake,
So breaks, through use, the lust of watering chaps
And craveth plainness: do I so ? Perhaps;
But that's my secret. Find me such a man
As Lippo yonder, built upon the plan
Of heavy storage, double-navelled, fat
From his own giblets' oil, an Ararat
Uplift o'er water, sucking rosy draughts
From Noah's vineyard,— . . . crisp, enticing wafts
Yon kitchen now emits, which to your sense
Somewhat abate the fear of old events,
Qualms to the stomach,—I, you see, am slow
Unnecessary duties to forgo,—
You understand ? A venison haunch, *haut goût,*
Ducks that in Cimbrian olives mildly stew,
And sprigs of anise, might one's teeth provoke
To taste, and so we wear the complex yoke
Just as it suits,—my liking, I confess,
More to receive, and to partake no less,
Still more obese, while through thick adipose
Sensation shoots, from testing tongue to toes
Far-off, dim-conscious, at the body's verge,
Where the froth-whispers of its waves emerge
On the untasting sand. Stay, now ! a seat
Is bare: I, Angelo, will sit and eat.

THE SHRIMP-GATHERERS.

(JEAN INGELOW)

SCARLET spaces of sand and ocean,
  Gulls that circle and winds that blow;
Baskets and boats and men in motion,
  Sailing and scattering to and fro.

Girls are waiting, their wimples adorning
  With crimson sprinkles the broad grey flood;
And down the beach the blush of the morning
  Shines reflected from moisture and mud.

Broad from the yard the sails hang limpy;
  Lightly the steersman whistles a lay;
Pull with a will, for the nets are shrimpy,
  Pull with a whistle, our hearts are gay !

Tuppence a quart; there are more than fifty !
  Coffee is certain, and beer galore:
Coats are corduroy, and minds are thrifty,
  Won't we go it on sea and shore !

See, behind, how the hills are freckled
  With low white huts, where the lasses bide !
See, before, how the sea is speckled
  With sloops and schooners that wait the tide !

Yarmouth fishers may rail and roister,
  Tyne-side boys may shout, ' Give way !'
Let them dredge for the lobster and oyster,
  Pink and sweet are our shrimps to-day !

Shrimps and the delicate periwinkle,
  Such are the sea-fruits lasses love:
Ho ! to your nets till the blue stars twinkle,
  And the shutterless cottages gleam above !

CIMABUELLA.

(D. G. ROSSETTI)

I.

FAIR-TINTED cheeks, clear eyelids drawn
  In crescent curves above the light
Of eyes, whose dim, uncertain dawn
  Becomes not day: a forehead white
Beneath long yellow heaps of hair:
She is so strange she must be fair.

II.

Had she sharp, slant-wise wings outspread,
    She were an angel; but she stands
With flat dead gold behind her head,
    And lilies in her long thin hands:
Her folded mantle, gathered in,
Falls to her feet as it were tin.

III.

Her nose is keen as pointed flame;
    Her crimson lips no thing express;
And never dread of saintly blame
    Held down her heavy eyelashes:
To guess what she were thinking of,
Precludeth any meaner love.

IV.

An azure carpet, fringed with gold,
    Sprinkled with scarlet spots, I laid
Before her straight, cool feet unrolled:
    But she nor sound nor movement made
(Albeit I heard a soft, shy smile,
Printing her neck a moment's while);

V.

And I was shamed through all my mind
    For that she spake not, neither kissed,
But stared right past me.   Lo ! behind
    Me stood, in pink and amethyst,
Sword-girt and velvet-doubleted,
A tall, gaunt youth, with frowzy head,

VI.

Wide nostrils in the air, dull eyes,
    Thick lips that simpered, but, ah me !
I saw, with most forlorn surprise,
    He was the Thirteenth Century,
I but the Nineteenth: then despair
Curdled beneath my curling hair.

VII.

O, Love and Fate! How could she choose
  My rounded outlines, broader brain,
And my resuscitated Muse?
  Some tears she shed, but whether pain
Or joy in him unlocked their source,
I could not fathom which, of course.

VIII.

But I from missals, quaintly bound,
  With cither and with clavichord
Will sing her songs of sovran sound:
  Belike her pity will afford
Such faint return as suits a saint
So sweetly done in verse and paint.

FROM 'THE TAMING OF THEMISTOCLES'

(WILLIAM MORRIS)

' HE must be holpen; yet how help shall I,
Steeped to the lips in ancient misery,
And by the newer grief apparellèd?
If that I throw these ashes on mine head,
Do this thing for thee,—while about my way
A shadow gathers, and the piteous day,
So wan and bleak for very loneliness,
Turneth from sight of such untruthfulness?'
Therewith he caught an arrow from the sheaf,
And brake the shaft in witlessness of grief;
But Chiton's vest, such dismal fear she had,
Shook from the heart that sorely was a-drad,
And she began, withouten any pause,
To say: ' Why break the old Ætolian laws?
Send this man forth, that never harm hath done,
Between the risen and the setten sun.'

And next, they wandered to a steepy hill,
Whence all the land was lying grey and still,
And not a living creature there might be
From the cold mountains to the salt, cold sea;

Only, within a little cove, one sail
Shook, as it whimpered at the cruel gale,
And the mast moaned from chafing of the rope;
So all was pain: they saw not any hope.

ALL OR NOTHING.

(EMERSON)

WHOSO answers my questions
    Knoweth more than me;
Hunger is but knowledge
    In a less degree:
Prophet, priest, and poet
    Oft prevaricate,
And the surest sentence
    Hath the greatest weight.

When upon my gaiters
    Drops the morning dew,
Somewhat of Life's riddle
    Soaks my spirit through.
I am buskined by the goddess
    Of Monadnock's crest,
And my wings extended
    Touch the East and West.

Or ever coal was hardened
    In the cells of earth,
Or flowed the founts of Bourbon,
    Lo ! I had my birth.
I am crowned coeval
    With the Saurian eggs,
And my fancy firmly
    Stands on its own legs.

Wouldst thou know the secret
    Of the barberry-bush,
Catch the slippery whistle
    Of the moulting thrush,

Dance upon the mushrooms,
　　Dive beneath the sea,
Or anything else remarkable,
　　Thou must follow me !

THE BALLAD OF HIRAM HOVER.

(WHITTIER)

WHERE the Moosatockmaguntic
Pours its waters in the Skuntic,
　　Met, along the forest-side,
　　Hiram Hover, Huldah Hyde.

She, a maiden fair and dapper,
He, a red-haired, stalwart trapper,
　　Hunting beaver, mink, and skunk,
　　In the woodlands of Squeedunk.

She, Pentucket's pensive daughter,
Walked beside the Skuntic water,
　　Gathering, in her apron wet,
　　Snakeroot, mint, and bouncing-bet.

' Why,' he murmured, loath to leave her,
' Gather yarbs for chills and fever,
　　When a lovyer, bold and true,
　　Only waits to gather you ?'

' Go,' she answered, ' I'm not hasty;
I prefer a man more tasty:
　　Leastways, one to please me well
　　Should not have a beasty smell.'

' Haughty Huldah !' Hiram answered;
' Mind and heart alike are cancered:
　　Jest look here ! these peltries give
　　Cash, wherefrom a pair may live.

' I, you think, am but a vagrant,
Trapping beasts by no means fragrant:
    Yet—I'm sure it's worth a thank—
    I've a handsome sum in bank.'

Turned and vanished Hiram Hover;
And, before the year was over,
    Huldah, with the yarbs she sold,
    Bought a cape, against the cold.

Black and thick the furry cape was;
Of a stylish cut the shape was,
    And the girls, in all the town,
    Envied Huldah up and down.

Then, at last, one winter morning,
Hiram came, without a warning:
    ' Either,' said he, ' you are blind,
    Huldah, or you've changed your mind.

' Me you snub for trapping varmints,
Yet you take the skins for garments:
    Since you wear the skunk and mink,
    There's no harm in me, I think.'

' Well,' she said, ' we will not quarrel,
Hiram: I accept the moral,
    Now the fashion's so, I guess
    I can't hardly do no less.'

Thus the trouble all was over
Of the love of Hiram Hover;
    Thus he made sweet Huldah Hyde
    Huldah Hover as his bride.

Love employs, with equal favour,
Things of good and evil savour;
    That, which first appeared to part,
    Warmed, at last, the maiden's heart.

Under one impartial banner,
Life, the hunter, Love, the tanner,
    Draw, from every beast they snare,
    Comfort for a wedded pair !

THE SEWING-MACHINE.

(LONGFELLOW)

A STRANGE vibration from the cottage window
    My vagrant steps delayed,
And half abstracted, like an ancient Hindoo,
    I paused beneath the shade.

What is, I said, this unremitted humming,
    Louder than bees in spring ?
As unto prayer the murmurous answer coming,
    Shed from Sandalphon's wing.

Is this the sound of unimpeded labour,
    That now usurpeth play ?
Our harsher substitute for pipe and tabor,
    Ghittern and virelay ?

Or, is it yearning for a higher vision,
    By spiritual hearing heard ?
Nearer I drew, to listen with precision,
    Detecting not a word.

Then, peering through the pane, as men of sin do,
    Myself the while unseen,
I marked a maiden seated by the window,
    Sewing with a machine.

Her gentle foot propelled the tireless treadle,
    Her gentle hand the seam :
My fancy said, it were a bliss to peddle
    Those shirts, as in a dream !

Her lovely fingers lent to yoke and collar
    Some imperceptible taste;
The rural swain, who buys it for a dollar.
    By beauty is embraced.

O fairer aspect of the common mission !
    Only the Poet sees
The true significance, the high position
    Of such small things as these.

Not now doth Toil, a brutal Boanerges,
    Deform the maiden's hand;
Her implement its soft sonata merges
    In songs of sea and land.

And thus the hum of the unspooling cotton,
    Blent with her rhythmic tread,
Shall still be heard, when virelays are forgotten,
    And troubadours are dead.

MORTIMER COLLINS.

IF.

(SWINBURNE)

IF life were never bitter,
  And love were always sweet,
Then who would care to borrow
A moral from to-morrow—
If Thames would always glitter,
  And joy would ne'er retreat,
If life were never bitter,
  And love were always sweet ?

If Care were not the waiter
  Behind a fellow's chair,
When easy-going sinners
Sit down to Richmond dinners,
And life's swift stream flows straighter—
  By Jove, it would be rare
If Care were not the waiter
  Behind a fellow's chair.

If wit were always radiant,
  And wine were always iced,
And bores were kicked out straightway
Through a convenient gateway;
Then down the years' long gradient
  'Twere sad to be enticed;
If wit were always radiant,
  And wine were always iced.

SALAD.

(SWINBURNE)

Brow.

O COOL in the summer is salad,
  And warm in the winter is love;
And a poet shall sing you a ballad
  Delicious thereon and thereof.

A singer am I, if no sinner,
My Muse has a marvellous wing,
And I willingly worship at dinner
The Sirens of Spring.

Take endive . . . like love it is bitter;
Take beet . . . for like love it is red;
Crisp leaf of the lettuce shall glitter,
And cress from the rivulet's bed;
Anchovies foam-born, like the Lady
Whose beauty has maddened this bard;
And olives, from groves that are shady;
And eggs—boil 'em hard.

(R. BROWNING)

Beard.

WAITRESS, with eyes so marvellous black,
And the blackest possible lustrous gay tress,
This is the month of the Zodiac
When I want a pretty deft-handed waitress.
Bring a china-bowl, you merry young soul;
Bring anything green, from worsted to celery;
Bring pure olive-oil, from Italy's soil . . .
Then your china-bowl we'll well array.
When the time arrives chip choicest chives,
And administer quietly chili and capsicum . . .
(Young girls do not quite know what 's what
Till as a Poet into their laps I come).
Then a lobster fresh as fresh can be
(When it screams in the pot I feel a murderer);
After which I fancy we
Shall want a few bottles of Heidsieck or Roederer.

(TENNYSON)

Hair.

KING ARTHUR, growing very tired indeed
Of wild Tintagel, now that Lancelot
Had gone to Jersey or to Jericho,
And there was nobody to make a rhyme,

And Cornish girls were christened Jennifer,
And the Round Table had grown rickety,
Said unto Merlin (who had been asleep
For a few centuries in Broceliande,
But woke, and had a bath, and felt refreshed):
' What shall I do to pull myself together ?'
Quoth Merlin, ' Salad is the very thing,
And you can get it at the " Cheshire Cheese." '
King Arthur went there: *verily*, I believe
That he has dined there every day since then.
Have you not marked the portly gentleman
In his cool corner, with his plate of greens ?
The great knight Lancelot prefers the ' Cock,'
Where port is excellent (in pints), and waiters
Are portlier than kings, and steaks are tender,
And poets have been known to meditate . . .
Ox-fed orating ominous octastichs.

ROBERT BARNABAS BROUGH.

I'M A SHRIMP.

(' I'M AFLOAT, I'M AFLOAT ')

I'M a shrimp ! I'm a shrimp, of diminutive size:
Inspect my antennæ, and look at my eyes;
I'm a natural syphon, when dipped in a cup,
For I drain the contents to the latest drop up.
I care not for craw-fish, I heed not the prawn,
From a flavour especial my fame has been drawn;
Nor e'en to the crab or the lobster do yield,
When I'm properly cook'd and efficiently peeled.
Quick! quick! pile the coals—let your saucepan be deep,
For the weather is warm, and I'm sure not to keep;
Off, off with my head—split my shell into three—
I'm a shrimp ! I'm a shrimp—to be eaten with tea.

DANTE GABRIEL ROSSETTI.

MACCRACKEN.

(TENNYSON)

GETTING his pictures, like his supper, cheap,
  Far, far away in Belfast by the sea,
His watchful one-eyed uninvaded sleep
  MacCracken sleepeth.   While the P.R.B.
Must keep the shady side, he walks a swell
  Through spungings of perennial growth and height :
  And far away in Belfast out of sight,
By many an open do and secret sell,
Fresh daubers he makes shift to scarify,
  And fleece with pliant shears the slumbering 'green.'
There he has lied, though aged, and will lie,
Fattening on ill-got pictures in his sleep,
Till some Preraphael prove for him too deep.
  Then, once by Hunt and Ruskin to be seen,
Insolvent he will turn, and in the Queen's Bench die.

THE BROTHERS.

By a Scotch Bard and English Reviewer.

(TENNYSON)

I AM two brothers with one face,
So which is the real man who can trace ?
  (My wrongs are raging inside of me.)
Here are some poets and they sell,
Therefore revenge becomes me well.
  (Oh Robert-Thomas is dread to see.)

Of course you know it's a burning shame,
But of my last books the press makes game !
  (My wrongs are boiling inside of me.)

So at least all other bards I'll slate
Till no one sells but the Laureate.
   (Oh Robert-Thomas is dread to see.)

I took a beast of a poet's tome
And nailed a cheque, and brought them home;
   (My wrongs were howling inside of me.)
And after supper, in lieu of bed,
I wound wet towels round my head.
   (Oh Robert-Thomas is dread to see.)

Of eyelids kissed and all the rest,
And rosy cheeks that lie on one's breast,
   (My wrongs were yelling inside of me.)
I told the worst that pen can tell,—
And Strahan and Company loved me well.
   (Oh Robert-Thomas is dread to see.)

I crowed out loud in the silent night,
I made my digs so sharp and bright:
   (My wrongs were gnashing inside of me.)
In our Contemptible Review
I struck the beggar through and through.
   (Oh Robert-Thomas is dread to see.)

I tanned his hide and combed his head,
And that bard, for one, I left for dead.
   (My wrongs are hooting inside of me.)
And now he's wrapped in a printer's sheet,
Let's fling him at our Public's feet.
   (Oh Robert-Thomas is dread to see.)

CHARLES STUART CALVERLEY.

ODE TO TOBACCO.

(LONGFELLOW)

THOU who, when fears attack,
Bid'st them avaunt, and Black
Care, at the horseman's back
    Perching, unseatest;
Sweet when the morn is grey;
Sweet, when they've cleared away
Lunch; and at close of day
    Possibly sweetest:

I have a liking old
For thee, though manifold
Stories, I know, are told,
    Not to thy credit;
How one (or two at most)
Drops make a cat a ghost—
Useless, except to roast—
    Doctors have said it:

How they who use fusees
All grow by slow degrees
Brainless as chimpanzees,
    Meagre as lizards;
Go mad, and beat their wives;
Plunge (after shocking lives)
Razors and carving knives
    Into their gizzards.

Confound such knavish tricks!
Yet know I five or six
Smokers who freely mix
    Still with their neighbours;
Jones—who, I'm glad to say,
Asked leave of Mrs. J.—
Daily absorbs a clay
    After his labours.

Cats may have had their goose
Cooked by tobacco-juice;
Still why deny its use
    Thoughtfully taken?
We're not as tabbies are:
Smith, take a fresh cigar!
Jones, the tobacco-jar!
    Here's to thee, Bacon!

BEER.

(BYRON)

IN those old days which poets say were golden—
    (Perhaps they laid the gilding on themselves:
And, if they did, I'm all the more beholden
    To those brown dwellers in my dusty shelves,
Who talk to me 'in language quaint and olden'
    Of gods and demigods and fauns and elves,
Pan with his pipes, and Bacchus with his leopards,
And staid young goddesses who flirt with shepherds:)

In those old days, the Nymph called Etiquette
    (Appalling thought to dwell on) was not born.
They had their May, but no Mayfair as yet,
    No fashions varying as the hues of morn.
Just as they pleased they dressed and drank and ate,
    Sang hymns to Ceres (their John Barleycorn)
And danced unchaperoned, and laughed unchecked,
And were no doubt extremely incorrect.

Yet do I think their theory was pleasant:
    And oft, I own, my 'wayward fancy roams'
Back to those times, so different from the present;
    When no one smoked cigars, nor gave At-homes,
Nor smote a billiard-ball, nor winged a pheasant,
    Nor 'did' their hair by means of long-tailed combs,
Nor migrated to Brighton once a year,
Nor—most astonishing of all—drank Beer.

No, they did not drink Beer, ' which brings me to '
   (As Gilpin said) ' the middle of my song.'
Not that ' the middle ' is precisely true,
   Or else I should not tax your patience long:
If I had said ' beginning ' it might do;
   But I have a dislike to quoting wrong:
I was unlucky—sinned against, not sinning—
When Cowper wrote down ' middle ' for ' beginning.'

So to proceed. That abstinence from Malt
   Has always struck me as extremely curious.
The Greek mind must have had some vital fault,
   That they should stick to liquors so injurious—
(Wine, water, tempered p'raps with Attic salt)—
   And not at once invent that mild, luxurious,
And artful beverage, Beer. How the digestion
Got on without it, is a startling question.

Had they digestions ? and an actual body
   Such as dyspepsia might make attacks on ?
Were they abstract ideas—(like Tom Noddy
   And Mr. Briggs)—or men, like Jones and Jackson ?
Then Nectar—was that beer, or whisky-toddy ?
   Some say the Gaelic mixture, I the Saxon:
I think a strict adherence to the latter
Might make some Scots less pigheaded, and fatter.

Besides, Bon Gaultier definitely shows
   That the real beverage for feasting gods on
Is a soft compound, grateful to the nose
   And also to the palate, known as ' Hodgson.'
I know a man—a tailor's son—who rose
   To be a peer: and this I would lay odds on,
(Though in his Memoirs it may not appear,)
That that man owed his rise to copious Beer.

O Beer ! O Hodgson, Guinness, Allsopp, Bass !
   Names that should be on every infant's tongue !
Shall days and months and years and centuries pass,
   And still your merits be unrecked, unsung ?
Oh ! I have gazed into my foaming glass,
   And wished that lyre could yet again be strung

Which once rang prophet-like through Greece, and
    taught her
Misguided sons that ' the best drink was water.'

How would he now recant that wild opinion,
    And sing—as would that I could sing—of you !
I was not born (alas !) the ' Muses' minion,'
    I'm not poetical, not even blue:
And he (we know) but strives with waxen pinion,
    Whoe'er he is that entertains the view
Of emulating Pindar, and will be
Sponsor at last to some now nameless sea.

Oh ! when the green slopes of Arcadia burned
    With all the lustre of the dying day,
And on Cithaeron's brow the reaper turned,
    (Humming, of course, in his delightful way,
How Lycidas was dead, and how concerned
    The Nymphs were when they saw his lifeless clay;
And how rock told to rock the dreadful story
That poor young Lycidas was gone to glory:)

What would that lone and labouring soul have given,
    At that soft moment, for a pewter pot !
How had the mists that dimmed his eye been riven,
    And Lycidas and sorrow all forgot !
If his own grandmother had died unshriven,
    In two short seconds he'd have recked it not;
Such power hath Beer. The heart which Grief hath
    canker'd
Hath one unfailing remedy—the Tankard.

Coffee is good, and so no doubt is cocoa;
    Tea did for Johnson and the Chinamen:
When ' Dulce est desipere in loco '
    Was written, real Falernian winged the pen.
When a rapt audience has encored ' Fra Poco '
    Or ' Casta Diva,' I have heard that then
The Prima Donna, smiling herself out,
Recruits her flagging powers with bottled stout.

But what is coffee, but a noxious berry,
    Born to keep used-up Londoners awake ?

What is Falernian, what is Port or Sherry,
　But vile concoctions to make dull heads ache ?
Nay stout itself—(though good with oysters, very) —
　Is not a thing your reading man should take.
He that would shine, and petrify his tutor,
Should drink draught Allsopp in its ' native pewter.'

But hark ! a sound is stealing on my ear—
　A soft and silvery sound—I know it well.
Its tinkling tells me that a time is near
　Precious to me—it is the Dinner Bell.
O blessed Bell ! Thou bringest beef and beer,
　Thou bringest good things more than tongue may
　　tell:
Seared is (of course) my heart—but unsubdued
Is, and shall be, my appetite for food.

I go. Untaught and feeble is my pen:
　But on one statement I may safely venture:
That few of our most highly gifted men
　Have more appreciation of the trencher.
I go. One pound of British beef, and then
　What Mr. Swiveller called ' a modest quencher ';
That, home-returning, I may ' soothly say,'
' Fate cannot touch me: I have dined to-day.'

WANDERERS.

(TENNYSON)

As o'er the hill we roam'd at will,
　My dog and I together,
We mark'd a chaise, by two bright bays
　Slow-moved along the heather:

Two bays arch-neck'd, with tails erect
　And gold upon their blinkers;
And by their side an ass I spied;
　It was a travelling tinker's.

The chaise went by, nor aught cared I;
  Such things are not in my way;
I turn'd me to the tinker, who
  Was loafing down a by-way:

I ask'd him where he lived—a stare
  Was all I got in answer,
As on he trudged: I rightly judged
  The stare said, ' Where I can, sir.'

I ask'd him if he'd take a whiff
  Of 'bacco; he acceded;
He grew communicative too,
  (A pipe was all he needed,)
Till of the tinker's life. I think,
  I knew as much as he did.

    ' I loiter down by thorp and town,
      For any job I'm willing;
    Take here and there a dusty brown,
      And here and there a shilling.

    ' I deal in every ware in turn,
      I've rings for buddin' Sally
    That sparkle like those eyes of her'n;
      I've liquor for the valet.

    ' I steal from th' parson's strawberry-plots,
      I hide by th' squire's covers;
    I teach the sweet young housemaids what's
      The art of trapping lovers.

    ' The things I've done 'neath moon and stars
      Have got me into messes:
    I've seen the sky through prison bars,
      I've torn up prison dresses:

    ' I've sat, I've sigh'd, I've gloom'd, I've glanced
      With envy at the swallows
    That through the window slid, and danced
      (Quite happy) round the gallows;

    ' But out again I come, and show
      My face nor care a stiver,
    For trades are brisk and trades are slow,
      But mine goes on for ever.'

Thus on he prattled like a babbling brook.
Then I, ' The sun hath slipped behind the hill,
And my aunt Vivian dines at half-past six.'
So in all love we parted; I to the Hall,
They to the village. It was noised next noon
That chickens had been miss'd at Syllabub Farm.

PROVERBIAL PHILOSOPHY.

(TUPPER)

INTRODUCTORY.

ART thou beautiful, O my daughter, as the budding
  rose of April ?
Are all thy motions music, and is poetry throned in
  thine eye ?
Then hearken unto me; and I will make the bud a
  fair flower,
I will plant it upon the bank of Elegance, and water
  it with the water of Cologne;
And in the season it shall ' come out,' yea bloom, the
  pride of the parterre;
Ladies shall marvel at its beauty, and a Lord shall
  pluck it at the last.

OF PROPRIETY.

Study first Propriety: for she is indeed the Polestar
Which shall guide the artless maiden through the mazes
  of Vanity Fair;
Nay, she is the golden chain which holdeth together
  Society;
The lamp by whose light young Psyche shall approach
  unblamed her Eros.
Verily Truth is as Eve, which was ashamed being naked;
Wherefore doth Propriety dress her with the fair foliage
  of artifice:
And when she is drest, behold ! she knoweth not herself
  again.—
I walked in the Forest; and above me stood the yew,

Stood like a slumbering giant, shrouded in impenetrable
    shade;
Then I pass'd into the citizen's garden, and marked a
    tree clipt into shape,
(The giant's locks had been shorn by the Dalilah-shears
    of Decorum;)
And I said, ' Surely nature is goodly; but how much
    goodlier is Art !'
I heard the wild notes of the lark floating far over the
    blue sky,
And my foolish heart went after him, and, lo ! I blessed
    him as he rose;
Foolish ! for far better is the trained boudoir bullfinch,
Which pipeth the semblance of a tune, and mechanically
    draweth up water:
And the reinless steed of the desert, though his neck
    be clothed with thunder,
Must yield to him that danceth and ' moveth in the
    circles ' at Astley's.
For verily, O my daughter, the world is a masquerade,
And God made thee one thing, that thou mightest make
    thyself another:
A maiden's heart is as champagne, ever aspiring and
    struggling upwards,
And it needed that its motions be checked by the
    silvered cork of Propriety:
He that can afford the price, his be the precious treasure,
Let him drink deeply of its sweetness, nor grumble if
    it tasteth of the cork.

OF FRIENDSHIP.

Choose judiciously thy friends; for to discard them is
    undesirable,
Yet it is better to drop thy friends, O my daughter,
    than to drop thy ' H's.'
Dost thou know a wise woman ? yea, wiser than the
    children of light ?
Hath she a position ? and a title ? and are her parties
    in the *Morning Post ?*
If thou dost, cleave unto her, and give up unto her
    thy body and mind;

Think with her ideas, and distribute thy smiles at her
    bidding:
So shalt thou become like unto her; and thy manners
    shall be ' formed,'
And thy name shall be a Sesame, at which the doors
    of the great shall fly open:
Thou shalt know every Peer, his arms, and the date
    of his creation,
His pedigree and their intermarriages, and cousins to
    the sixth remove:
Thou shalt kiss the hand of Royalty, and lo ! in next
    morning's papers,
Side by side with rumours of wars, and stories of ship-
    wrecks and sieges,
Shall appear thy name, and the minutiæ of thy head-
    dress and petticoat,
For an enraptured public to muse upon over their
    matutinal muffin.

Of Reading.

Read not Milton, for he is dry; nor Shakespeare, for he
    wrote of common life:
Nor Scott, for his romances, though fascinating, are
    yet intelligible:
Nor Thackeray, for he is a Hogarth, a photographer
    who flattereth not:
Nor Kingsley, for he shall teach thee that thou shouldest
    not dream, but do.
Read incessantly thy Burke; that Burke who, nobler
    than he of old,
Treateth of the Peer and Peeress, the truly Sublime
    and Beautiful:
Likewise study the ' creations ' of ' the Prince of modern
    Romance ';
Sigh over Leonard the Martyr, and smile on Pelham the
    puppy:
Learn how ' love is the dram-drinking of existence ';
And how we ' invoke, in the Gadara of our still closets,
The beautiful ghost of the Ideal, with the simple wand
    of the pen.'

Listen how Maltravers and the orphan ' forgot all but
  love,'
And how Devereux's family chaplain ' made and un-
  made kings ':
How Eugene Aram, though a thief, a liar, and a murderer,
Yet, being intellectual, was amongst the noblest of
  mankind.
So shalt thou live in a world peopled with heroes and
  master-spirits;
And if thou canst not realize the Ideal, thou shalt at
  least idealize the Real.

THE COCK AND THE BULL.

(BROWNING)

You see this pebble-stone ? It's a thing I bought
Of a bit of a chit of a boy i' the mid o' the day—
I like to dock the smaller parts-o'-speech,
As we curtail the already cur-tail'd cur
(You catch the paronomasia, play 'po' words ?),
Did, rather, i' the pre-Landseerian days.
Well, to my muttons. I purchased the concern,
And clapt it i' my poke, having given for same
By way o' chop, swop, barter or exchange—
' Chop ' was my snickering dandiprat's own term—
One shilling and fourpence, current coin o' the realm.
O-n-e one and f-o-u-r four
Pence, one and fourpence—you are with me, sir ?—
What hour it skills not: ten or eleven o' the clock,
One day (and what a roaring day it was
Go shop or sight-see—bar a spit o' rain !)
In February, eighteen sixty nine,
Alexandrina Victoria, Fidei
Hm—hm—how runs the jargon ? being on throne.

Such, sir, are all the facts, succinctly put,
The basis or substratum—what you will—
Of the impending eighty thousand lines.

'Not much in 'em either,' quoth perhaps simple Hodge.
But there's a superstructure. Wait a bit.
Mark first the rationale of the thing:
Hear logic rivel and levigate the deed.
That shilling—and for matter o' that, the pence—
I had o' course upo' me—wi' me say—
(*Mecum's* the Latin, make a note o' that)
When I popp'd pen i' stand, scratch'd ear, wip'd snout,
(Let everybody wipe his own himself)
Sniff'd—tch!—at snuffbox; tumbled up, he-heed,
Haw-haw'd (not hee-haw'd, that's another guess thing:)
Then fumbled at, and stumbled out of, door,
I shoved the timber ope wi' my omoplat;
And *in vestibulo,* i' the lobby to-wit,
(Iacobi Facciolati's rendering, sir,)
Donn'd galligaskins, antigropeloes,
And so forth; and, complete with hat and gloves,
One on and one a-dangle i' my hand,
And ombrifuge (Lord love you!), case o' rain,
I flopp'd forth, 'sbuddikins! on my own ten toes,
(I do assure you there be ten of them,)
And went clump-clumping up hill and down dale
To find myself o' the sudden i' front o' the boy.
Put case I hadn't 'em on me, could I ha' bought
This sort-o'-kind-o'-what-you-might-call toy,
This pebble-thing, o' the boy-thing? Q.E.D.
That's proven without aid from mumping Pope,
Sleek porporate or bloated Cardinal.
(Isn't it, old Fatchaps? You're in Euclid now.)
So, having the shilling—having i' fact a lot—
And pence and halfpence, ever so many o' them,
I purchased, as I think I said before,
The pebble (*lapis, lapidis, -di, -dem, -de*—
What nouns 'crease short i' the genitive, Fatchaps, eh?)
O' the boy, a bare-legg'd beggarly son of a gun,
For one-and-fourpence. Here we are again.

Now Law steps in, bigwigg'd, voluminous-jaw'd;
Investigates and re-investigates.
Was the transaction illegal? Law shakes head.
Perpend, sir, all the bearings of the case.

At first the coin was mine, the chattel his.
But now (by virtue of the said exchange
And barter) *vice versa* all the coin,
Per juris operationem, vests
I' the boy and his assigns till ding o' doom;
(*In sæcula sæculo-o-o-orum ;*
I think I hear the Abate mouth out that.)
To have and hold the same to him and them. . . .
Confer some idiot on Conveyancing.
Whereas the pebble and every part thereof,
And all that appertaineth thereunto,
Quodcunque pertinet ad eam rem,
(I fancy, sir, my Latin's rather pat)
Or shall, will, may, might, can, could, would or should,
(*Subaudi cætera*—clap we to the close—
For what's the good of law in a case o' the kind)
Is mine to all intents and purposes.
This settled, I resume the thread o' the tale.

Now for a touch o' the vendor's quality.
He says a gen'lman bought a pebble of him,
(This pebble i' sooth, sir, which I hold i' my hand)—
And paid for 't, *like* a gen'lman, on the nail.
'Did I o'ercharge him a ha'penny ? Devil a bit.
Fiddlepin's end ! Get out, you blazing ass !
Gabble o' the goose. Don't bugaboo-baby *me !*
Go double or quits ? Yah ! tittup ! what's the odds ?'
—There's the transaction view'd i' the vendor's light.

Next ask that dumpled hag, stood snuffling by,
With her three frowsy blowsy brats o' babes,
The scum o' the kennel, cream o' the filth-heap—Faugh !
Aie, aie, aie, aie ! ὀτοτοτοτοτοῖ,
('Stead which we blurt out Hoighty toighty now)—
And the baker and candlestickmaker, and Jack and Gill,
Blear'd Goody this and queasy Gaffer that.
Ask the schoolmaster. Take schoolmaster first.

He saw a gentleman purchase of a lad
A stone, and pay for it *rite,* on the square,
And carry it off *per saltum,* jauntily,

Propria quæ maribus, gentleman's property now
(Agreeably to the law explain'd above),
In proprium usum, for his private ends.
The boy he chuck'd a brown i' the air, and bit
I' the face the shilling: heaved a thumping stone
At a lean hen that ran cluck clucking by,
(And hit her, dead as nail i' post o' door,)
Then *abiit*—what's the Ciceronian phrase ?—
Excessit, evasit, erupit—off slogs boy;
Off like bird, *avi similis*—(you observed
The dative ?   Pretty i' the Mantuan !)—Anglice,
Off in three flea skips. *Hactenus*, so far,
So good, *tam bene.   Bene, satis, male*—,
Where was I with my trope 'bout one in a quag ?
I did once hitch the syntax into verse:
Verbum personale, a verb personal,
Concordat—ay, ' agrees,' old Fatchaps—*cum
Nominativo*, with its nominative,
Genere, i' point o' gender, *numero*,
O' number, *et persona*, and person.   *Ut,*
Instance: *Sol ruit*, down flops sun, *et* and,
Montes umbrantur, out flounce mountains.   Pah !
Excuse me, sir, I think I'm going mad.
You see the trick on 't though, and can yourself
Continue the discourse *ad libitum*.
It takes up about eighty thousand lines,
A thing imagination boggles at;
And might, odds-bobs, sir ! in judicious hands,
Extend from here to Mesopotamy.

LOVERS, AND A REFLECTION.

(JEAN INGELOW)

IN moss-prankt dells which the sunbeams flatter
(And heaven it knoweth what that may mean;
Meaning, however, is no great matter)
Where woods are a-tremble, with rifts atween;

Through God's own heather we wonned together,
  I and my Willie (O love my love):
I need hardly remark it was glorious weather,
  And flitterbats wavered alow, above:

Boats were curtseying, rising, bowing
  (Boats in that climate are so polite),
And sands were a ribbon of green endowing,
  And O the sundazzle on bark and bight!

Through the rare red heather we danced together,
  (O love my Willie!) and smelt for flowers:
I must mention again it was gorgeous weather,
  Rhymes are so scarce in this world of ours:—

By rises that flushed with their purple favours,
  Through becks that brattled o'er grasses sheen,
We walked and waded, we two young shavers,
  Thanking our stars we were both so green.

We journeyed in parallels, I and Willie,
  In fortunate parallels! Butterflies,
Hid in weltering shadows of daffodilly
  Or marjoram, kept making peacock eyes:

Songbirds darted about, some inky
  As coal, some snowy (I ween) as curds;
Or rosy as pinks, or as roses pinky—
  They reck of no eerie To-come, those birds!

But they skim over bents which the millstream washes,
  Or hang in the lift 'neath a white cloud's hem;
They need no parasols, no goloshes;
  And good Mrs. Trimmer she feedeth them.

Then we thrid God's cowslips (as erst His heather)
  That endowed the wan grass with their golden blooms
And snapped—(it was perfectly charming weather)—
  Our fingers at Fate and her goddess-glooms:

                                                        x

And Willie 'gan sing (O, his notes were fluty;
   Wafts fluttered them out to the white-winged sea)—
Something made up of rhymes that have done much
   duty
   Rhymes (better to put it) of ' ancientry ':

Bowers of flowers encountered showers
   In William's carol—(O love my Willie !)
Then he bade sorrow borrow from blithe to-morrow
   I quite forget what—say a daffodilly:

A nest in a hollow, ' with buds to follow,'
   I think occurred next in his nimble strain;
And clay that was ' kneaden ' of course in Eden—
   A rhyme most novel, I do maintain:

Mists, bones, the singer himself, love-stories,
   And all least furlable things got ' furled ';
Not with any design to conceal their ' glories,'
   But simply and solely to rhyme with ' world.'

     .   .   .   .   .

O if billows and pillows and hours and flowers,
   And all the brave rhymes of an elder day,
Could be furled together, this genial weather,
   And carted, or carried on ' wafts ' away,
Nor ever again trotted out—ah me !
How much fewer volumes of verse there'd be !

BALLAD.

(JEAN INGELOW)

THE auld wife sat at her ivied door,
   (*Butter and eggs and a pound of cheese*)
A thing she had frequently done before;
   And her spectacles lay on her aproned knees.

The piper he piped on the hill-top high,
   (*Butter and eggs and a pound of cheese*)
Till the cow said ' I die,' and the goose asked ' Why ?'
   And the dog said nothing, but searched for fleas.

The farmer he strove through the square farmyard;
  (*Butter and eggs and a pound of cheese*)
His last brew of ale was a trifle hard—
  The connexion of which with the plot one sees.

The farmer's daughter hath frank blue eyes;
  (*Butter and eggs and a pound of cheese*)
She hears the rooks caw in the windy skies,
  As she sits at her lattice and shells her peas.

The farmer's daughter hath ripe red lips;
  (*Butter and eggs and a pound of cheese*)
If you try to approach her, away she skips
  Over tables and chairs with apparent ease.

The farmer's daughter hath soft brown hair;
  (*Butter and eggs and a pound of cheese*)
And I met with a ballad, I can't say where,
  Which wholly consisted of lines like these.

PART II.

She sat, with her hands 'neath her dimpled cheeks,
  (*Butter and eggs and a pound of cheese*)
And spake not a word. While a lady speaks
  There is hope, but she didn't even sneeze.

She sat, with her hands 'neath her crimson cheeks,
  (*Butter and eggs and a pound of cheese*)
She gave up mending her father's breeks,
  And let the cat roll in her new chemise.

She sat, with her hands 'neath her burning cheeks,
  (*Butter and eggs and a pound of cheese*)
And gazed at the piper for thirteen weeks;
  Then she followed him out o'er the misty leas.

Her sheep followed her, as their tails did them.
  (*Butter and eggs and a pound of cheese*)
And this song is considered a perfect gem,
  And as to the meaning, it's what you please.

CHARLES LUTWIDGE DODGSON (' LEWIS CARROLL ')

HOW DOTH THE LITTLE CROCODILE

(ISAAC WATTS)

How doth the little crocodile
 Improve his shining tail,
And pour the waters of the Nile
 On every golden scale !

How cheerfully he seems to grin,
 How neatly spreads his claws,
And welcomes little fishes in,
 With gently smiling jaws !

'TIS THE VOICE OF THE LOBSTER.

(ISAAC WATTS)

'TIS the voice of the Lobster; I heard him declare,
' You have baked me too brown, I must sugar my
 hair.'
As a duck with its eyelids, so he with his nose
Trims his belt and his buttons, and turns out his toes.

TWINKLE, TWINKLE, LITTLE BAT.

(JANE TAYLOR)

TWINKLE, twinkle, little bat !
How I wonder what you're at !
Up above the world you fly,
Like a tea-tray in the sky.

YOU ARE OLD, FATHER WILLIAM.

(SOUTHEY)

'You are old, Father William,' the young man said,
  'And your hair has become very white;
And yet you incessantly stand on your head—
  Do you think, at your age, it is right?'

'In my youth,' Father William replied to his son,
  'I feared it might injure the brain;
But now that I'm perfectly sure I have none,
  Why, I do it again and again.'

'You are old,' said the youth, 'as I mentioned before,
  And have grown most uncommonly fat;
Yet you turned a back-somersault in at the door—
  Pray, what is the reason of that?'

'In my youth,' said the sage, as he shook his grey locks,
  'I kept all my limbs very supple
By the use of this ointment—one shilling the box-
  Allow me to sell you a couple.'

'You are old,' said the youth, 'and your jaws are too
      weak
  For anything tougher than suet;
Yet you finished the goose, with the bones and the beak—
  Pray how did you manage to do it?'

'In my youth,' said his father, 'I took to the law,
  And argued each case with my wife;
And the muscular strength, which it gave to my jaw,
  Has lasted the rest of my life.'

'You are old,' said the youth, 'one would hardly suppose
  That your eye was as steady as ever;
Yet you balanced an eel on the end of your nose—
  What made you so awfully clever?'

'I have answered three questions, and that is enough,'
  Said his father; 'don't give yourself airs!
Do you think I can listen all day to such stuff?
  Be off, or I'll kick you downstairs!'

HIAWATHA'S PHOTOGRAPHING.

(LONGFELLOW)

In an age of imitation, I can claim no sort of merit for this slight attempt at doing what is known to be so easy. Anyone who knows what verse is, with the slightest ear for rhythm, can throw off a composition in the easy running metre of 'The Song of Hiawatha.' Having, then, distinctly stated that I challenge no attention, in the following little poem, to its merely verbal jingle, I must beg the candid reader, to confine his criticism to its treatment of the subject.

FROM his shoulder Hiawatha
Took the camera of rosewood,
Made of sliding, folding rosewood;
Neatly put it all together.
In its case it lay compactly,
Folded into nearly nothing;
But he opened out the hinges,
Pushed and pulled the joints and hinges,
Till it looked all squares and oblongs,
Like a complicated figure
In the second book of Euclid.

This he perched upon a tripod,
And the family in order
Sat before him for their pictures.
Mystic, awful was the process.

First a piece of glass he coated
With Collodion, and plunged it
In a bath of Lunar Caustic
Carefully dissolved in water:
There he left it certain minutes.

Secondly, my Hiawatha
Made with cunning hand a mixture
Of the acid Pyro-gallic,
And of Glacial Acetic,
And of Alcohol and water:
This developed all the picture.

Finally, he fixed each picture
With a saturate solution
Of a certain salt of Soda—
Chemists call it Hyposulphite.
(Very difficult the name is

For a metre like the present,
But periphrasis has done it.)
   All the family in order
Sat before him for their pictures.
Each in turn, as he was taken,
Volunteered his own suggestions,
His invaluable suggestions.
   First the Governor, the Father:
He suggested velvet curtains
Looped about a massy pillar;
And the corner of a table,
Of a rosewood dining-table.
He would hold a scroll of something,
Hold it firmly in his left-hand;
He would keep his right-hand buried
(Like Napoleon) in his waistcoat;
He would contemplate the distance
With a look of pensive meaning,
As of ducks that die in tempests.
   Grand, heroic was the notion:
Yet the picture failed entirely:
Failed, because he moved a little,
Moved, because he couldn't help it.
   Next, his better half took courage;
She would have her picture taken:
She came dressed beyond description,
Dressed in jewels and in satin
Far too gorgeous for an empress.
Gracefully she sat down sideways,
With a simper scarcely human,
Holding in her hand a nosegay
Rather larger than a cabbage.
All the while that she was taking,
Still the lady chattered, chattered,
Like a monkey in the forest.
' Am I sitting still ? ' she asked him.
' Is my face enough in profile ?
Shall I hold the nosegay higher ?
Will it come into the picture ? '
And the picture failed completely.
   Next the Son, the Stunning-Cantab:
He suggested curves of beauty,

Curves pervading all his figure,
Which the eye might follow onward,
Till they centred in the breast-pin,
Centred in the golden breast-pin.
He had learnt it all from Ruskin
(Author of ' The Stones of Venice,'
' Seven Lamps of Architecture,'
' Modern Painters,' and some others);
And perhaps he had not fully
Understood his author's meaning;
But, whatever was the reason,
All was fruitless, as the picture
Ended in an utter failure.

Next to him the eldest daughter:
She suggested very little;
Only asked if he would take her
With her look of ' passive beauty.'

Her idea of passive beauty
Was a squinting of the left-eye,
Was a drooping of the right-eye,
Was a smile that went up sideways
To the corner of the nostrils.

Hiawatha, when she asked him,
Took no notice of the question,
Looked as if he hadn't heard it;
But, when pointedly appealed to,
Smiled in his peculiar manner,
Coughed and said it ' didn't matter,'
Bit his lip and changed the subject.

Nor in this was he mistaken,
As the picture failed completely.

So in turn the other sisters.
Last, the youngest son was taken:
Very rough and thick his hair was,
Very round and red his face was,
Very dusty was his jacket,
Very fidgetty his manner.
And his overbearing sisters
Called him names he disapproved of:
Called him Johnny, ' Daddy's Darling,'
Called him Jacky, ' Scrubby School-boy.'
And, so awful was the picture,

In comparison the others
Might be thought to have succeeded,
To have partially succeeded.
   Finally my Hiawatha
Tumbled all the tribe together,
' Grouped ' is not the right expression,)
And, as happy chance would have it,
Did at last obtain a picture
Where the faces all succeeded:
Each came out a perfect likeness.
   Then they joined and all abused it,
Unrestrainedly abused it,
As ' the worst and ugliest picture
They could possibly have dreamed of.
Giving one such strange expressions !
Sulkiness, conceit, and meanness !
Really any one would take us
(Any one that did not know us)
For the most unpleasant people !'
(Hiawatha seemed to think so,
Seemed to think it not unlikely.)
All together rang their voices,
Angry, loud, discordant voices,
As of dogs that howl in concert,
As of cats that wail in chorus.
   But my Hiawatha's patience,
His politeness and his patience,
Unaccountably had vanished,
And he left that happy party.
Neither did he leave them slowly,
With that calm deliberation,
That intense deliberation
Which photographers aspire to :
But he left them in a hurry,
Left them in a mighty hurry,
Vowing that he would not stand it.
   Hurriedly he packed his boxes,
Hurriedly the porter trundled
On a barrow all his boxes;
Hurriedly he took his ticket,
Hurriedly the train received him:
Thus departed Hiawatha.

THE THREE VOICES.

(TENNYSON)

The First Voice.

WITH hands tight clenched through matted hair,
He crouched in trance of dumb despair:
There came a breeze from out the air.

It passed athwart the glooming flat—
It fanned his forehead as he sat—
It lightly bore away his hat,

All to the feet of one who stood
Like maid enchanted in a wood,
Frowning as darkly as she could.

With huge umbrella, lank and brown,
Unerringly she pinned it down,
Right through the centre of the crown.

Then, with an aspect cold and grim,
Regardless of its battered rim,
She took it up and gave it him.

Awhile like one in dreams he stood,
Then faltered forth his gratitude,
In words just short of being rude:

For it had lost its shape and shine,
And it had cost him four-and-nine,
And he was going out to dine.

With grave indifference to his speech,
Fixing her eyes upon the beach,
She said ' Each gives to more than each.'

He could not answer yea or nay:
He faltered ' Gifts may pass away.'
Yet knew not what he meant to say.

' If that be so,' she straight replied,
' Each heart with each doth coincide.
What boots it ? For the world is wide.'

And he, not wishing to appear
Less wise, said ' This Material Sphere
Is but Attributive Idea.'

But when she asked him ' Wherefore so ?'
He felt his very whiskers glow,
And frankly owned ' I do not know.'

While, like broad waves of golden grain,
Or sunlit hues on cloistered pane,
His colour came and went again.

Pitying his obvious distress,
Yet with a tinge of bitterness,
She said ' The More exceeds the Less.'

' A truth of such undoubted weight,
He urged, ' and so extreme in date,
It were superfluous to state.'

Roused into sudden passion, she
In tone of cold malignity:
' To others, yes: but not to thee.'

But when she saw him quail and quake,
And when he urged ' For pity's sake !'
Once more in gentle tone she spake.

' Thought in the mind doth still abide;
That is by Intellect supplied,
And within that Idea doth hide.

' And he, that yearns the truth to know,
Still further inwardly may go,
And find Idea from Notion flow.

' And thus the chain, that sages sought,
Is to a glorious circle wrought,
For Notion hath its source in Thought.'

When he, with racked and whirling brain,
Feebly implored her to explain,
She simply said it all again.

Wrenched with an agony intense,
He spake, neglecting Sound and Sense,
And careless of all consequence:

' Mind—I believe—is Essence—Ent—
Abstract—that is—an Accident—
Which we—that is to say—I meant—'

When, with quick breath and cheeks all flushed,
At length his speech was somewhat hushed,
She looked at him, and he was crushed.

It needed not her calm reply:
She fixed him with a stony eye,
And he could neither fight nor fly,

While she dissected, word by word,
His speech, half guessed at and half heard,
As might a cat a little bird.

Then, having wholly overthrown
His views, and stripped them to the bone,
Proceeded to unfold her own.

So passed they on with even pace,
Yet gradually one might trace
A shadow growing on his face.

The Second Voice.

They walked beside the wave-worn beach,
Her tongue was very apt to teach,
And now and then he did beseech

She would abate her dulcet tone,
Because the talk was all her own,
And he was dull as any drone.

She urged ' No cheese is made of chalk ':
And ceaseless flowed her dreary talk,
Tuned to the footfall of a walk.

Her voice was very full and rich,
And, when at length she asked him ' Which ?'
It mounted to its highest pitch.

He a bewildered answer gave,
Drowned in the sullen moaning wave,
Lost in the echoes of the cave.

He answered her he knew not what:
Like shaft from bow at random shot:
He spoke, but she regarded not.

She waited not for his reply,
But with a downward leaden eye
Went on as if he were not by.

Sound argument and grave defence,
Strange questions raised on ' Why ?' and
   ' Whence ?'
And weighted down with common sense.

' Shall Man be Man ? And shall he miss
Of other thoughts no thought but this,
Harmonious dews of sober bliss ?

' What boots it ? Shall his fevered eye
Through towering nothingness descry
The grisly phantom hurry by ?

' And hear dumb shrieks that fill the air;
See mouths that gape, and eyes that stare
And redden in the dusky glare ?

' The meadows breathing amber light,
The darkness toppling from the height,
The feathery train of granite Night ?

' Shall he, grown gray among his peers,
Through the thick curtain of his tears
Catch glimpses of his earlier years,

' And hear the sounds he knew of yore,
Old shufflings on the sanded floor,
Old knuckles tapping at the door ?

' Yet still before him as he flies
One pallid form shall ever rise,
And, bodying forth in glassy eyes

' The vision of a vanished good,
Low peering through the tangled wood,
Shall freeze the current of his blood.'

Still from each fact, with skill uncouth
And savage rapture, like a tooth
She wrenched a slow reluctant truth.

Till, like some silent water-mill,
When summer suns have dried the rill,
She reached a full stop, and was still.

Dead calm succeeded to the fuss,
As when the loaded omnibus
Has reached the railway terminus:

When, for the tumult of the street,
Is heard the engine's stifled beat,
The velvet tread of porters' feet.

With glance that ever sought the ground,
She moved her lips without a sound,
And every now and then she frowned.

He gazed upon the sleeping sea,
And joyed in its tranquillity,
And in that silence dead, but she

To muse a little space did seem,
Then, like the echo of a dream,
Harped back upon her threadbare theme.

Still an attentive ear he lent,
But could not fathom what she meant:
She was not deep, nor eloquent.

He marked the ripple on the sand:
The even swaying of her hand
Was all that he could understand.

He left her, and he turned aside:
He sat and watched the coming tide
Across the shores so newly dried.

He wondered at the waters clear,
The breeze that whispered in his ear,
The billows heaving far and near;

And why he had so long preferred
To hang upon her every word;
' In truth,' he said, ' it was absurd.'

The Third Voice.

Not long this transport held its place:
Within a little moment's space
Quick tears were raining down his face.

His heart stood still, aghast with fear;
A wordless voice, nor far nor near,
He seemed to hear and not to hear.

' Tears kindle not the doubtful spark:
If so, why not ?   Of this remark
The bearings are profoundly dark.'

' Her speech,' he said, ' hath caused this pain;
Easier I count it to explain
The jargon of the howling main,

' Or, stretched beside some sedgy brook,
To con, with inexpressive look,
An unintelligible book.'

Low spake the voice within his head,
In words imagined more than said,
Soundless as ghost's intended tread:

' If thou art duller than before,
Why quittedst thou the voice of lore ?
Why not endure, expecting more ?'

' Rather than that,' he groaned aghast,
' I'd writhe in depths of cavern vast,
Some loathly vampire's rich repast.'

' 'Twere hard,' it answered, ' themes immense
To coop within the narrow fence
That rings *thy* scant intelligence.'

' Not so,' he urged, ' nor once alone:
But there was that within her tone
Which chilled me to the very bone.

' Her style was anything but clear,
And most unpleasantly severe;
Her epithets were very queer.

' And yet, so grand were her replies,
I could not choose but deem her wise;
I did not dare to criticise;

' Nor did I leave her, till she went
So deep in tangled argument
That all my powers of thought were spent.'

A little whisper inly slid;
' Yet truth is truth: you know you did—'
A little wink beneath the lid.

And, sickened with excess of dread,
Prone to the dust he bent his head,
And lay like one three-quarters dead.

Forth went the whisper like a breeze;
Left him amid the wondering trees,
Left him by no means at his ease.

Once more he weltered in despair,
With hands, through denser-matted hair,
More tightly clenched than then they were.

When, bathed in dawn of living red,
Majestic frowned the mountain head,
' Tell me my fault,' was all he said.

When, at high noon, the blazing sky
Scorched in his head each haggard eye,
Then keenest rose his weary cry.

And when at eve the unpitying sun
Smiled grimly on the solemn fun,
' Alack,' he sighed, ' what *have* I done ?'

But saddest, darkest was the sight,
When the cold grasp of leaden Night
Dashed him to earth, and held him tight.

Tortured, unaided, and alone,
Thunders were silence to his groan,
Bagpipes sweet music to its tone:

' What ?   Ever thus, in dismal round,
Shall Pain and Misery profound
Pursue me like a sleepless hound,

' With crimson-dashed and eager jaws,
Me, still in ignorance of the cause,
Unknowing what I brake of laws ?'

The whisper to his ear did seem
Like echoed flow of silent stream,
Or shadow of forgotten dream;

The whisper trembling in the wind:
' Her fate with thine was intertwined,'
So spake it in his inner mind:

' Each orbed on each a baleful star,
Each proved the other's blight and bar,
Each unto each were best, most far:

' Yea, each to each was worse than foe,
Thou, a scared dullard, gibbering low,
And she, an avalanche of woe.'

BEAUTIFUL SOUP.

(UNCERTAIN)

BEAUTIFUL Soup, so rich and green,
Waiting in a hot tureen!
Who for such dainties would not stoop?
Soup of the evening, beautiful Soup!
Soup of the evening, beautiful Soup!
   Beau—ootiful Soo—oop!
   Beau—ootiful Soo—oop!
Soo—oop of the e—e—evening,
   Beautiful, beautiful Soup!

Beautiful Soup! who cares for fish,
Game, or any other dish?
Who would not give all else for two p
ennyworth only of beautiful Soup?
Pennyworth only of beautiful Soup?
   Beau—ootiful Soo—oop!
   Beau—ootiful Soo—oop!
Soo—oop of the e—e—evening
   Beautiful, beauti—FUL SOUP!

THOMAS HOOD THE YOUNGER.

RAVINGS.

(BY E., A POE-T)

THE autumn upon us was rushing,
  The Parks were deserted and lone—
  The streets were unpeopled and lone;
My foot through the sere leaves was brushing,
  That over the pathway were strown—
  By the wind in its wanderings strown.
I sighed—for my feelings were gushing
  Round Mnemosyne's porphyry throne,
Like lava liquescent lay gushing,
  And rose to the porphyry throne—
To the filigree footstool were gushing,
  That stands on the steps of that throne—
  On the stolid stone steps of that throne!

I cried—' Shall the winter-leaves fret us ?'
  Oh, turn—we must turn to the fruit,
  To the freshness and force of the fruit !
To the gifts wherewith Autumn has met us—
  Her music that never grows mute
  (That maunders but never grows mute),
The tendrils the vine branches net us,
  The lily, the lettuce, the lute—
The esculent, succulent lettuce,
  And the languishing lily, and lute;—
Yes;—the lotos-like leaves of the lettuce;
  Late lily and lingering lute.

Then come—let us fly from the city !
  Let us travel in orient isles—
  In the purple of orient isles—
Oh, bear me—yes, bear me in pity
  To climes where a sun ever smiles—
  Ever smoothly and speciously smiles !

Where the swarth-browed Arabian's wild ditty
  Enhances pyramidal piles:
Where his wild, weird, and wonderful ditty
  Awakens pyramidal piles—
Yes :—his pointless perpetual ditty
  Perplexes pyramidal piles !

IN MEMORIAM TECHNICAM.

(TENNYSON)

I count it true which sages teach—
  That passion sways not with repose,
  That love, confounding these with those,
Is ever welding each with each.

And so when time has ebbed away,
  Like childish wreaths too lightly held,
  The song of immemorial eld
Shall moan about the belted bay,

Where slant Orion slopes his star
  To swelter in the rolling seas,
  Till slowly widening by degrees,
The grey climbs upward from afar,

And golden youth and passion stray
  Along the ridges of the strand—
  Not far apart, but hand in hand—
With all the darkness danced away !

THE WEDDING.

(' OWEN MEREDITH ')

Lady Clara Vere de Vere !
I hardly know what I must say,
But I'm to be Queen of the May, mother
I'm to be Queen of the May !
I am half-crazed; I don't feel grave,
  Let me rave !

Whole weeks and months, early and late,
To win his love I lay in wait.
　Oh, the Earl was fair to see,
　As fair as any man could be:—
　The wind is howling in turret and tree !

We two shall be wed to-morrow morn,
　And I shall be the Lady Clare,
And when my marriage morn shall fall
　I hardly know what I shall wear.
　　But I shan't say ' my life is dreary,'
　　　And sadly hang my head,
　　With the remark, ' I'm very weary,
　　　And wish that I were dead.'

But on my husband's arm I'll lean,
　And roundly waste his plenteous gold,
Passing the honeymoon serene
　In that new world which is the old.
For down we'll go and take the boat
Beside St. Katherine's Docks afloat,
Which round about its prow has wrote—
　' The Lady of Shalotter '
(Mondays and Thursdays—Captain Foat),
　Bound for the Dam of Rotter.

　　　　　(From *Ten Hours, or the Warbling Wag'ner*.
　　　　　By OWING MERRYTHIEF.)

POETS AND LINNETS.

(BROWNING)

WHERE'ER there's a thistle to feed a linnet
And linnets are plenty, thistles rife—
Or an acorn-cup to catch dew-drops in it
There's ample promise of further life.
Now, mark how we begin it.

For linnets will follow, if linnets are minded,
As blows the white-feather parachute;

And ships will reel by the tempest blinded—
Aye, ships and shiploads of men to boot !
How deep whole fleets you'll find hid.

And we blow the thistle-down hither and thither
Forgetful of linnets, and men, and God.
The dew ! for its want an oak will wither—
By the dull hoof into the dust is trod,
And then who strikes the cither ?

But thistles were only for donkeys intended,
And that donkeys are common enough is clear,
And that drop ! what a vessel it might have befriended,
Does it add any flavour to Glugabib's beer ?
Well, there's my musing ended.

WALTER WILLIAM SKEAT.

A CLERK THER WAS OF CAUNTEBRIGGE ALSO.

(CHAUCER)

A CLERK ther was of Cauntebrigge also,
That unto rowing haddè long y-go.
Of thinnè shidès[1] wolde he shippès makè,
And he was nat right fat, I undertakè.
And whan his ship he wrought had attè fullè,
Right gladly by the river wolde he pullè,
And eek returne as blythly as he wentè.
Him rekkèd nevere that the sonne him brentè,[2]
Ne stinted he his cours for reyn ne snowè;
It was a joyè for to seen him rowè!
Yit was him lever, in his shelves newè,
Six oldè textès,[3] clad in greenish hewè,
Of Chaucer and his oldè poesyè
Than ale, or wyn of Lepe,[4] or Malvoisyè.
And therwithal he wex a philosofre;
And peyned him to gadren gold in cofre
Of sundry folk; and al that he mighte hentè[5]
On textès and emprinting he it spentè;
And busily gan bokès to purveyè
For hem that yeve him wherwith to scoleyè.[6]
Of glossaryès took he hede and curè[7];
And when he spyèd had, by aventurè,
A word that semèd him or strange or rarè,
To henten[8] it anon he noldè sparè,[9]
But wolde it on a shrede[10] of paper wrytè,
And in a cheste he dide his shredès whytè,
And preyèd every man to doon the samè;
Swich maner study was to him but gamè.

[1] Thin boards.   [2] Burnt.
[3] See the 'six-text' edition of Chaucer.   [4] A town in Spain.
[5] Acquire.   [6] For those that gave him the means to study with.
[7] Care.   [8] Seize upon.   [9] Would not hesitate.
[10] All quotations for the 'Oxford Dictionary' illustrating special uses of English words were written on pieces of paper of a particular size.

And on this wysè many a yeer he wroughtè,
Ay storing every shreed that men him broughtè,
Til, attè lastè, from the noble pressè
Of Clarendoun, at Oxenforde, I gessè,
Cam stalking forth the Gretè Dictionárie
That no man wel may pinche at[1] ne contrárie.
But for to tellen alle his queintè gerès,[2]
They wolden occupye wel seven yerès;
Therefore I passe as lightly as I may;
Ne speke I of his hatte or his array,
Ne how his berd by every wind was shakè
When as, for hete, his hat he wolde of takè.
Souning in[3] Erly English was his spechè,
' And gladly wolde he lerne, and gladly techè.

[1] Find fault with.   [2] Curious ways.   [3] In accordance with.

HENRY SAMBROOKE LEIGH.

ONLY SEVEN.

(A PASTORAL STORY, AFTER WORDSWORTH)

I MARVELLED why a simple child
   That lightly draws its breath
Should utter groans so very wild,
   And look as pale as Death.

Adopting a parental tone,
   I asked her why she cried;
The damsel answered, with a groan,
   ' I've got a pain inside.

' I thought it would have sent me mad
   Last night about eleven;'
Said I, ' What is it makes you bad?
How many apples have you had?'
   She answered, ' Only seven!'

' And are you sure you took no more,
   My little maid?' quoth I.
' Oh! please, sir, mother gave me four,
   But *they* were in a pie!'

' If that's the case,' I stammered out,
   ' Of course you've had eleven;'
The maiden answered, with a pout,
   ' I ain't had more nor seven!'

I wondered hugely what she meant,
   And said, ' I'm bad at riddles,
But I know where little girls are sent
   For telling tarradiddles.

'Now, if you don't reform,' said I,
  'You'll never go to heaven.'
But all in vain; each time I try,
That little idiot makes reply,
  'I ain't had more nor seven!'

POSTSCRIPT.

To borrow Wordsworth's name was wrong,
  Or slightly misapplied;
And so I'd better call my song,
  'Lines after *Ache-inside*.'

CHATEAUX D'ESPAGNE.

(A REMINISCENCE OF 'DAVID GARRICK' AND 'THE BATTLE
OF ANDALUSIA.')

(E. A. POE)

ONCE upon an evening weary, shortly after Lord Dun-
    dreary
With his quaint and curious humour set the town in
    such a roar,
With my shilling I stood rapping—only very gently
    tapping—

For the man in charge was napping—at the money-
    taker's door.
It was Mr. Buckstone's playhouse, where I lingered at
    the door;
  Paid half price and nothing more.

Most distinctly I remember, it was just about Sep-
    tember—
Though it might have been in August, or it might have
    been before—
Dreadfully I fear'd the morrow.   Vainly had I sought to
    borrow;
For (I own it to my sorrow) I was miserably poor,
And the heart is heavy laden when one's miserably poor;
  (I have been so once before.)

I was doubtful and uncertain, at the rising of the
    curtain,
If the piece would prove a novelty, or one I'd seen
    before;
For a band of robbers drinking in a gloomy cave, and
    clinking
With their glasses on the table, I had witness'd o'er
    and o'er;
Since the half-forgotten period of my innocence was
    o'er;
    Twenty years ago or more.

Presently my doubt grew stronger. I could stand the
    thing no longer;
'Miss,' said I, 'or Madam, truly your forgiveness I
    implore.
Pardon my apparent rudeness. Would you kindly have
    the goodness
To inform me if this drama is from Gaul's enlightened
    shore ?'
For I know that plays are often brought us from the
    Gallic shore;
    Adaptations—nothing more !

So I put the question lowly: and my neighbour answer'd
    slowly,
'It's a British drama wholly, written quite in days of
    yore.
'Tis an Andalusian story of a castle old and hoary,
And the music is delicious, though the dialogue be
    poor !'
(And I could not help agreeing that the dialogue *was*
    poor;
    Very flat, and nothing more.)

But at last a lady entered, and my interest grew
    centred
In her figure, and her features, and the costume that
    she wore.

And the slightest sound she utter'd was like music; so
  I mutter'd
To my neighbour, ' Glance a minute at your play-bill,
  I implore.
Who's that rare and radiant maiden ?   Tell, oh, tell
  me ! I implore !'
  Quoth my neighbour. ' Nelly Moore !'

Then I ask'd in quite a tremble—it was useless to
  dissemble—
' Miss, or Madam, do not trifle with my feelings any
  more;
Tell me who, then, was the maiden, that appear'd so
  sorrow laden
In the room of David Garrick, with a bust above the
  door ?'
  Quoth my neighbour, ' Nelly Moore.'

   *   *   *   *   *

I've her photograph from Lacy's; that delicious little
  face is
Smiling on me as I'm sitting (in a draught from yonder
  door),
And often in the nightfalls, when a precious little light
  falls
From the wretched tallow candles on my gloomy second-
  floor,
(For I have not got the gaslight on my gloomy second-
  floor)
  Comes an echo, ' Nelly Moore !'

ROBERT HENRY NEWELL.

('ORPHEUS C. KERR')

REJECTED NATIONAL ANTHEMS.

I.

(BRYANT)

THE sun sinks softly to his evening post,
  The sun swells grandly to his morning crown;
Yet not a star our flag of Heav'n has lost,
  And not a sunset stripe with him goes down.

So thrones may fall; and from the dust of those,
  New thrones may rise, to totter like the last;
But still our country's nobler planet glows
  While the eternal stars of Heaven are fast.

II.

(EMERSON)

SOURCE immaterial of material naught,
  Focus of light infinitesimal,
Sum of all things by sleepless Nature wrought,
  Of which the abnormal man is decimal.

Refract, in prism immortal, from thy stars
  To the stars blent incipient on our flag,
The beam translucent, neutrifying death;
  And raise to immortality the rag.

III.

(WILLIS)

ONE hue of our flag is taken
  From the cheeks of my blushing Pet,
And its stars beat time and sparkle
  Like the studs on her chemisette.
Its blue is the ocean shadow
  That hides in her dreamy eyes,
It conquers all men, like her,
  And still for a Union flies.

IV.

(LONGFELLOW)

BACK in the years when Phlagstaff, the Dane, was
monarch
  Over the sea-ribb'd land of the fleet-footed Norse-
men,
Once there went forth young Ursa to gaze at the
heavens—
  Ursa, the noblest of all the Vikings and horsemen.

Musing, he sat in his stirrups and viewed the horizon,
  Where the Aurora lapt stars in a North-polar manner,
Wildly he started—for there in the heavens before him
  Flutter'd and flew the original Star-Spangled Banner.

V.

(WHITTIER)

MY native land, thy Puritanic stock
Stills finds its roots firm-bound in Plymouth Rock,
And all thy sons unite in one grand wish—
To keep the virtues of Preservéd Fish.

Preservéd Fish the Deacon stern and true
Told our New England what her sons should do,
And should they swerve from loyalty and right,
Then the whole land were lost indeed in night.

VI.

(HOLMES)

A DIAGNOSIS of our hist'ry proves
Our native land a land its native loves;
Its birth a deed obstetric without peer,
Its growth a source of wonder far and near.

To love it more behold, how foreign shores
Sink into nothingness beside its stores;
Hyde Park at best—though counted ultra-grand—
The ' Boston Common ' of Victoria's land.

VII.

(STODDARD)

BEHOLD the flag ! Is it not a flag ?
  Deny it, man, if you dare;
And midway spread, 'twixt earth and sky,
  It hangs like a written prayer.

Would impious hand of foe disturb
  Its memories' holy spell,
And blight it with a dew of blood ?
  Ha, tr-r-aitor ! ! . . . . It is well.

VIII.

(ALDRICH)

THE little brown squirrel hops in the corn
  The cricket quaintly sings;
The emerald pigeon nods his head,
  And the shad in the river springs,
The dainty sunflower hangs its head
  On the shore of the summer sea;
And better far that I were dead,
  If Maud did not love me.

I love the squirrel that hops in the corn,
  And the cricket that quaintly sings;
And the emerald pigeon that nods his head,
  And the shad that gaily springs.
I love the dainty sunflower, too,
  And Maud with her snowy breast;
I love them all;—but I love—I love—
  I love my country best.

ALGERNON CHARLES SWINBURNE.

THE POET AND THE WOODLOUSE

(E. B. BROWNING)

SAID a poet to a woodlouse — ' Thou art certainly my
    brother;
  I discern in thee the markings of the fingers of the
    Whole;
And I recognize, in spite of all the terrene smut and
    smother,
  In the colours shaded off thee, the suggestions of a
    soul.

' Yea,' the poet said, ' I smell thee by some passive
    divination,
  . I am satisfied with insight of the measure of thine
    house;
What had happened I conjecture, in a blank and
    rhythmic passion,
  Had the æons thought of making thee a man, and me
    a louse.

' The broad lives of upper planets, their absorption and
    digestion,
  Food and famine, health and sickness, I can scrutinize
    and test;
Through a shiver of the senses comes a resonance of
    question,
  And by proof of balanced answer I decide that I
    am best.

' Man, the fleshly marvel, alway feels a certain kind of
    awe stick
  To the skirts of contemplation, cramped with nympho-
    leptic weight:
Feels his faint sense charred and branded by the touch
    of solar caustic,
  On the forehead of his spirit feels the footprint of a
    Fate.'

' Notwithstanding which, O poet,' spake the wood-
    louse, very blandly,
    ' I am likewise the created,—I the equipoise of thee;
I the particle, the atom, I behold on either hand lie
    The inane of measured ages that were embryos of
    me.

' I am fed with intimations, I am clothed with conse-
    quences,
    And the air I breathe is coloured with apocalyptic
    blush:
Ripest-budded odours blossom out of dim chaotic
    stenches,
    And the Soul plants spirit-lilies in sick leagues of
    human slush.

' I am thrilled half cosmically through by cryptophantic
    surgings,
    Till the rhythmic hills roar silent through a spon-
    gious kind of blee:
And earth's soul yawns disembowelled of her pan-
    creatic organs,
    Like a madrepore if mesmerized, in rapt catalepsy.

' And I sacrifice, a Levite—and I palpitate, a poet;—
    Can I close dead ears against the rush and resonance
    of things ?
Symbols in me breathe and flicker up the heights of
    the heroic;
    Earth's worst spawn, you said, and cursed me ? look !
    approve me ! I have wings.

' Ah, men's poets ! men's conventions crust you round
    and swathe you mist-like,
    And the world's wheels grind your spirits down the
    dust ye overtrod:
We stand sinlessly stark-naked in effulgence of the
    Christlight,
    And our polecat chokes not cherubs; and our skunk
    smells sweet to God.

                                                      z

' For He grasps the pale Created by some thousand
  vital handles,
 Till a Godshine, bluely winnowed through the sieve
 of thunderstorms,
Shimmers up the non-existent round the churning feet
 of angels;
 And the atoms of that glory may be seraphs, being
 worms.

' Friends, your nature underlies us and your pulses
 overplay us;
 Ye, with social sores unbandaged, can ye sing right
 and steer wrong ?
For the transient cosmic, rooted in imperishable chaos,
 Must be kneaded into drastics as material for a song.

' Eyes once purged from homebred vapours through
 humanitarian passion
 See that monochrome a despot through a democratic
 prism;
Hands that rip the soul up, reeking from divine evis-
 ceration,
 Not with priestlike oil anoint him, but a stronger-
 smelling chrism.

' Pass, O poet, retransfigured ! God, the psychometric
 rhapsode,
 Fills with fiery rhythms the silence, stings the dark
 with stars that blink;
All eternities hang round him like an old man's clothes
 collapsèd,
 While he makes his mundane music—AND HE WILL
 NOT STOP, I THINK.'

THE PERSON OF THE HOUSE.

IDYL CCCLXVI. THE KID.

(PATMORE)

MY spirit, in the doorway's pause,
 Fluttered with fancies in my breast;
Obsequious to all decent laws,
 I felt exceedingly distressed.

I knew it rude to enter there
  With Mrs. V. in such a state;
And, 'neath a magisterial air,
  Felt actually indelicate.
I knew the nurse began to grin;
  I turned to greet my Love. Said she—
' Confound your modesty, come in !
  —What shall we call the darling, V. ?'
(There are so many charming names !
  Girls'—Peg, Moll, Doll, Fan, Kate, Blanche, Bab:
Boys'—Mahershalal-hashbaz, James,
  Luke, Nick, Dick, Mark, Aminadab.)

Lo, as the acorn to the oak,
  As well-heads to the river's height,
As to the chicken the moist yolk,
  As to high noon the day's first white—
Such is the baby to the man.
  There, straddling one red arm and leg,
Lay my last work, in length a span,
  Half hatched, and conscious of the egg.
A creditable child, I hoped;
  And half a score of joys to be
Through sunny lengths of prospect sloped
  Smooth to the bland futurity.
O, fate surpassing other dooms,
  O, hope above all wrecks of time !
O, light that fills all vanquished glooms,
  O, silent song o'ermastering rhyme !
I covered either little foot,
  I drew the strings about its waist;
Pink as the unshell'd inner fruit,
  But barely decent, hardly chaste,
Its nudity had startled me;
  But when the petticoats were on,
' I know,' I said; ' its name shall be
  Paul Cyril Athanasius John.'
' Why,' said my wife, ' the child's a girl.'
  My brain swooned, sick with failing sense;
With all perception in a whirl,
  How could I tell the difference ?

' Nay,' smiled the nurse, ' the child's a boy.'
  And all my soul was soothed to hear
That so it was: then startled Joy
  Mocked Sorrow with a doubtful tear.
And I was glad as one who sees
  For sensual optics things unmeet:
As purity makes passion freeze,
  So faith warns science off her beat.
Blessed are they that have not seen,
  And yet, not seeing, have believed:
To walk by faith, as preached the Dean,
  And not by sight, have I achieved.
Let love, that does not look, believe;
  Let knowledge, that believes not, look:
Truth pins her trust on falsehood's sleeve,
  While reason blunders by the book.
Then Mrs. Prig addressed me thus:
  ' Sir, if you'll be advised by me,
You'll leave the blessed babe to us;
  It's my belief he wants his tea.'

NEPHELIDIA.

(SWINBURNE)

FROM the depth of the dreamy decline of the dawn
    through a notable nimbus of nebulous noonshine,
  Pallid and pink as the palm of the flag-flower that
    flickers with fear of the flies as they float,
Are they looks of our lovers that lustrously lean from
    a marvel of mystic miraculous moonshine,
  These that we feel in the blood of our blushes that
    thicken and threaten with throbs through the throat ?
Thicken and thrill as a theatre thronged at appeal of
    an actor's appalled agitation,
  Fainter with fear of the fires of the future than pale
    with the promise of pride in the past;
Flushed with the famishing fullness of fever that reddens
    with radiance of rathe recreation,
  Gaunt as the ghastliest of glimpses that gleam through
    the gloom of the gloaming when ghosts go aghast ?

Nay, for the nick of the tick of the time is a tremulous
touch on the temples of terror,
Strained as the sinews yet strenuous with strife of
the dead who is dumb as the dust-heaps of death:
Surely no soul is it, sweet as the spasm of erotic emo-
tional exquisite error,
Bathed in the balms of beatified bliss, beatific itself
by beatitude's breath.
Surely no spirit or sense of a soul that was soft to the
spirit and soul of our senses
Sweetens the stress of suspiring suspicion that sobs
in the semblance and sound of a sigh;
Only this oracle opens Olympian, in mystical moods
and triangular tenses—
' Life is the lust of a lamp for the light that is dark
till the dawn of the day when we die.'
Mild is the mirk and monotonous music of memory,
melodiously mute as it may be,
While the hope in the heart of a hero is bruised by
the breach of men's rapiers, resigned to the rod;
Made meek as a mother whose bosom-beats bound with
the bliss-bringing bulk of a balm-breathing baby,
As they grope through the graveyard of creeds, under
skies growing green at a groan for the grimness of
God.
Blank is the book of his bounty beholden of old, and its
binding is blacker than bluer:
Out of blue into black is the scheme of the skies, and
their dews are the wine of the bloodshed of things;
Till the darkling desire of delight shall be free as a fawn
that is freed from the fangs that pursue her,
Till the heart-beats of hell shall be hushed by a
hymn from the hunt that has harried the kennel of
kings.

FRANCIS BRET HARTE.

A GEOLOGICAL MADRIGAL.

(SHENSTONE)

I HAVE found out a gift for my fair;
  I know where the fossils abound,
Where the footprints of *Aves* declare
  The birds that once walked on the ground;
Oh, come, and—in technical speech—
  We'll walk this Devonian shore,
Or on some Silurian beach
  We'll wander, my love, evermore.

I will show thee the sinuous track
  By the slow-moving annelid made,
Or the Trilobite that, farther back,
  In the old Potsdam sandstone was laid;
Thou shalt see, in his Jurassic tomb,
  The Plesiosaurus embalmed;
In his Oolitic prime and his bloom,
  Iguanodon safe and unharmed !

You wished—I remember it well,
  And I loved you the more for that wish—
For a perfect cystedian shell,
  And a *whole* holocephalic fish.
And oh, if Earth's strata contains
  In its lowest Silurian drift,
Or palæozoic remains
  The same,—'tis your lover's free gift !

Then come, love, and never say nay,
  But calm all your maidenly fears;
We'll note, love, in one summer's day
  The record of millions of years;
And though the Darwinian plan
  Your sensitive feelings may shock,
We'll find the beginning of man,—
  Our fossil ancestors, in rock !

MRS. JUDGE JENKINS.

[Being the only genuine sequel to ' Maud Muller.']

(WHITTIER)

MAUD MULLER all that summer day
Raked the meadows sweet with hay;

Yet, looking down the distant lane,
She hoped the judge would come again.

But when he came, with smile and bow,
Maud only blushed, and stammered, ' Ha-ow ?'

And spoke of her ' pa,' and wondered whether
He'd give consent they should wed together.

Old Muller burst in tears, and then
Begged that the judge would lend him ' ten ';

For trade was dull, and wages low,
And the ' craps ' this year were somewhat slow.

And ere the languid summer died,
Sweet Maud became the judge's bride.

But on the day that they were mated
Maud's brother Bob was intoxicated;

And Maud's relations, twelve in all,
Were very drunk at the judge's hall.

And when the summer came again,
The young bride bore him babies twain.

And the judge was blest, but thought it strange
That bearing children made such a change:

For Maud grew broad and red and stout:
And the waist that his arm once clasped about

Was more than he now could span; and he
Sighed as he pondered, ruefully,

How that which in Maud was native grace
In Mrs. Jenkins was out of place;

And thought of the twins, and wished that they
Looked less like the man who raked the hay

On Muller's farm, and dreamed with pain
Of the day he wandered down the lane,

And, looking down that dreary track,
He half·regretted that he came back.

For, had he waited, he might have wed
Some maiden fair and thoroughbred;

For there be women fair as she,
Whose verbs and nouns do more agree.

Alas for maiden! alas for judge!
And the sentimental,—that's one-half ' fudge ';

For Maud soon thought the judge a bore,
With all his learning and all his lore.

And the judge would have bartered Maud's fair face
For more refinement and social grace.

If, of all words of tongue and pen,
The saddest are, ' It might have been,'

More sad are these we daily see:
' It is, but hadn't ought to be.'

THE WILLOWS.

(POE)

THE skies they were ashen and sober,
    The streets they were dirty and drear;
It was night in the month of October,
    Of my most immemorial year;

Like the skies I was perfectly sober,
  As I stopped at the mansion of Shear,—
At the Nightingale,—perfectly sober,
  And the willowy woodland, down here.

Here, once in an alley Titanic
  Of Ten-pins, I roamed with my soul,—
  Of Ten-pins,—with Mary, my soul;
They were days when my heart was volcanic,
  And impelled me to frequently roll,
  And make me resistlessly roll,
Till my ten-strikes created a panic
  In the realms of the Boreal pole,
Till my ten-strikes created a panic
  With the monkey atop of his pole.

I repeat, I was perfectly sober,
  But my thoughts they were palsied and sere,—
  My thoughts were decidedly queer;
For I knew not the month was October,
  And I marked not the night of the year,
I forgot that sweet *morceau* of Auber
  That the band oft performèd down here,
And I mixed the sweet music of Auber
  With the Nightingale's music by Shear.

And now as the night was senescent,
  And the star-dials pointed to morn,
  And car-drivers hinted of morn,
At the end of the path a liquescent
  And bibulous lustre was born;
'Twas made by the bar-keeper present,
  Who mixéd a duplicate horn,—
His two hands describing a crescent
  Distinct with a duplicate horn.

And I said: ' This looks perfectly regal,
  For it's warm, and I know I feel dry,—
  I am confident that I feel dry;
We have come past the emu and eagle,
  And watched the gay monkey on high;

Let us drink to the emu and eagle,—
  To the swan and the monkey on high,—
  To the eagle and monkey on high;
For this bar-keeper will not inveigle,—
  Bully boy with the vitreous eye;
He surely would never inveigle,—
  Sweet youth with the crystalline eye.'

But Mary, uplifting her finger,
  Said, ' Sadly this bar I mistrust,—
  I fear that this bar does not trust.
O hasten ! O let us not linger !
  O fly,—let us fly,—ere we must !'
In terror she cried, letting sink her
  Parasol till it trailed in the dust,—
In agony sobbed, letting sink her
  Parasol till it trailed in the dust,—
  Till it sorrowfully trailed in the dust.

Then I pacified Mary and kissed her,
  And tempted her into the room,
  And conquered her scruples and gloom;
And we passed to the end of the vista,
  But were stopped by the warning of doom,—
  By some words that were warning of doom;
And I said, ' What is written, sweet sister,
  At the opposite end of ●the room ?'
She sobbed, as she answered, ' All liquors
  Must be paid for ere leaving the room.'

Then my heart it grew ashen and sober,
  As the streets were deserted and drear,—
  For my pockets were empty and drear;
And I cried, ' It was surely October,
  On this very night of last year,
  That I journeyed—I journeyed down here,—
  That I brought a fair maiden down here,
  On this night of all nights in the year.
  Ah ! to me that inscription is clear;
Well I know now, I'm perfectly sober,
  Why no longer they credit me here,—
Well I know now that music of Auber,
  And this Nightingale, kept by one Shear.'

HENRY DUFF TRAILL.

VERS DE SOCIÉTÉ.

(LOCKER-LAMPSON)

THERE, pay it, James ! 'tis cheaply earned;
  My conscience ! how one's cabman charges !
But never mind, so I'm returned
  Safe to my native street of Clarges.
I've just an hour for one cigar
  (What style these Reinas have, and *what* ash !)
One hour to watch the evening star
  With just one Curaçao-and-potash.

Ah me ! that face beneath the leaves
  And blossoms of its piquant bonnet !
Who would have thought that forty thieves
  Of years had laid their fingers on it !
Could you have managed to enchant
  At Lord's to-day old lovers simple,
Had Robber Time not played gallant,
  And spared you every youthful dimple !

That Robber bold, like courtier Claude,
  Who danced the gay coranto jesting,
By your bright beauty charmed and awed,
  Has bowed and passed you unmolesting.
No feet of many-wintered crows
  Have traced about your eyes a wrinkle;
Your sunny hair has thawed the snows
  That other heads with silver sprinkle.

I wonder if that pair of gloves
  I won of you you'll ever pay me !
I wonder if our early loves
  Were wise or foolish, cousin Amy ?
I wonder if our childish tiff
  Now seems to you, like me, a blunder !
I wonder if you wonder if
  I ever wonder if you wonder.

I wonder if you'd think it bliss
    Once more to be the fashion's leader !
I wonder if the trick of this
    Escapes the unsuspecting reader !
And as for him who does or can
    Delight in it, I wonder whether
He knows that almost any man
    Could reel it off by yards together !

I wonder if— What's that ? a knock ?
    Is that you, James ? Eh ? What ? God bless me !
How time has flown ! It's eight o'clock,
    And here's my fellow come to dress me.
Be quick, or I shall be the guest
    Whom Lady Mary never pardons;
I trust you, James, to do your best
    To save the soup at Grosvenor Gardens.

FROM 'THE PUSS AND THE BOOTS.'

(BROWNING)

Put case I circumvent and kill him: good.
Good riddance—wipes at least from book o' th' world
The ugly admiration-note-like blot—
Gives honesty more elbow-room by just
The three dimensions of one wicked knave.
But then slips in the plaguy After-voice.
' Wicked ? Holloa ! my friend, whither away
So fast ? Who made you, Moses-like, a judge
And ruler over men to spare or slay ?
A blot wiped off forsooth ! Produce forthwith
Credentials of your mission to erase
The ink-spots of mankind—t' abolish ill
For being what it is, is bound to be,
Its nature being so—cut wizards off
In flower of their necromantic lives
For being wizards, when 'tis plain enough
That they have no more wrought their wizardship
Than cats their cathood.' Thus the plaguy Voice,
Puzzling withal not overmuch, for thus

I turn the enemy's flank: ' Meseems, my friend,
Your argument's a thought too fine of mesh,
And catches what you would not. Every mouse
Trapped i' the larder by the kitchen wench
Might reason so—but scarcely with effect.
Methinks 'twould little serve the captured thief
To plead, " The fault's Dame Nature's, guiltless I.
Am I to blame that in the parcelling-out
Of my ingredients the Great Chemist set
Just so much here, there so much, and no more
(Since 'tis but question, after all is said,
Of mere proportion 'twixt the part that feels
And that which guides), so much proclivity
To nightly cupboard-breaking, so much lust
Of bacon-scraps, such tendency to think
Old Stilton-rind the noblest thing on earth ?
Then the *per contra*—so much power to choose
The right and shun the wrong; so much of force
Of uncorrupted will to stoutly bar
The sensory inlets of the murine soul,
And, when by night the floating rare-bit fume
Lures like a siren's song, stop nostrils fast
With more than Odusseian sailor-wax:
Lastly so much of wholesome fear of trap
To keep self-abnegation sweet. Then comes
The hour of trial, when lo ! the suadent scale
Sinks instant, the deterrent kicks the beam,
The heavier falls, the lighter mounts (as much
A thing of law with motives as with plums),
And I, forsooth, must die simply because
Dame Nature, having chosen so to load
The dishes, did not choose suspend for me
The gravitation of the moral world."
How would the kitchen-wench reply ? Why thus
(If given, as scullions use, to logic-fence
And keen retorsion of dilemmata
In speeches of a hundred lines or so):
" Grant your plea valid. Good. There's mine to hear.
'Twas Nature made you ? well: and me, no less;
You she by forces past your own control
Made a cheese-stealer ? Be it so: of me
By forces as resistless and her own

She made a mouse-killer. Thus, either plays
A rôle in no wise chosen of himself,
But takes what part the great Stage Manager
Cast him for, when the play was set afoot.
Remains we act ours—without private spite,
But still with spirit and fidelity,
As fits good actors: you I blame no whit
For nibbling cheese—simply I throw you down
Unblamed—nay, even morally assoiled,
To pussy there: blame thou not me for that."
Or say perhaps the girl is slow of wit,
Something inapt at ethics—why, then thus.
" Enough of prating, little thief ! This talk
Of ' fate, free-will, foreknowledge absolute,'
Is hugely out of place ! What next indeed,
If all the casuistry of the schools
Be prayed in aid by every pilfering mouse
That's caught i' th' trap ?   See here, my thieving friend,.
Thus I resolve the problem. We prefer
To keep our cheeses for our own behoof,
And eat them with our proper jaws; and so,
Having command of mouse-traps, we will catch
Whatever mice we can, and promptly kill
Whatever mice we catch. *Entendez vous ?*
Aye, and we *will*, though all the mice on earth
Pass indignation votes, obtest the faith
Of gods and men, and make the welkin ring
With world-resounding dissonance of squeak !" '

But hist ! here comes my wizard ! Ready then
My nerves—and talons—for the trial of strength !:
A stout heart, feline cunning, and—who knows ?

AFTER DILETTANTE CONCETTI.

(ROSSETTI)

' WHY do you wear your hair like a man,.
             Sister Helen ?
This week is the third since you began.'

' I'm writing a ballad; be still if you can,
                         Little   brother.
            (*O Mother Carey, mother !*
What chickens are these between sea and heaven ?)"

' But why does your figure appear so lean,
                         Sister Helen?
And why do you dress in sage, sage green ?"
' Children should never·be heard, if seen,
                         Little brother.
            (*O Mother Carey. mother !*
What fowls are a-wing in the stormy heaven !)"

' But why is your face so yellowy white,
                         Sister Helen ?
And why are your skirts so funnily tight ?'
' Be quiet, you torment, or how can I write,
                         Little brother ?
            (*O Mother Carey, mother !*
How gathers thy train to the sea from the heaven !)

' And who's Mother Carey, and what is her train,
                         Sister Helen ?
And why do you call her again and again ?'
' You troublesome boy, why that's the refrain,
                         Little brother.
            (*O Mother Carey, mother !*
What work is toward in the startled heaven ?)'

' And what's a refrain ?   What a curious word,
                         Sister Helen !
Is the ballad you're writing about a sea-bird ?'
' Not at all; why should it be ?   Don't be absurd,
                         Little brother.
            (*O Mother Carey, mother !*
Thy brood flies lower as lowers the heaven.)'

            (*A big brother speaketh :*)
' The refrain you've studied a meaning had,
                         Sister Helen !
It gave strange force to a weird ballàd,

But refrains have become a ridiculous " fad,"
                                        Little brother.
            And *Mother Carey, mother,*
Has a bearing on nothing in earth or heaven.

' But the finical fashion has had its day,
                                        Sister Helen.
And let's try in the style of a different lay
To bid it adieu in poetical way,
                                        Little brother.
            So, Mother Carey, mother !
Collect your chickens and go to—heaven.'
    (*A pause.   Then the big brother singeth, accom-
        panying himself in a plaintive wise on the
        triangle :*)

' Look in my face.   My name is Used-to-was,
    I am also called Played-out and Done-to-death,
    And It-will-wash-no-more.   Awakeneth
Slowly, but sure awakening it has,
The common-sense of man; and I, alas !
    The ballad-burden trick, now known too well,
    Am turned to scorn, and grown contemptible—
A too transparent artifice to pass.

' What a cheap dodge I am !   The cats who dart
    Tin-kettled through the streets in wild surprise
    Assail judicious ears not otherwise;
And yet no critics praise the urchin's " art,"
Who to the wretched creature's caudal part
    Its foolish empty-jingling " burden " ties.'

ANDREW LANG.

'OH, NO, WE NEVER MENTION HER.'

(ROSSETTI)

LOVE spake to me and said:
 ' O lips, be mute;
Let that one name be dead,
That memory flown and fled,
 Untouched that lute !
Go forth,' said Love, ' with willow in thy hand,
 And in thy hair
 Dead blossoms wear,
Blown from the sunless land.

' Go forth,' said Love; ' thou never more shalt see
Her shadow glimmer by the trysting tree;
 But *she* is glad,
 With roses crowned and clad,
Who hath forgotten thee !'
 But I made answer: ' Love !
 Tell me no more thereof,
For she has drunk of that same cup as I.
Yea, though her eyes be dry,
 She garners there for me
 Tears salter than the sea,
Even till the day she die.'
So gave I Love the lie.

BALLADE OF CRICKET.

To T. W. Lang.

(SWINBURNE)

THE burden of hard hitting: slog away !
Here shalt thou make a ' five ' and there a ' four,'
And then upon thy bat shalt lean, and say,
That thou art in for an uncommon score.
Yea, the loud ring applauding thee shall roar,
And thou to rival THORNTON shalt aspire,
When lo, the Umpire gives thee ' leg before,'—
' This is the end of every man's desire !'

The burden of much bowling, when the stay
Of all thy team is ' collared,' swift or slower,
When ' bailers ' break not in their wonted way,
And ' yorkers ' come not off as here-to-fore,
When length balls shoot no more, ah never more,
When all deliveries lose their former fire,
When bats seem broader than the broad barn-door,—
' This is the end of every man's desire !'

The burden of long fielding, when the clay
Clings to thy shoon in sudden shower's downpour,
And running still thou stumblest, or the ray
Of blazing suns doth bite and burn thee sore,
And blind thee till, forgetful of thy lore,
Thou dost most mournfully misjudge a ' skyer,'
And lose a match the Fates cannot restore,—
' This is the end of every man's desire !'

ENVOY.

Alas, yet liefer on Youth's hither shore
Would I be some poor Player on scant hire,
Than King among the old, who play no more,—
' *This* is the end of every man's desire !'

BRAHMA.

(EMERSON)

IF the wild bowler thinks he bowls,
  Or if the batsman thinks he's bowled,
They know not, poor misguided souls,
  They, too, shall perish unconsoled.
I am the batsman and the bat,
  I am the bowler and the ball,
The umpire, the pavilion cat,
  The roller, pitch, and stumps, and all.

THE PALACE OF BRIC-À-BRAC.

(SWINBURNE)

HERE, where old Nankin glitters,
  Here, where men's tumult seems
As faint as feeble twitters
  Of sparrows heard in dreams,
We watch Limoges enamel,
An old chased silver camel,
A shawl, the gift of Schamyl,
  And manuscripts in reams.

Here, where the hawthorn pattern
  On flawless cup and plate
Need fear no housemaid slattern,
  Fell minister of fate,
'Mid webs divinely woven,
And helms and hauberks cloven,
On music of Beethoven
  We dream and meditate.

We know not, and we need not
  To know how mortals fare,
Of Bills that pass, or speed not,
  Time finds us unaware.

Yea, creeds and codes may crumble,
And Dilke and Gladstone stumble.
And eat the pie that's humble,
  We neither know nor care!

Can kings or clergies alter
  The crackle on one plate?
Can creeds or systems palter
  With what is truly great?
With Corots and with Millets,
With April daffodillies,
Or make the maiden lilies
  Bloom early or bloom late?

Nay, here 'midst Rhodian roses,
  'Midst tissues of Cashmere,
The Soul sublime reposes,
  And knows not hope nor fear;
Here all she sees her own is,
And musical her moan is,
O'er Caxtons and Bodonis,
  Aldine and Elzevir!

'GAILY THE TROUBADOUR.'

(MORRIS)

SIR RALPH he is hardy and mickle of might,
  Ha, la belle blanche aubépine!
Soldans seven hath he slain in fight,
  Honneur à la belle Isoline!

Sir Ralph he rideth in riven mail,
  Ha, la belle blanche aubépine!
Beneath his nasal is his dark face pale,
  Honneur à la belle Isoline!

His eyes they blaze as the burning coal,
  Ha, la belle blanche aubépine!
He smiteth a stave on his gold citole,
  'Honneur à la belle Isoline!'

From her mangonel she looketh forth,
Ha, la belle blanche aubépine !
' Who is he spurreth so late to the north ?'
Honneur à la belle Isoline !

Hark ! for he speaketh a knightly name,
Ha, la belle blanche aubépine !
And her wan cheek glows as a burning flame,
Honneur à la belle Isoline !

For Sir Ralph he is hardy and mickle of might,
Ha, la belle blanche aubépine !
And his love shall ungirdle his sword to-night,
Honneur à la belle Isoline !

ARTHUR CLEMENT HILTON.

THE VULTURE AND THE HUSBANDMAN.

By Louisa Caroline.

('LEWIS CARROLL')

N.B.—A *Vulture* is a rapacious and obscene bird, which destroys its prey by *plucking* it limb from limb with its powerful beak and talons.

A *Husbandman* is a man in a low position of life, who supports himself by the use of the *plough.—Johnson's Dictionary.*

> The rain was raining cheerfully,
>   As if it had been May;
> The Senate-House appeared inside
>   Unusually gay;
> And this was strange, because it was
>   A Viva-Voce day.
>
> The men were sitting sulkily,
>   Their paper work was done;
> They wanted much to go away
>   To ride or row or run;
> 'It's very rude,' they said, 'to keep
>   Us here, and spoil our fun.'
>
> The papers they had finished lay
>   In piles of blue and white.
> They answered everything they could,
>   And wrote with all their might,
> But, though they wrote it all by rote,
>   They did not write it right.
>
> The Vulture and the Husbandman
>   Beside these piles did stand,
> They wept like anything to see
>   The work they had in hand,
> 'If this were only finished up,'
>   Said they, 'it would be grand!'

'If seven D's or seven C's
    We give to all the crowd,
Do you suppose,' the Vulture said,
    ' That we could get them ploughed ?'
' I think so,' said the Husbandman,
    ' But pray don't talk so loud.'

' O undergraduates, come up,'
    The Vulture did beseech,
' And let us see if you can learn
    As well as we can teach;
We cannot do with more than two
    To have a word with each.'

Two Undergraduates came up,
    And slowly took a seat,
They knit their brows, and bit their thumbs,
    As if they found them sweet,
And this was odd, because you know
    Thumbs are not good to eat.

' The time has come,' the Vulture said,
    ' To talk of many things,
Of Accidence and Adjectives,
    And names of Jewish kings,
How many notes a sackbut has,
    And whether shawms have strings.'

' Please, sir,' the Undergraduates said,
    Turning a little blue,
' We did not know that was the sort
    Of thing we had to do.'
' We thank you much,' the Vulture said,
    ' Send up another two.'

Two more came up, and then two more;
    And more, and more, and more;
And some looked upwards at the roof,
    Some down upon the floor,
But none were any wiser than
    The pair that went before.

'I weep for you,' the Vulture said,
  'I deeply sympathize !'
With sobs and tears he gave them all
  D's of the largest size,
While at the Husbandman he winked
  One of his streaming eyes.

'I think,' observed the Husbandman,
  'We're getting on too quick.
Are we not putting down the D's
  A little bit too thick ?'
The Vulture said with much disgust
  'Their answers make me sick.'

'Now, Undergraduates,' he cried,
  'Our fun is nearly done,
Will anybody else come up ?'
  But answer came there none;
And this was scarcely odd, because
  They'd ploughed them every one !

THE HEATHEN PASS-EE.

BEING THE STORY OF A PASS EXAMINATION. BY BRED HARD.

(BRET HARTE)

WHICH I wish to remark,
  And my language is plain,
That for plots that are dark
  And not always in vain,
The heathen Pass-ee is peculiar,
  And the same I would rise to explain.

I would also premise
  That the term of Pass-ee
Most fitly applies,
  As you probably see,
To one whose vocation is passing
  The 'ordinary B.A. degree.'

Tom Crib was his name,
  And I shall not deny
In regard to the same
  What that name might imply,
But his face it was trustful and childlike,
  And he had the most innocent eye.

Upon April the First
  The Little-Go fell,
And that was the worst
  Of the gentleman's sell,
For he fooled the Examining Body
  In a way I'm reluctant to tell.

The candidates came
  And Tom Crib soon appeared;
It was Euclid. The same
  Was ' the subject he feared,'
But he smiled as he sat by the table
  With a smile that was wary and weird.

Yet he did what he could,
  And the papers he showed
Were remarkably good,
  And his countenance glowed
With pride when I met him soon after
  As he walked down the Trumpington Road.

We did not find him out,
  Which I bitterly grieve,
For I've not the least doubt
  That he'd placed up his sleeve
Mr. Todhunter's excellent Euclid,
  The same with intent to deceive.

But I shall not forget
  How the next day at two
A stiff paper was set
  By Examiner U . . .
On Euripides' tragedy, Bacchae.
  A subject Tom ' partially knew.'

But the knowledge displayed
  By that heathen Pass-ee,
And the answers he made
  Were quite frightful to see,
For he rapidly floored the whole paper
  By about twenty minutes to three.

Then I looked up at U . . .
  And he gazed upon me.
I observed, ' This won't do.'
  He replied, ' Goodness me !
We are fooled by this artful young person,'
  And he sent for that heathen Pass-ee.

The scene that ensued
  Was disgraceful to view,
For the floor it was strewed
  With a tolerable few
Of the ' tips ' that Tom Crib had been hiding
  For the ' subject he partially knew.'

On the cuff of his shirt
  He had managed to get
What we hoped had been dirt,
  But which proved, I regret,
To be notes on the rise of the Drama,
  A question invariably set.

In his various coats
  We proceeded to seek,
Where we found sundry notes
  And—with sorrow I speak—
One of Bohn's publications, so useful
  To the student of Latin or Greek.

In the crown of his cap
  Were the Furies and Fates,
And a delicate map
  Of the Dorian States,
And we found in his palms which were hollow,
  What are frequent in palms,—that is dates.

Which is why I remark,
  And my language is plain,
That for plots that are dark
  And not always in vain,
The heathen Pass-ee is peculiar,
  Which the same I am free to maintain.

OCTOPUS.[1]

BY ALGERNON CHARLES SIN-BURN.

(SWINBURNE)

STRANGE beauty, eight-limbed and eight-handed,
  Whence camest to dazzle our eyes ?
With thy bosom bespangled and banded
  With the hues of the seas and the skies;
Is thy home European or Asian,
  O mystical monster marine ?
Part molluscous and partly crustacean,
  Betwixt and between.

Wast thou born to the sound of sea-trumpets ?
  Hast thou eaten and drunk to excess
Of the sponges—thy muffins and crumpets,
  Of the seaweed—thy mustard and cress ?
Wast thou nurtured in caverns of coral,
  Remote from reproof or restraint ?
Art thou innocent, art thou immoral,
  Sinburnian or Saint ?

Lithe limbs, curling free, as a creeper
  That creeps in a desolate place,
To enrol and envelop the sleeper
  In a silent and stealthy embrace,
Cruel beak craning forward to bite us,
  Our juices to drain and to drink,
Or to whelm us in waves of Cocytus,
  Indelible ink !

Written at the Crystal Palace Aquarium.

O breast, that 'twere rapture to writhe on !
   O arms 'twere delicious to feel
Clinging close with the crush of the Python,
   When she maketh her murderous meal !
In thy eight-fold embraces enfolden,
   Let our empty existence escape;
Give us death that is glorious and golden,
   Crushed all out of shape !

Ah ! thy red lips, lascivious and luscious,
   With death in their amorous kiss !
Cling round us, and clasp us, and crush us,
   With bitings of agonized bliss;
We are sick with the poison of pleasure,
   Dispense us the potion of pain;
Ope thy mouth to its uttermost measure
   And bite us again !

HENRY CUYLER BUNNER.

HOME, SWEET HOME, WITH VARIATIONS.

BEING SUGGESTIONS OF THE VARIOUS STYLES IN WHICH
AN OLD THEME MIGHT HAVE BEEN TREATED BY
CERTAIN METRICAL COMPOSERS.

FANTASIA.

1.

THE ORIGINAL THEME, AS JOHN HOWARD PAYNE WROTE IT:

'MID pleasures and palaces though we may roam,
Be it ever so humble, there's no place like home!
A charm from the skies seems to hallow us there,
Which, seek through the world, is not met with else-
    where.
        Home, Home! Sweet, Sweet Home!
        There's no place like Home!

An exile from home, splendour dazzles in vain!
Oh, give me my lowly thatched cottage again!
The birds singing gaily that came at my call!
Give me them! and the peace of mind dearer than all.
        Home, Home! Sweet, Sweet Home!
        There's no place like Home!

II.

AS ALGERNON CHARLES SWINBURNE MIGHT HAVE WRAPPED IT UP
IN VARIATIONS:

['*Mid pleasures and palaces*—]

As sea-foam blown of the winds, as blossom of brine
    that is drifted
Hither and yon on the barren breast of the breeze,
Though we wander on gusts of a god's breath shaken
    and shifted,
The salt of us stings, and is sore for the sobbing seas.

For home's sake hungry at heart, we sicken in pillared
    porches
Of bliss, made sick for a life that is barren of bliss,
For the place whereon is a light out of heaven that sears
    not nor scorches,
Nor elsewhere than this.

[*An exile from home, splendour dazzles in vain*—]
For here we know shall no gold thing glisten,
    No bright thing burn, and no sweet thing shine;
Nor Love lower never an ear to listen
    To words that work in the heart like wine.
        What time we are set from our land apart,
        For pain of passion and hunger of heart,
Though we walk with exiles fame faints to christen,
    Or sing at the Cytherean's shrine.

[VARIATION: *An exile from home*—]
        Whether with him whose head
        Of gods is honourèd,
    With song made splendent in the sight of men—
        Whose heart most sweetly stout,
        From ravished France cast out,
    Being firstly hers, was hers most wholly then—
        Or where on shining seas like wine
        The dove's wings draw the drooping Erycine.

[*Give me my lowly thatched cottage*—]
            For Joy finds Love grow bitter,
            And spreads his wings to quit her,
            At thought of birds that twitter
                Beneath the roof-tree's straw—
            Of birds that come for calling,
            No fear or fright appalling,
            When dews of dusk are falling,
                Or daylight's draperies draw.

[*Give me them, and the peace of mind*—]
        Give me these things then back, though the giving
            Be at cost of earth's garner of gold;

There is no life without these worth living,
No treasure where these are not told.
For the heart give the hope that it knows not,
Give the balm for the burn of the breast—
For the soul and the mind that repose not,
O, give us a rest!

III.

As Mr. Francis Bret Harte might have Woven it into
a Touching Tale of a Western Gentleman
in a Red Shirt:

Brown o' San Juan,
Stranger, I'm Brown.
Come up this mornin' from 'Frisco—
Be'n a-saltin' my specie-stacks down.

Be'n a-knockin' around,
Fer a man from San Juan,
Putty consid'able frequent—
Jes' catch onter that streak o' the dawn!

Right thar lies my home—
Right thar in the red—
I could slop over, stranger, in po'try
Would spread out old Shakspoke cold dead.

Stranger, you freeze to this: there ain't no kinder gin-
palace.
Nor no variety-show lays over a man's own rancho.
Maybe it hain't no style, but the Queen in the Tower o'
London
Ain't got naathin' I'd swop for that house over thar on
the hill-side.

Thar is my ole gal, 'n' the kids, 'n' the rest o' my live
stock;
Thar my Remington hangs, and thar there's a griddle-
cake br'ilin'—
For the two of us, pard—and thar, I allow, the heavens
Smile more friendly-like than on any other locality.

Stranger, nowhere else I don't take no satisfaction.
Gimme my ranch, 'n' them friendly old Shanghai
    chickens—
I brung the original pair f'm the States in eighteen-'n'-
    fifty—
Gimme them and the feelin' of solid domestic comfort.

        Yer parding, young man—
          But this landscape a kind
        Er flickers—I 'low 'twuz the po'try—
          I thought thet my eyes hed gone blind.

      *   *   *   *   *

        Take that pop from my belt !
          Hi, thar—gimme yer han'—
        Or I'll kill myself—Lizzie !—she's left me—
          Gone off with a purtier man !

        Thar, I'll quit—the ole gal
          An' the kids—run away !
        I be derned ! Howsomever, come in, pard—
          The griddle-cake's thar, anyway.

IV.

As Austin Dobson might have Translated it from Horace,
if it had ever occurred to Horace to write it :

RONDEAU.

    Palatiis in remotis voluptates
    Si quæris . . .
        Flaccus, 2. Horatius, *Carmina, Lib. V.,* 1

At home alone, O Nomades,
Although Maecenas' marble frieze
    Stand not between you and the sky,
    Nor Persian luxury supply
Its rosy surfeit, find ye ease.

Tempt not the far Ægean breeze;
With home-made wine and books that please,
To duns and bores the door deny
    At home, alone.

Strange joys may lure. Your deities
Smile here alone. Oh, give me these:
  Low eaves, where birds familiar fly,
  And peace of mind, and, fluttering by,
My Lydia's graceful draperies,
    At home, *alone.*

v.

As it might have been Constructed in 1744,
Oliver Goldsmith, at 19, Writing the
First Stanza, and Alexander Pope,
at 52, the Second:

Home ! at the word, what blissful visions rise;
Lift us from earth, and draw toward the skies !
'Mid mirag'd towers, or meretricious joys,
Although we roam, one thought the mind employs:
Or lowly hut, good friend, or loftiest dome,
Earth knows no spot so holy as our Home.
There, where affection warms the father's breast,
There is the spot of heav'n most surely blest.
Howe'er we search, though wandering with the wind
Through frigid Zembla, or the heats of Ind,
Not elsewhere may we seek, nor elsewhere know,
The light of heav'n upon our dark below.

When from our dearest hope and haven reft,
Delight nor dazzles, nor is luxury left,
We long, obedient to our nature's law,
To see again our hovel thatched with straw:
See birds that know our avenaceous store
Stoop to our hand, and thence repleted soar:
But, of all hopes the wanderer's soul that share,
His pristine peace of mind 's his final prayer.

VI.

As Walt Whitman might have Written all around it:

1.

You over there, young man with the guide-book, red-
bound, covered flexibly with red linen,
Come here, I want to talk with you; I, Walt, the Man-
hattanese, citizen of these States, call you.
Yes, and the courier, too, smirking, smug-mouthed,
with oil'd hair; a garlicky look about him generally;
him, too, I take in, just as I would a coyote, or a
king, or a toad-stool, or a ham-sandwich, or anything or anybody else in the world.
Where are you going?
You want to see Paris, to eat truffles, to have a good
time; in Vienna, London, Florence, Monaco, to have
a good time; you want to see Venice.
Come with me. I will give you a good time; I will
give you all the Venice you want, and most of the
Paris.
I, Walt, I call to you. I am all on deck! Come and
loaf with me! Let me tote you around by your
elbow and show you things.
You listen to my ophicleide!
Home!
Home, I celebrate. I elevate my fog-whistle, inspir'd
by the thought of home.
Come in!—take a front seat; the jostle of the crowd
not minding; there is room enough for all of you.
This is my exhibition—it is the greatest show on earth
—there is no charge for admission.
All you have to pay me is to take in my romanza.

2.

1. The brown-stone house; the father coming home
    worried from a bad day's business; the wife meets
    him in the marble-pav'd vestibule; she throws
    her arms about him; she presses him close to her;

she looks him full in the face with affectionate
eyes; the frown from his brow disappearing.

Darling, she says, *Johnny has fallen down and cut
his head ; the cook is going away, and the boiler
leaks.*

2. The mechanic's dark little third story room, seen in
a flash from the Elevated Railway train; the
sewing-machine in a corner; the small cook-stove;
the whole family eating cabbage around a kero-
sene lamp; of the clatter and roar and groaning
wail of the Elevated train unconscious; of the
smell of the cabbage unconscious.

Me, passant, in the train, of the cabbage not quite
so unconscious.

3. The French flat ; the small rooms, all right angles,
unindividual ; the narrow halls ; the gaudy cheap
decorations everywhere.

The janitor and the cook exchanging compliments
up and down the elevator-shaft; the refusal to
send up more coal, the solid splash of the water
upon his head, the language he sends up the shaft,
the triumphant laughter of the cook, to her
kitchen retiring.

4. The widow's small house in the suburbs of the city;
the widow's boy coming home from his first day
down town; he is flushed with happiness and
pride; he is no longer a school-boy, he is earning
money; he takes on the airs of a man and talks
learnedly of business.

5. The room in the third-class boarding-house; the
mean little hard-coal fire, the slovenly Irish ser-
vant-girl making it, the ashes on the hearth, the
faded furniture, the private provender hid away
in the closet, the dreary back-yard out the window; the young girl at the glass, with her mouth
full of hair-pins, doing up her hair to go downstairs and flirt with the young fellows in the
parlour.

6. The kitchen of the old farm-house; the young convict just return'd from prison—it was his first
offence, and the judges were lenient to him.

He is taking his first meal out of prison; he has

been receiv'd back, kiss'd, encourag'd to start
again; his lungs, his nostrils expand with the big
breaths of free air ; with shame, with wonderment, with a trembling joy, his heart too ex-
panding.

The old mother busies herself about the table; she
has ready for him the dishes he us'd to like; the
father sits with his back to them, reading the
newspaper, the newspaper shaking and rustling
much; the children hang wondering around the
prodigal——they have been caution'd: *Do not ask
where our Jim has been ; only say you are glad to
see him.*

The elder daughter is there, pale-fac'd, quiet; her
young man went back on her four years ago; his
folks would not let him marry a convict's sister.
She sits by the window, sewing on the children's
clothes, the clothes not only patching up; her
hunger for children of her own invisibly patching
up.

The brother looks up; he catches her eye, he fearful,
apologetic; she smiles back at him, not reproach-
fully smiling, with loving pretence of hope smiling
—it is too much for him; he buries his face in the
folds of the mother's black gown.

7. The best room of the house, on the Sabbath only
open'd; the smell of horse-hair furniture and
mahogany varnish; the ornaments on the what-
not in the corner; the wax-fruit, dusty, sunken,
sagged in, consumptive-looking, under a glass
globe; the sealing-wax imitation of coral; the
cigar boxes with shells plastered over; the per-
forated card-board motto.

The kitchen; the housewife sprinkling the clothes
for the fine ironing to-morrow—it is Third-day
night, and the plain things are already iron'd, now
in cupboards, in drawers stowed away.

The wife waiting for the husband—he is at the
tavern, jovial, carousing; she, alone in the kitchen
sprinkling clothes—the little red wood clock with
peaked top, with pendulum wagging behind a
pane of gaily painted glass, strikes twelve.

The sound of the husband's voice on the still night
  air—he is singing: *We won't go home till morning !*
  —the wife arising, toward the wood-shed hastily
  going, stealthily entering, the voice all the time
  coming nearer, inebriate, chantant.
The wood-shed; the club behind the door of the
  wood-shed; the wife annexing the club; the husband approaching, always inebriate, chantant.
The husband passing the door of the wood-shed;
  the club over his head, now with his head in con-
  tact; the sudden cessation of the song; the tem-
  perance pledge signed the next morning; the
  benediction of peace over the domestic foyer
  temporarily resting.

3.

I sing the soothing influences of home.
You, young man, thoughtlessly wandering, with
  courier, with guide-book wandering,
You hearken to the melody of my steam-calliope.
Yawp !

JAMES KENNETH STEPHEN.

ODE ON A RETROSPECT OF ETON COLLEGE.

(GRAY)

YE bigot spires, ye Tory towers,
   That crown the watery lea,
Where grateful science still adores
   The aristocracy:
A happy usher once I strayed
Beneath your lofty elm trees' shade,
   With mind untouched by guilt or woe:
But mad ambition made me stray
Beyond the round of work and play
   Wherein we ought to go.

My office was to teach the young
   Idea how to shoot:
But, ah! I joined with eager tongue
   Political dispute:
I ventured humbly to suggest
That all things were not for the best
   Among the Irish peasantry:
And finding all the world abuse
My simple unpretending views,
   I thought I'd go and see.

I boldly left the College bounds:
   Across the sea I went,
To probe the economic grounds
   Of Irish discontent.
My constant goings to and fro
Excited some alarm; and so
   Policemen girded up their loins,
And, from his innocent pursuits,—
Morose unsympathetic brutes,—
   They snatched a fearful Joynes.

Escaped, I speedily returned
To teach the boys again:
But ah, my spirit inly burned
To think on Ireland's pain.
Such wrongs must out: and then, you see,
My own adventures might not be
Uninteresting to my friends:
I therefore ventured to prepare
A little book, designed with care,
To serve these humble ends.

Our stern head-master spoke to me
Severely:—' You appear
(*Horresco referens*) to be
A party pamphleteer.
If you *must* write, let Cæsar's page
Or Virgil's poetry engage
Your all too numerous leisure hours:
But now annihilate and quash
This impious philanthropic bosh:
Or quit these antique towers.'

It seems that he who dares to write
Is all unfit to teach:
And literary fame is quite
Beyond an usher's reach.
I dared imprisonment in vain:
The little bantling of my brain
I am compelled to sacrifice.
The moral, after all, is this:—
That here, where ignorance is bliss,
'Tis folly to be wise.

A SONNET.

(WORDSWORTH)

Two voices are there: one is of the deep;
It learns the storm-cloud's thunderous melody,
Now roars, now murmurs with the changing sea,
Now bird-like pipes, now closes soft in sleep:
And one is of an old half-witted sheep
Which bleats articulate monotony,
And indicates that two and one are three,
That grass is green, lakes damp, and mountains steep:
And, Wordsworth, both are thine: at certain times
Forth from the heart of thy melodious rhymes,
The form and pressure of high thoughts will burst:
At other times—good Lord! I'd rather be
Quite unacquainted with the ABC
Than write such hopeless rubbish as thy worst.

SINCERE FLATTERY OF R. B.

(BROWNING)

Birthdays? yes, in a general way;
For the most if not for the best of men:
You were born (I suppose) on a certain day:
So was I: or perhaps in the night: what then?

Only this: or at least, if more,
You must know, not think it, and learn, not speak:
There is truth to be found on the unknown shore,
And many will find where few will seek.

For many are called and few are chosen,
And the few grow many as ages lapse:
But when will the many grow few: what dozen
Is fused into one by Time's hammer-taps?

A bare brown stone in a babbling brook:—
It was wanton to hurl it there, you say:
And the moss, which clung in the sheltered nook
(Yet the stream runs cooler), is washed away.

That begs the question: many a prater
Thinks such a suggestion a sound ' stop thief !'
Which, may I ask, do you think the greater,
Sergeant-at-arms or a Robber Chief ?

And if it were not so ? still you doubt ?
Ah ! yours is a birthday indeed if so.
That were something to write a poem about,
If one thought a little. I only know.

P.S.

There 's a Me Society down at Cambridge,
Where my works, *cum notis variorum,*
Are talked about; well, I require the same bridge
That Euclid took toll at as *Asinorum :*

And, as they have got through several ditties
I thought were as stiff as a brick-built wall,
I've composed the above, and a stiff one·*it* is,
A bridge to stop asses at, once for all.

SINCERE FLATTERY OF W. W. (AMERICANUS).

(WHITMAN)

THE clear cool note of the cuckoo which has ousted the
    legitimate nest-holder,
The whistle of the railway guard dispatching the train
    to the inevitable collision,
The maiden's monosyllabic reply to a polysyllabic
    proposal,
The fundamental note of the last trump, which is
    presumably D natural;
All of these are sounds to rejoice in, yea to let your
    very ribs re-echo with:
But better than all of them is the absolutely last chord
    of the apparently inexhaustible pianoforte player.

TO A. T. M.

(F. W. H. MYERS)

SEE where the K., in sturdy self-reliance,
  Thoughtful and placid as a brooding dove,
Stands, firmly sucking, in the cause of science,
  Just such a peppermint as schoolboys love.

Suck, placid K.: the world will be thy debtor;
  Though thine eyes water and thine heart grow faint,
Suck: and the less thou likest it the better;
  Suck for our sake, and utter no complaint.

Near thee a being, passionate and gentle,
  Man's latest teacher, wisdom's pioneer,
Calmly majestically monumental,
  Stands: the august Telepathist is here.

Waves of perception, subtle emanations,
  Thrill through the ether, circulate amain;
Delicate soft impalpable sensations,
  Born of thy palate, quiver in his brain.

Lo ! with a voice unspeakably dramatic,
  Lo ! with a gesture singularly fine,
He makes at last a lucid and emphatic
  Statement of what is in that mouth of thine.

He could detect that peppermint's existence,
  He read its nature in the book of doom;
Standing at some considerable distance;
  Standing, in fact, in quite another room.

Was there a faint impenetrable essence
  Wafted towards him from the sucking K.?
Did some pale ghost inform him of its presence ?
  Or did it happen in some other way ?

These are the questions nobody can answer,
  These are the problems nobody can solve;
Only we know that Man is an Advancer:
  Only we know the Centuries revolve.

FRANCIS THOMPSON.

WAKE! FOR THE RUDDY BALL HAS TAKEN FLIGHT.

(EDWARD FITZGERALD)

I.

WAKE! for the Ruddy Ball has taken flight
That scatters the slow Wicket of the Night;
   And the swift Batsman of the Dawn has driven
Against the Star-spiked Rails a fiery Smite.

Wake, my Belovèd! take the Bat that clears
The sluggish Liver, and Dyspeptics cheers:
   To-morrow? Why, to-morrow I may be
Myself with Hambledon and all its Peers.

To-day a Score of Batsmen brings, you say?
Yes, but where leaves the Bats of yesterday?
   And this same summer day that brings a Knight
May take the Grace and Ranjitsinjh away.

Willsher the famed is gone with all his 'throws,'
And Alfred's Six-foot Reach where no man knows;
   And Hornby—that great hitter—his own Son
Plays in his place, yet recks not the Red Rose.

And Silver Billy, Fuller Pilch and Small,
Alike the pigmy Briggs and Ulyett tall,
   Have swung their Bats an hour or two before,
But none played out the last and silent Ball.

Well, let them Perish! What have we to do
With Gilbert Grace the Great, or that Hindu?
   Let Hirst and Spooner slog them as they list,
Or Warren bowl his 'snorter'; care not you!

With me along the Strip of Herbage strown,
That is not laid or watered, rolled or sown,
   Where name of Lord's and Oval is forgot,
And peace to Nicholas on his bomb-girt Throne.

A level Wicket, as the Ground allow,
A driving Bat, a lively Ball, and thou
  Before me bowling on the Cricket-Pitch—
O Cricket-pitch were Paradise enow!

II.

I listened where the Grass was shaven small,
And heard the Bat that groaned against the Ball:
  Thou pitchest Here and There, and Left and Right,
Nor deem I where the Spot thou next may'st Fall.

Forward I play, and Back, and Left and Right,
And overthrown at once, or stay till Night:
  But this I know, where nothing else I know,
The last is Thine, how so the Bat shall smite.

This thing is sure, where nothing else is sure,
The boldest Bat may but a Space endure;
  And he who One or who a Hundred hits
Falleth at ending to thy Force or Lure.

Wherefore am I allotted but a Day
To taste Delight, and make so brief a stay;
  For Meed of all my Labour laid aside,
Ended alike the Player and the Play?

Behold, there is an Arm behind the Ball,
Nor the Bat's Stroke of its own Striking all;
  And who the Gamesters, to what end the Game,
I think thereof our Willing is but small.

Against the Attack and Twist of Circumstance
Though I oppose Defence and shifty Glance,
  What Power gives Nerve to me, and what Assaults,—
This is the Riddle. Let dull bats cry 'Chance.'

Is there a Foe that [domineers] the Ball?
And one that Shapes and wields us Willows all?
  Be patient if Thy Creature in Thy Hand
Break, and the so-long-guarded Wicket fall!

Thus spoke the Bat. Perchance a foolish Speech
And wooden, for a Bat has straitened Reach :
   Yet thought I, I had heard Philosophers
Prate much on this wise, and aspire to Teach.

Ah, let us take our Stand, and play the Game,
But rather for the Cause than for the Fame ;
   Albeit right evil is the Ground, and we
Know our Defence thereon will be but lame.

O Love, if thou and I could but Conspire
Against this Pitch of Life, so false with Mire,
   Would we not Doctor it afresh, and then
Roll it out smoother to the Bat's Desire ?

ROBERT FULLER MURRAY.

THE POET'S HAT.

(TENNYSON)

THE rain had fallen, the Poet arose,
  He passed through the doorway into the street,
A strong wind lifted his hat from his head,
  And he uttered some words that were far from sweet.
And then he started to follow the chase,
  ·And put on a spurt that was wild and fleet,
It made the people pause in a crowd,
  And lay odds as to which would beat.

The street cad scoffed as he hunted the hat,
  The errand-boy shouted hooray !
The scavenger stood with his broom in his hand,
  And smiled in a very rude way;
And the clergyman thought, ' I have heard many
    words,
  But never, until to-day,
Did I hear any words that were quite so bad
  As I heard that young man say.'

A TENNYSONIAN FRAGMENT.

[Inserted by special permission of the Proprietors of *Punch*.]

(TENNYSON)

So in the village inn the poet dwelt.
His honey-dew was gone; only the pouch,
His cousin's work, her empty labour, left.
But still he sniffed it, still a fragrance clung
And lingered all about the broidered flowers.
Then came his landlord, saying in broad Scotch
'Smoke plug, mon,' whom he looked at doubtfully.
Then came the grocer, saying, 'Hae some twist
At tippence,' whom he answered with a qualm.

But when they left him to himself again,
Twist, like a fiend's breath from a distant room
Diffusing through the passage, crept; the smell
Deepening had power upon him, and he mixt
His fancies with the billow-lifted bay
Of Biscay and the rollings of a ship.

And on that night he made a little song,
And called his song 'The Song of Twist and Plug,'
And sang it; scarcely could he make or sing.

'Rank is black plug, though smoked in wind and rain;
And rank is twist, which gives no end of pain;
I know not which is ranker, no, not I.

'Plug, art thou rank? then milder twist must be;
Plug, thou art milder: rank is twist to me.
O twist, if plug be milder, let me buy.

'Rank twist that seems to make me fade away,
Rank plug, that navvies smoke in loveless clay,
I know not which is ranker, no, not I.

'I fain would purchase flake, if that could be;
I needs must purchase plug, ah, woe is me!
Plug and a cutty, a cutty, let me buy.'

ANDREW M'CRIE.

(FROM THE UNPUBLISHED REMAINS OF EDGAR ALLAN POE)

IT was many and many a year ago,
  In a city by the sea,
That a man there lived whom I happened to know
  By the name of Andrew M'Crie;
And this man he slept in another room,
  But ground and had meals with me.

I was an ass and he was an ass,
  In this city by the sea;
But we ground in a way which was more than a grind,
  I and Andrew M'Crie;
In a way that the idle semis next door
  Declared was shameful to see.

And this was the reason that, one dark night,
  In this city by the sea,
A stone flew in at the window, hitting
  The milk-jug and Andrew M'Crie.
And once some low-bred tertians came,
  And bore him away from me,
And shoved him into a private house
  Where the people were having tea.

Professors, not half so well up in their work,
  Went envying him and me—
Yes!—that was the reason, I always thought
  (And Andrew agreed with me),
Why they ploughed us both at the end of the year,
  Chilling and killing poor Andrew M'Crie.

But his ghost is more terrible far than the ghosts
  Of many more famous than he—
  Of many more gory than he—
And neither visits to foreign coasts,
  Nor tonics, can ever set free
Two well-known Profs from the haunting wraith
  Of the injured Andrew M'Crie.

For at night, as they dream, they frequently scream,
  ' Have mercy, Mr. M'Crie !'
And at morn they will rise with bloodshot eyes,
  And the very first thing they will see.
When they dare to descend to their coffee and rolls,
Sitting down by the scuttle, the scuttle of coals,
  With a volume of notes on its knee,
  Is the spectre of Andrew M'Crie.

UNKNOWN.

THE TOWN LIFE

(ROGERS)

MINE is a house at Notting Hill:
  The Indian's tum-tum smites my ear;
A crowd enjoys a casual ' mill '
  With no policeman lingering near.

The thief attempts the chain and watch
  Conspicuous in my spacious vest;
Their balls of brass the tumblers catch,
  In soiled and spangled garments dressed.

Around my steps street-organs bring
  The dirtiest brats that can be seen;
And boys turn wheels, and niggers sing
  To banjo and to tambourine.

The dustman bawls; the beggars tease
  When coppers are not duly given;
Whilst papers, flowers, and fusees,
  Annoy me six days out of seven.

FISH HAVE THEIR TIMES TO BITE.

(MRS. HEMANS)

FISH have their times to bite—
The bream in summer, and the trout in spring,
  What time the hawthorn buds are white,
And streams are clear, and winds low-whispering.

The pike bite free when fall
The autumn leaves before the north-wind's breath,
  And tench in June, but there are all—
There are all seasons for the gudgeon's death.

The trout his ambush keeps
Crafty and strong, in Pangbourne's eddying pools,
  And patient still in Marlow deeps
For the shy barbel wait expectant fools.

Many the perch but small
That swim in Basildon, and Thames hath nought
  Like Cookham's pike, but, oh! in all—
Yes, in all places are the gudgeon caught.

The old man angles still
For roach, and sits red-faced and fills his chair;
  And perch, the boy expects to kill,
And roves and fishes here and fishes there.

The child but three feet tall
For the gay minnows and the bleak doth ply
  His bending hazel, but by all—
Oh! by all hands the luckless gudgeon die.

ANOTHER ODE TO THE NORTH-EAST WIND

(KINGSLEY)

HANG thee, vile North Easter:
  Other things may be
Very bad to bear with,
  Nothing equals thee.
Grim and grey North Easter,
  From each Essex-bog,
From the Plaistow marshes,
  Rolling London fog—
' Tired we are of Summer '
  Kingsley may declare,
I give the assertion
  Contradiction bare,
I, in bed, this morning
  Felt thee, as I lay:
' There's a vile North Easter
  Out of doors to-day !'
Set the dust clouds blowing
  Till each face they strike,
With the blacks is growing
  Chimney-sweeper like.
Fill our rooms with smoke gusts
  From the chimney-pipe.
Fill our eyes with water,
  That defies the wipe.
Through the draughty passage
  Whistle loud and high,
Making doors and windows
  Rattle, flap and fly;
Mark, that vile North Easter
  Roaring up the vent,
Nipping soul and body,
  Breeding discontent !
Squall, my noisy children;
  Smoke, my parlour grate;

Scold, my shrewish partner;
  I accept my fate.
All is quite in tune with
  This North Eastern Blast;
Who can look for comfort
  Till this wind be past ?
If all goes contrary,
  Who can feel surprise,
With this Rude North Easter
  In his teeth and eyes ?
It blows much too often,
  Nine days out of ten,
Yet we boast our climate,
  Like true English men !
In their soft South Easters
  Could I bask at ease,
I'd let France and Naples
  Bully as they please,
But while this North Easter
  In one's teeth is hurled,
Liberty seems worth just
  Nothing in the world.
Come, as came our fathers
  Heralded by thee,
Blasting, blighting, burning
  Out of Normandy.
Come and flay and skin us,
  And dry up our blood—
All to have a Kingsley
  Swear it does him good !

A GIRTONIAN FUNERAL.

(BROWNING)

The *Academy* reports that the students of Girton College have dissolved their ' Browning Society,' and expended its remaining funds, two shillings and twopence, upon chocolate creams.

LET us begin and portion out these sweets,
    Sitting together.
Leave we our deep debates, our sage conceits,—
    Wherefore ? and whether ?
Thus with a fine that fits the work begun
    Our labours crowning,
For we, in sooth, our duty well have done
    By Robert Browning.
Have we not wrought at essay and critique,
    Scorning supine ease ?
Wrestled with clauses crabbed as Bito's Greek,
    Baffling as Chinese ?
Out the Inn Album's mystic heart we took,
    Lucid of soul, and
Threaded the mazes of the Ring and Book;
    Cleared up Childe Roland.
We settled Fifine's business—let her be—
    (Strangest of lasses;)
Watched by the hour some thick-veiled truth to see
    Where Pippa passes.
(Though, dare we own, secure in victors' gains,
    Ample to shield us ?
Red Cotton Night-cap Country for our pains
    Little would yield us.)
What then to do ? Our culture-feast drag out
    E'en to satiety ?
Oft such the fate that findeth, nothing doubt,
    Such a Society.
Oh, the dull meetings ! Some one yawns an *aye*,
    One gapes again a *yea*.
We girls determined not to yawn, but buy
    Chocolate Ménier.

Fry's creams are cheap, but Cadbury's excel,
    (Quick, Maud, for none wait)
Nay, now, 'tis Ménier bears away the bell,
    Sold by the ton-weight.
So, with unburdened brains and spirits light,
    Blithe did we troop hence,
All our funds voted for this closing rite,—
    Just two-and-two-pence.
Do—make in scorn, old Crœsus, proud and glum,
    Peaked eyebrow lift eye;
Put case one stick's a halfpenny; work the sum;
    Full two and fifty.
Off with the twine! who scans each smooth brown slab
    Yet not supposeth
What soft, sweet, cold, pure whiteness, bound in drab,
    Tooth's bite discloseth?
Are they not grand? Why (you may think it odd)
    Some power alchemic
Turns, as we munch, to Zeus-assenting nod
    Sneers Academic.
Till, when one cries, ' 'Ware hours that fleet like clouds,
    Time, deft escaper!'
We answer bold: ' Leave Time to Dons and Dowds;
    (Grace, pass the paper)
Say, boots it aught to evermore affect
    Raptures high-flying?
Though *we* choose chocolate, will the world suspect
    Genius undying?'

NOTES

P. 1. *Rejected Addresses.* First published anonymously in the autumn of 1812. The authors, James Smith (1775-1839) and Horace Smith (1779-1849) were brothers, the former a solicitor, the latter a stockbroker. James wrote a number of 'entertainments' for Charles Mathews, who described him as 'the only man in London who can write good nonsense.' Horace wrote more than a score of novels and collections of stories, of which, perhaps, *Lrambletye House* is the best remembered. It was of him that Shelley wrote, in the *Letter to Maria Gisborne :*

> Wit and sense,
> Virtue and human knowledge; all that might
> Make this dull world a business of delight,
> Are all combined in Horace Smith.

How the *Rejected Addresses* came to be written is told in the authors' prefaces:

PREFACE TO THE FIRST EDITION.

ON the 14th of August, 1812, the following advertisement appeared in most of the daily papers:—

' *Rebuilding of Drury Lane Theatre.*

' The Committee are desirous of promoting a free and fair competition for an Address to be spoken upon the opening of the Theatre, which will take place on the 10th of October next. They have, therefore, thought fit to announce to the public, that they will be glad to receive any such compositions, addressed to their Secretary, at the Treasury Office, in Drury Lane, on or before the 10th of September, sealed up; with a distinguishing word, number, or motto, on the cover, corresponding with the inscription on a separate sealed paper, containing the name of the author, which will not be opened unless containing the name of the successful candidate.'

Upon the propriety of this plan, men's minds were, as they usually are upon matters of moment, much divided. Some thought it a fair promise of the future intention of the Committee to abolish that phalanx of authors who usurp the stage, to the exclusion of a large assortment of dramatic talent blushing unseen in the background; while others contended, that the scheme would prevent men of real eminence from descending into an amphitheatre in which all Grub Street (that is to say, all London and Westminster) would be arrayed against them. The event has proved both parties to be in a degree right, and in a degree wrong. One hundred and twelve ' Addresses ' have been sent in, each sealed and signed, and mottoed, ' as per order,' some written by men of great, some by men of little, and some by men of no, talent.

Many of the public prints have censured the taste of the Committee, in thus contracting for ' Addresses,' as they would for nails— by the gross; but it is surprising that none should have censured their *temerity*. One hundred and eleven of the ' Addresses ' must, of course, be unsuccessful: to each of the authors, thus infallibly classed with the *genus irritabile*, it would be very hard to deny six staunch friends, who consider his the best of all possible ' Addresses,' and whose tongues will be as ready to laud him, as to hiss his adversary. These, with the potent aid of the Bard himself, make seven foes per Address; and thus will be created seven hundred and seventy-seven implacable auditors, prepared to condemn the strains of Apollo himself—a band of adversaries which no prudent manager would think of exasperating.

But, leaving the Committee to encounter the responsibility they have incurred, the public have at least to thank them for ascertaining and establishing one point, which might otherwise have admitted of controversy. When it is considered that many amateur writers have been discouraged from becoming competitors, and that few, if any, of the professional authors can afford to write for nothing, and, of course, have not been candidates for the honorary prize at Drury Lane, we may confidently pronounce that, as far as regards NUMBER, the present is undoubtedly the Augustan age of English poetry. Whether or not this distinction will be extended to the QUALITY of its productions, must be decided at the tribunal of posterity; though the natural anxiety of our authors on this score ought to be considerably diminished when they reflect how few will, in all probability, be had up for judgement.

It is not necessary for the Editor to mention the manner in which he became possessed of this ' fair sample of the present state of poetry in Great Britain.' It was his first intention to publish the whole; but a little reflection convinced him that, by so doing, he might depress the good, without elevating the bad. He has therefore culled what had the appearance of flowers, from what possessed the reality of weeds, and is extremely sorry that, in so doing, he has diminished his collection to twenty-one. Those which he has rejected may possibly make their appearance in a separate volume, or they may be admitted as volunteers in the files of some of the Newspapers; or, at all events, they are sure of being received among the awkward squad of the Magazines. In general, they bear a close resemblance to each other; thirty of them contain extravagant compliments to the immortal Wellington and the indefatigable Whitbread; and, as the last-mentioned gentleman is said to dislike praise in the exact proportion in which he deserves it, these laudatory writers may have been only building a wall against which they might run their own heads.

The Editor here begs leave to advance a few words in behalf of that useful and much abused bird the Phœnix; and in so doing he is biased by no partiality, as he assures the reader he not only never saw one, but (*mirabile dictu !*) never caged one in a simile in the whole course of his life. Not less than sixty-nine of the competitors have invoked the aid of this native of Arabia; but as, from their manner of using him after they had caught him, he does not by any means appear to have been a native of *Arabia Felix*, the Editor has left the proprietors to treat with Mr. Polito, and refused to receive this *rara avis*, or black swan, into the present collection. One exception occurs, in which the admirable treatment of this feathered incombustible, entitles the author to great praise; that address has been preserved, and was thought worthy of taking the lead.

Perhaps the reason why several of the subjoined productions of the MUSÆ LONDINENSES have failed of selection, may be discovered in their being penned in a metre unusual upon occasions of this sort, and in their not being written with that attention to stage effect, the want of which, like want of manners in the concerns of life, is more prejudicial than a deficiency of talent. There is an art of writing for the Theatre, technically called *touch and go*, which is indispensable when we consider the small quantum of patience which so motley an assemblage as a London audience can be expected to afford. All the contributors have been very exact in sending their initials and mottoes. Those belonging to the present collection have been carefully preserved, and each has been affixed to its respective poem. The letters that accompanied the Addresses having been honourably destroyed unopened, it is impossible to state the real authors with any certainty; but the ingenious reader, after comparing the initials with the motto, and both with the poem will form his own conclusions.

We do not anticipate any disapprobation from thus giving publicity to a small portion of the *Rejected Addresses ;* for unless we are widely mistaken in assigning the respective authors, the fame of each individual is established on much too firm a basis to be shaken by so trifling and evanescent a publication as the present:

> ——neque ego illi detrahere ausim
> Hærentem capiti multa cum laude coronam.

Of the numerous pieces already sent to the Committee for performance, we have only availed ourselves of three vocal Travesties, which we have selected, not for their merit, but simply for their brevity. Above one hundred spectacles, melodramas, operas, and pantomimes have been transmitted, besides the two first acts of one legitimate comedy. Some of these evince considerable smartness of manual dialogue, and several brilliant repartees of chairs, tables, and other inanimate wits; but the authors seem to have forgotten that in the new Drury Lane the audience can hear as well as see. Of late our theatres have been so constructed, that John Bull has been compelled to have very long ears, or none at all; to keep them dangling about his skull like discarded servants, while his eyes were gazing at piebalds and elephants, or else to stretch them out to an asinine length to catch the congenial sound of braying trumpets. An auricular revolution is, we trust, about to take place; and as many people have been much puzzled to define the meaning of the new era, of which we have heard so much, we venture to pronounce, that as far as regards Drury Lane Theat , the new era means the reign of ears. If the past affords any pledge for the future, we may confidently expect from the Committee of that House everything that can be accomplished by the union of taste and assiduity.

The text of the *Rejected Addresses* here given is that of the eighteenth edition with Horace Smith's annotations. The footnotes from the *Edinburgh Review* were taken from an article by Lord Jeffrey in the number for November, 1812. It may be mentioned that the actual addresses sent in to the Drury Lane Committee are preserved with their covering letters in the Manuscript Department of the British Museum, and that on the immediate success of the Smiths' parodies an enterprising publisher issued a volume of *Genuine Rejected Addresses* from the forty-three competitors who responded to his appeal for such. The following is from the Preface to the eighteenth edition:

Our first difficulty, that of selection, was by no means a light one. Some of our most eminent poets, such, for instance, as Rogers and Campbell, presented so much beauty, harmony, and proportion in their writings, both as to style and sentiment, that if we had attempted to caricature them, nobody would have recognized the likeness; and if we had endeavoured to give a servile copy of their manner, it would only have amounted, at best, to a tame and unamusing portrait, which it was not our object to present. Although fully aware that their names would, in the theatrical phrase, have conferred great strength upon our bill, we were reluctantly compelled to forgo them, and to confine ourselves to writers whose style and habit of thought, being more marked and peculiar, was more capable of exaggeration and distortion. To avoid politics and personality, to imitate the turn of mind, as well as the phraseology of our originals, and, at all events, to raise a harmless laugh, were our main objects: in the attainment of which united aims, we were sometimes hurried into extravagance, by attaching much more importance to the last than to the two first. In no instance were we thus betrayed into a greater injustice than in the case of Mr. Wordsworth—the touching sentiment, profound wisdom, and copious harmony of whose loftier writings we left unnoticed, in the desire of burlesquing them; while we pounced upon his popular ballads, and exerted ourselves to push their simplicity into puerility and silliness. With pride and pleasure do we now claim to be ranked among the most ardent admirers of this true poet; and if he himself could see the state of his works, which are ever at our right hand, he would, perhaps, receive the manifest evidences they exhibit of constant reference, and delighted re-perusal, as some sort of *amende honorable* for the unfairness of which we were guilty, when we were less conversant with the higher inspirations of his muse. To Mr. Coleridge, and others of our originals, we must also do a tardy act of justice, by declaring that our burlesque of their peculiarities, has never blinded us to those beauties and talents which are beyond the reach of all ridicule.

One of us had written a genuine Address for the occasion, which was sent to the Committee, and shared the fate it merited, in being rejected. To swell the bulk, or rather to diminish the tenuity of our little work, we added it to the Imitations; and prefixing the initials of S. T. P. for the purpose of puzzling the critics, were not a little amused, in the sequel, by the many guesses and conjectures into which we had ensnared some of our readers. We could even enjoy the mysticism, qualified as it was by the poor compliment, that our carefully written Address exhibited no 'very prominent trait of absurdity,' when we saw it thus noticed in the *Edinburgh Review* for November, 1812. ' An Address by S. T. P. we can make nothing of; and professing our ignorance of the author designated by these letters, we can only add, that the Address, though a little affected, and not very full of meaning, has no very prominent trait of absurdity, that we can detect; and might have been adopted and spoken, so far as we can perceive, without any hazard of ridicule. In our simplicity we consider it as a very decent, mellifluous, occasional prologue; and do not understand how it has found its way into its present company.'

Urged forward by hurry, and trusting to chance, two very bad coadjutors in any enterprise, we at length congratulated ourselves on having completed our task in time to have it printed and published by the opening of the theatre. But, alas ! our difficulties, so far from being surmounted, seemed only to be beginning. Strangers to the arcana of the bookseller's trade, and unacquainted with their almost invincible objection to single volumes of low price, especially when tendered by writers who have acquired no previous name, we little anticipated that they would refuse to publish our *Rejected Addresses*, even although we asked nothing for the copyright. Such however, proved to be the case. Our manuscript was perused and returned to us by several of the most eminent publishers. Well do we remember betaking ourselves to one of the craft in Bond Street, whom we found in a back parlour, with his gouty leg propped upon à cushion, in spite of which warning he diluted his luncheon with frequent glasses of Madeira. ' What have you already written ?' was his first question, an interrogatory to which we had been subjected in almost every instance. ' Nothing by which we can be known.' ' Then I am afraid to undertake the publication.' We presumed timidly to suggest that every writer must have a beginning, and that to refuse to publish for him until he had acquired a name, was to imitate the sapient mother who cautioned her son against going into the water until he could swim. ' An old joke—a regular Joe !' exclaimed our companion, tossing off another bumper. ' Still older than Joe Miller,' was our reply; ' for, if we mistake not, it is the very first anecdote in the facetiæ of Hierocles.' ' Ha, sirs !' resumed the bibliopolist, ' you are learned, are you ? So, soh !— Well, leave your manuscript with me; I will look it over to-night, and give you an answer to-morrow.' Punctual as the clock we presented ourselves at his door on the following morning, when our papers were returned to us with the observation—' These trifles are

really not deficient in smartness; they are well, vastly well for
beginners; but they will never do—never. They would not pay for
advertising, and without it I should not sell fifty copies.'

This was discouraging enough. If the most experienced publishers feared to be out of pocket by the work, it was manifest, *a
fortiori*, that its writers ran a risk of being still more heavy losers,
should they undertake the publication on their own account. We
had no objection to raise a laugh at the expense of others; but to
do it at our own cost, uncertain as we were to what extent we might
be involved, had never entered into our contemplation. In this
dilemma, our *Addresses*, now in every sense rejected, might probably
have never seen the light, had not some good angel whispered us to
betake ourselves to Mr. John Miller, a dramatic publisher, then
residing in Bow Street, Covent Garden. No sooner had this gentleman looked over our manuscript, than he immediately offered to
take upon himself all the risk of publication, and to give us half
the profits, *should there be any ;* a liberal proposition, with which
we gladly closed. So rapid and decided was its success, at which
none were more unfeignedly astonished than its authors, that Mr.
Miller advised us to collect some *Imitations of Horace*, which had
appeared anonymously in the *Monthly Mirror*, offering to publish
them upon the same terms. We did so accordingly; and as new
editions of the *Rejected Addresses* were called for in quick succession,
we were shortly enabled to sell our half copyright in the two works
to Mr. Miller, for one thousand pounds ! ! We have entered into
this unimportant detail, not to gratify any vanity of our own, but
to encourage such literary beginners as may be placed in similar
circumstances; as well as to impress upon publishers the propriety
of giving more consideration to the possible merit of the works
submitted to them, than to the mere magic of a name.

To the credit of the *genus irritabile* be it recorded, that not one
of those whom we had parodied or burlesqued ever betrayed the
least soreness on the occasion, or refused to join in the laugh that
we had occasioned. With most of them we subsequently formed
acquaintanceship; while some honoured us with an intimacy which
still continues, where it has not been severed by the rude hand of
Death. Alas ! it is painful to reflect, that of the twelve writers
whom we presumed to imitate, five are now no more; the list of
the deceased being unhappily swelled by the most illustrious of all,
the *clarum et venerabile nomen* of Sir Walter Scott ! From that
distinguished writer, whose transcendent talents were only to be
equalled by his virtues and his amiability, we received favours and
notice, both public and private, which it will be difficult to forget,
because we had not the smallest claim upon his kindness. ' I certainly must have written this myself !' said that fine-tempered man
to one of the authors, pointing to the description of the Fire,
' although I forget upon what occasion.' Lydia White, a literary
lady, who was prone to feed the lions of the day, invited one of us
to dinner; but, recollecting afterwards that William Spencer formed
one of the party, wrote to the latter to put him off; telling him that
a man was to be at her table whom he ' would not like to meet.'
' Pray who is this whom I should not like to meet ?' inquired the

poet. ' Oh !' answered the lady, ' one of those men who have made that shameful attack upon you !' ' The very man upon earth I should like to know !' rejoined the lively and careless bard. The two individuals accordingly met, and have continued fast friends ever since. Lord Byron, too, wrote thus to Mr. Murray from Italy— ' Tell him we forgive him, were he twenty times our satirist.'

It may not be amiss to notice, in this place, one criticism of a Leicestershire clergyman, which may be pronounced unique: ' I do not see why they should have been rejected,' observed the matter-of-fact annotator; ' I think some of them very good !'

P. 1. *Loyal Effusion.* By Horace Smith. Fitzgerald (1759 ?- 1829) was a ready versifier who was self-appointed laureate of public events for a number of years. He was especially notable for his persistent recital of patriotic lines at the annual dinners of the Royal Literary Fund. The piece of his which Smith possibly had more particularly in mind was the ' Address to every Loyal Briton on the Threatened Invasion of his Country.'

P. 2. *By Wyatt's trowel.* James Wyatt (1746-1813) was the architect of the rebuilt Drury Lane Theatre.

Let hoarse Fitzgerald bawl. Byron (*English Bards and Scotch Reviewers*, line 1) wrote ' shall,' not ' let.'

P. 4. *The Baby's Debut.* By James Smith.

P. 6. *the Young Betty mania.* William Henry West Betty (1791-1874) first appeared on the stage in his twelfth year, and retired with a fortune in his seventeenth. Though he occasionally reappeared on the boards in manhood, he never repeated his early success.

P. 7. *An Address without a Phœnix.* This was the genuine address which Horace Smith had sent in for competition (see p. 397).

P. 9. *Cui Bono.* The opening stanza by James, the rest by Horace Smith.

P. 13. *The Tradesman duns.* Originally, ' The plaintiff calls.'

P. 15. *To the Secretary* and *a Hampshire Farmer.* By James Smith. William Cobbett (1762-1835) became Member of Parliament for Oldham in 1832.

P. 16. *Mr. Whitbread.* Samuel Whitbread (1758-1815), brewer and politician, Member of Parliament for Bedford, was Chairman of the Committee for the rebuilding of Drury Lane Theatre.

P. 19. *The Living Lustres.* By Horace Smith.

The following three stanzas were originally included :—between the third and fourth :

> Each pillar that opens our stage to the circle is
> Verdant antique, like Ninon de l'Enclos;
> I'd ramble from them to the pillars of Hercules,
> Give me but Rosa wherever I go.

Between the fourth and fifth:

> Attun'd to the scene when the pale yellow moon is on
> Tower and tree they'd look sober and sage,
> And when they all winked their dear peepers in unison,
> Night, pitchy night would envelop the stage.

> Ah! could I some girl from yon box for her youth pick,
> I'd love her as long as she blossomed in youth;
> Oh! white is the ivory case of her toothpick,
> But when beauty smiles how much whiter the tooth!

P. 21. *The Rebuilding.* By James Smith.

P. 29. *Laura Matilda.* Horace Smith, the author of *Drury's Dirge*, wrote that 'the authors, as in gallantry bound, wish this lady to continue anonymous,' and as a consequence there have been several attempts to pierce the veil of anonymity. One annotator boldly 'assumes the lady to have been' Letitia Elizabeth Landon (1802-1836), who was ten years of age when the *Rejected Addresses* were published. The motto from *The Baviad* which stands at the head of the parody is sufficient indication that the original was to be found among the 'Della Cruscans,' whose 'namby-pamby' verses, after appearing in the *World*, were published in two volumes as *The British Album* in 1790 (see the note on p. 405). The chief lady among those sentimentals was 'Anna Matilda,' otherwise Hannah Cowley (1743-1809), a dramatist of considerable, and a poet of but little, ability. As Mrs. Cowley had died three years before the Addresses were sent in, it is probable either that the parodists did not know of her death or that they merely meant to make fun of the school of which she was a leader. The passage from Gifford's *Baviad* given by way of motto is taken from that part of the satire in which the writers of *The British Album* are more particularly castigated.

P. 32. *A Tale of Drury Lane.* By Horace Smith.

P. 38. *Johnson's Ghost.* By Horace Smith.

P. 42. *The Beautiful Incendiary.* By Horace Smith. Spencer's best-remembered work is the tragic ballad of *Beth Gelert.*

P. 46. *Fire and Ale.* By Horace Smith.

P. 49. *Playhouse Musings.* By James Smith.

P. 52. *Drury Lane Hustings.* By James Smith. The 'Pic-Nic Poet,' in parodying the popular songs of the day, seems a very good imitation of the improvisings for which Theodore Hook came to be famous. The description suggests, however, that no particular writer was aimed at in the parody. Both James and Horace Smith had ten years before been contributors to a short-lived magazine entitled the *Pic-Nic.*

P. 54. *Architectural Atoms.* By Horace Smith. Thomas Busby (1755-1838), organist, musical composer, and man of letters. By way of supplement to the authors' note it may be said that the Address printed in the newspapers at the time as that sent in by Dr. Busby, and parodied by Lord Byron (see p. 174), was not the Address actually sent in, for that (preserved in the British Museum) begins:

> Ye social Energies ! that link mankind
> In golden bonds—as potent as refined !

Byron used quotation effectively in *Don Juan*, Canto I., ccxxii.:

> ' Go, little book, from this my solitude !
> I cast thee on the waters—go thy ways !
> And if, as I believe, thy vein be good,
> The world will find thee after many days.'
> When Southey's read, and Wordsworth understood,
> I can't help putting in my claim to praise—
> The four first rhymes are Southey's, every line:
> For God's sake, reader ! take them not for mine !
>
> BYRON: Don Juan, Canto I., ccxxii.

P. 62. *Theatrical Alarm Bell.* By James Smith.

committee of O.P.'s, etc. Referring to the tumultuous scenes at Covent Garden Theatre in 1809, when for sixty-seven successive nights there was uproar due to the attempt of the management to raise the prices of admission. Both James and Horace Smith appear to have written verse contributions to the newspaper warfare which accompanied, and served to stimulate, the disturbance in the theatre in favour of Old Prices.

P. 64. *The Theatre.* By James Smith. Spencer, referred to in the footnote, is the writer of society verse parodied in *The Beautiful Incendiary* (p. 42).

P. 69. *To the Managing Committee, etc.* By James Smith.

The Hamlet Travestie. By John Poole. Was published in 1810, and acted at Drury Lane in 1813.

The Stranger, translated by Benjamin Thompson from *Menschenhass und Reue,* by August von Kotzebue (1761-1819)— one line is remembered: ' There is another and a better world '— and *George Barnwell,* by George Lillo (1693-1739), based on the ballad in Percy's *Reliques,* were sensational plays that enjoyed considerable popularity in the early part of the nineteenth century.

P. 72. *Mrs. Haller.* One of the principal characters in *The Stranger.*

P. 76. *Punch's Apotheosis.* By Horace Smith. Theodore Hook wrote a number of light plays and farces before he was out of his teens, and was long notable for the way in which he could improvise such false gallop of verses as is parodied in *Punch's Apotheosis.*

P. 82. *Can Bartolozzi's . . . Could Grignion's.* The work of the engravers, Francesco Bartolozzi (1725-1815) and Charles Grignion (1717-1810), was much in use for sumptuously illustrated books.

D D

The epic rage of Blackmore. Sir Richard Blackmore (d. 1729), a physician-poet, who wrote *Prince Arthur, an Heroick Poem ; Eliza, an Epic Poem ; Alfred, an Epic Poem ;* and various other works which the world has willingly let die.

P. 83. *With Griffiths, Langhorne, Kenrick, etc.* Ralph Griffiths (1720-1803) was founder, proprietor, publisher, and sometime editor of *The Monthly Review*, the contributors to which included John Langhorne (1735-1779), the translator of Plutarch, and William Kenrick (1725 ?-1779).

P. 86. The first lines are an imitation of Pope's *Dunciad :*

> The mighty Mother, and her son, who brings
> The Smithfield Muses to the ears of Kings, etc.

Lo ! the poor toper is imitated from Pope's *Essay on Man :*

> Lo, the poor Indian ! whose untutor'd mind
> Sees God in clouds, and hears Him in the wind, etc.

P. 87. *Catherine Fanshawe.* The parody on Gray was sent by Miss Fanshawe to her friend, Miss Berry (one of Walpole's Misses Berry), with a letter purporting to be a letter of thanks to her for permission to read the verses, which, it was pretended, had been sent by Miss Berry, their author, to Miss Fanshawe for approval. The reference to Sydney Smith is to his lectures on 'Moral Philosophy' delivered at the Royal Institution, 1804-1806. Payne was a fashionable milliner of the period.

P. 92. *A Fable.* Dryden's *The Hind and the Panther :*

> A milk-white Hind, immortal and unchanged,
> Fed on the lawns and in the forest ranged.

The Course of Time. Robert Pollok's poem, despite this parody, was so popular that from its first publication in 1827 to 1868 it attained a sale of 78,000 copies.

P. 93. *Canning and Frere. The Poetry of the Anti-Jacobin,* 1852 and 1854, has been followed in attributing the authorship of the various parodies to Canning and others. The authority consists of Canning's own copy of the *Anti-Jacobin*, that of Lord Burghersh, that of Wright the publisher, and information given by Upcott.

Inscription. Southey's poem was an 'inscription for the apartment in Chepstow Castle where Henry Marten, the regicide, was imprisoned for thirty years.'

> For thirty years secluded from mankind,
> Here Marten linger'd.

It was written in 1795, but Southey excluded it from later editions of his works issued when he was no longer in sympathy with the French Revolution. Mrs. Brownrigg, the wife of a house-painter, was hanged at Tyburn for murder.

P. 94. *The Soldier's Wife.* Southey's *The Soldier's Wife :*

> Weary way-wanderer, languid and sick at heart,
> Travelling painfully over the rugged road;
> Wild-visaged wanderer ! Ah, for thy heavy chance.

Coleridge wrote the third stanza, indicated by asterisks in the second imitation. Southey finally suppressed this poem also.

Dilworth and Dyche. A reference to Thomas Dilworth's *Guide to the English Tongue* (1761) and Thomas Dyche's *Guide to the English Tongue* (1709).

P. 95. *Sapphics.* Southey's *The Widow :*

> Cold was the night wind, drifting fast the snow fell;
> Wide were the downs and shelterless and naked,
> When a poor wanderer struggled on her journey,
> Weary and way-sore.

George Tierney was the 'Friend of Humanity.' The original shared the fate of the other two poems in being finally suppressed.

P. 97. *The Loves of the Triangles.* Darwin's *Loves of the Plants.* Frere wrote the first lines to 'And liveried lizards wait upon her call' (p. 99); Ellis from that point to 'Twine round his struggling heart, and bind with endless chain' (p. 101); Canning, Ellis, and Frere were the joint-authors of the portion from 'Thus, happy France' to 'And folds the parent-monarch to her breast' (p. 102), Canning alone being responsible for the following twelve lines; and the trio finished the parody together. As a rule only portions of this masterpiece *sui generis* have hitherto been reprinted.

P. 104. *Lodi's blood-stained Bridge.* Napoleon beat the Austrians at Lodi on May 10, 1796.

P. 105. *Muir, Ashley, etc.* Thomas Muir (1765-1798) was a Parliamentary reformer; Thomas Paine (1737-1809), author of the *Rights of Man ;* Archibald Hamilton Rowan (1751-1834), a prominent United Irishman; Ashley and Barlow evade identification.

P. 107. *Song by Rogero.* *The Rovers, or the Double Arrangement*, was a travesty of German drama, in particular of Schiller's *Robbers*, Kotzebue's *The Stranger*, and Goethe's *Stella*, and it was performed at the Haymarket Theatre in 1811. It is the work of Canning, Ellis, and Frere, but only the first two wrote this 'song' (according to some authorities Pitt is credited with the last verse), having in mind Pitt's friend, Sir Robert Adair, who was educated at Göttingen. The editors of the *Anti-Jacobin* say: 'The song of Rogero with which the first act concludes is admitted on almost all hands to be in the very first taste, and if no German original is to be found for it, so much the worse for the credit of German literature.' This parody has itself often been parodied—by, among others, R. H. Barham, whose topic was the newly established London University.

P. 109. James Hogg. The Ettrick Shepherd's *Poetic Mirror, or the Living Bards of Great Britain,* was published anonymously in 1816, and it is generally admitted that his parodies of style are among the finest in the language. They are, however, overlong, and we have been obliged to be content with the 'song' alone from the parody of Scott, which, complete, would occupy more than seventy pages.

P. 115. The light-heel'd author of the Isle of Palms. John Wilson ('Christopher North') who published *The Isle of Palms and other Poems* in 1812.

P. 124. Joan I chose. Southey's *Joan of Arc* was published in 1796.

The next, a son, I bred a Mussulman. Thalaba the Destroyer, 1801.

A tiny thing . . . from the north . . . with vengeful spite was probably meant for the *Edinburgh Review.*

P. 125. My third, a Christian and a warrior true. Madoc, 1805.

And next, his brother, a supreme Hindu. The Curse of Kehama, 1810.

P. 128. The Curse. The closing lines are a faithful imitation of 'the Curse' in *The Curse of Kehama,* which ends:

> Thou shalt live in thy pain
> While Kehama shall reign,
> With a fire in thy heart,
> And a fire in thy brain;
> And Sleep shall obey me,
> And visit thee never
> And the Curse shall be on thee
> For ever and ever.

P. 128. And C—t—e shun thee. Possibly Cottle, the publisher and friend of Southey.

P. 129. The Gude Greye Katt. A parody of Hogg's own narrative, *The Witch of Fyfe.*

P. 142. Sonnets Attempted, etc. These appeared originally in the second number of the *Monthly Magazine* in November, 1797, with the signature of 'Nehemiah Higginbottom.' Coleridge described them as written—

in ridicule of my own Poems, and Charles Lloyd's and Lamb's, etc,, etc., exposing that affectation of unaffectedness, of jumping and misplaced accent in commonplace epithets, flat lines forced into poetry by italics (signifying how well and mouthishly the author would read them), puny pathos, etc., etc. The instances were almost all taken from myself and Lloyd and Lamb.'

The first sonnet, Coleridge said,

had for its object to excite a good-natured laugh at the spirit of doleful egotism and at the recurrence of favourite phrases, with the double object of being at once trite and licentious. The second was on low creeping language and thoughts under the pretence of *simplicity*. [Lamb had written some months earlier, ' Cultivate simplicity, Coleridge.'] The third, the phrases of which were borrowed entirely from my own poems, on the indiscriminate use of elaborate and swelling language and imagery . . . So general at that time and so decided was the opinion concerning the characteristic vices of my style that a celebrated physician (now, alas ! no more) speaking of me in other respects with his usual kindness to a gentleman who was about to meet me at a dinner-party could not, however, resist giving him a hint not to mention *The House that Jack Built* in my presence, for that I was as sore as a boil about that sonnet, he not knowing that I was myself the author of it. (*See* the Oxford Coleridge.)

P. 144. *Amatory Poems*. It is curious that Southey, who had taken offence at Coleridge's sonnet *To Simplicity*, signed ' Nehemiah Higginbottom,' believing it directed against himself, should himself have turned parodist and adopted the similar name of ' Abel Shufflebottom ' a couple of years later. Coleridge wrote, so he declared, that he might do the young poets good; Southey, it may be believed, merely to make fun of that band of vain and foolish versifiers who came to be known as ' the Della Cruscans.' Haunters of the bookstalls may yet occasionally light upon two small volumes entitled *The British Album, containing the Poems of Della Crusca, Anna Matilda, Arley, Benedict, the Bard, etc., etc. Which were originally published under the Title of the Poetry of the World, revised and corrected by the Respective Authors.* The second edition was dated 1790, and the work was still current when the brothers Smith gave their Laura Matilda parody in the *Rejected Addresses* (see p. 29). A few stanzas of one of ' Della Crusca's ' poems addressed to ' Anna Matilda ' will suffice to indicate the stuff which Southey was satirising:

> While the *dear Songstress* had melodious stole
>   O'er ev'ry sense, and charm'd each nerve to rest,
> *Thy Bard* in silent ecstasy of soul,
>   Had strain'd the *dearer Woman* to his breast.
>
> Or had she said, that *War's the worthiest grave*,
>   He would have felt his proud heart burn the while,
> Have dar'd, perhaps, to rush among the brave,
>   Have gain'd, perhaps, the glory—of a smile.
>
> And 'tis most true, while Time's relentless hand,
>   With sickly grasp drags *others* to the tomb,
> The Soldier scorns to wait the dull command,
>   But springs impatient to a nobler doom.

Tho' on the plain *he* lies, outstretch'd, and pale,
  Without one friend his steadfast eyes to close,
Yet on his honour'd corse shall many a gale,
  Waft the moist fragrance of the weeping rose.

O'er that dread spot, the melancholy Moon
  Shall pause a while, a sadder beam to shed,
And starry Night, amidst her awful noon,
  Sprinkle light dews upon his hallow'd head.

There too the solitary Bird shall swell
  With long-drawn melody her plaintive throat,
While distant echo from responsive cell,
  Shall oft with fading force return the note.

Such recompense be Valour's due alone !
  To me, no proffer'd meed must e'er belong,
To me, who trod the vale of life unknown,
  Whose proudest boast was but an idle song.

'Della Crusca,' the chief of the band, was Robert Merry (1755-
1798). The 'Della Cruscans' may be said to have been killed
by ridicule by Gifford's *Baviad* and *Maeviad*.

  P. 151. *Epicedium*. This appeared originally under the title
'Gone or Going' in Hone's *Table Book* (1827), and was reprinted by Lamb in his *Album Verses*. It is an echo rather
than a close parody of Michael Drayton's *Ballad of Agincourt*,
of which the fifth stanza runs:

> And for myself (quoth he)
> This my full rest shall be,
> England ne'er mourn for me,
>   Nor more esteem me.
> Victor I will remain,
> Or on this earth lie slain,
> Never shall she sustain
>   Loss to redeem me.

  P. 153. *Hypochondriacus*. This formed part of some imitations (mostly prose) which Lamb described as *Curious Fragments
extracted from a Commonplace Book which belonged to Robert
Burton, the famous Author of the Anatomy of Melancholy* (1801).
Though it is parody of matter more than of manner, it has
echoes of Burton's *Abstract of Melancholy*, which prefaces the
Anatomy.

  P. 154. *Nonsense Verses*. Here Lamb parodies the sentiment
which had inspired his own poem, *Angel Help*, written on a
picture showing a girl who had been spinning so long for the
support of a bed-ridden mother that she had fallen asleep, while
angels were shown finishing her work and watering a lily.

P. 155. *The Numbering of the Clergy.* Sir Charles Hanbury Williams's—

> Come, Chloe, and give me sweet kisses,
> For sweeter sure never girl gave;
> But why, in the midst of my blisses,
> Do you ask me how many I'd have ?

P. 156. *Peacock.* All these parodies but the last (the Byron) are from Peacock's *Paper Money Lyrics* published in 1837, but written ten or twelve years earlier ' during the prevalence of an influenza to which the beautiful fabric of paper-credit is periodically subject.'

P. 160. *Præmium of an Epic.* Southey's *Thalaba the Destroyer :* ' How beautiful is night !'

P. 165. *Song by Mr. Cypress.* The quintessence of Byron as distilled by Peacock into what Swinburne calls ' the two consummate stanzas which utter or exhale the lyric agony of Mr. Cypress.' The lines occur in *Nightmare Abbey.*

P. 166. *The Patriot's Progress.* Shakespeare, *As You Like It,* Act II., Scene 7.

P. 167. *Our Parodies are Ended. The Tempest,* Act. IV., Sc. 1.

P. 167. *Fashion.* Milton's *L'Allegro.*

P. 171. *Verses.* The ' Editor ' was Leigh Hunt, editor of the *Examiner,* imprisoned for two years (1814-15) in Surrey Gaol for libelling the Prince Regent. The authorship of this parody is often wrongfully attributed.

Never hear Mr. Br——m make a speech. Henry, afterwards Lord, Brougham.

Law. Edward Law Baron Ellenborough, Lord Chief Justice.

P. 172. *But Cobbett has got his discharge.* William Cobbett had been imprisoned for two years (1810-12) for his strictures on the Government of the day.

To Mr. Murray. John Murray was ' Bookseller to the Admiralty and the Board of Longitude.' He had possessed, and parted with, a share in *Blackwood's Magazine.*

Strahan, Tonson, Lintot, the publishers and booksellers of the eighteenth century.

P. 174. *Busby.* Dr. Busby had been one of the unsuccessful writers of an Address for the opening of Drury Lane (see p. 54 and note). The lines and words in inverted commas were from the Address which Busby printed as having been sent in, not from the one that he did send in, which is preserved in the British Museum.

As if Sir Fretful. Sir Fretful Plagiary, of course, from Sheridan's *The Critic.*

P. 176. *Margate.* Two stanzas, complete in themselves, from Mr. Peters's story, ' The Bagman's Dog,' in the *Ingoldsby Legends.* Byron's *Childe Harold*, Canto IV.

P. 177. *Not a sous had he got.* Barham notes that during the controversy in 1824 as to the authorship of ' The Burial of Sir John Moore,' a—

claimant started up in the person of a *soi-disant* ' Dr. Marshall,' who turned out to be a Durham blacksmith and his pretensions a hoax. It was then that a certain ' Doctor Peppercorn ' put forth *his* pretensions, to what he averred was the ' true and original ' version—the somewhat vulgar parody reprinted from *The Ingoldsby Legends.*

Hos ego versiculos feci, tulit alter honores.—VIRGIL.

I wrote these lines— . . . owned them—he told stories !
THOMAS INGOLDSBY.

P. 178. *The Demolished Farce.* Bayly's own popular song:
> Oh no, we never mention her,
> Her name is never heard.

See also Andrew Lang's parody, p. 353.

P. 179. *Peter Bell the Third.* Mrs. Shelley felt constrained to note that—

nothing personal to the author of *Peter Bell* is intended in this poem. No man ever admired Wordsworth's poetry more;—he read it perpetually, and taught others to appreciate its beauties. . . . His idea was that a man gifted, even as transcendently as the author of *Peter Bell*, with the highest qualities of genius, must, if he fostered such errors, be infected with dullness. This poem was written as a warning—not as a narration of reality. He was unacquainted personally with Wordsworth, or with Coleridge (to whom he alludes in the fifth part of the poem), and therefore, I repeat, his poem is purely ideal ;—it contains something of criticism on the compositions of those great poets, but nothing injurious to the men themselves.

P. 186. * * * Mr. H. Buxton Forman says : 'All seems to me to point to Eldon as the name left out here.'

(*See* note to p. 219.)

Byron was less respectful:
> There's something in a stupid ass,
> And something in a heavy dunce,
>   But never since I went to school
>   I heard or saw so damned a fool
> As William Wordsworth is for once.

> And now I've seen so great a fool
> As William Wordsworth is for once,
>   I really wish that Peter Bell
>   And he who wrote it, were in hell,
> For writing nonsense for the nonce.

P. 201. *A long poem in blank verse.* This reference in the note is to Wordsworth's *Excursion*, the lines indicated being:

> And, verily, the silent creatures made
> A splendid sight, together thus exposed;
> Dead—but not sullied or deformed by death,
> That seemed to pity what he could not spare.
>
> Book VIII., lines 568-571.

P. 202. *As the Prince Regent did with Sherry—i.e.*, Richard Brinsley Sheridan.

'Twould make George Colman melancholy. George Colman was author of *Broad Grins* and other humorous work.

P. 203. *May Carnage and slaughter.* The reference here is to lines in Wordsworth's *Thanksgiving Ode on the Battle of Waterloo* (later *Ode*, 1815), as originally published:

> But Thy most dreaded instrument
> In working out a pure intent,
> Is Man—arrayed for mutual slaughter.
> —Yea, Carnage is thy daughter!

P. 205. *The immortal Described by Swift.* Presumably a reference to the undying Struldbrugs of *Gulliver's Travels*, 'despised and hated by all sorts of people.'

P. 206. *'Twould have made Guatimozin doze.* Guatimozin or Cuauhtemoc was the last of the Aztec emperors, executed with circumstances of great cruelty by Cortes.

P. 206. *Like those famed Seven who slept three ages—i.e.*, the Seven Sleepers of Ephesus who, according to a Syrian legend, hid themselves in a cave during the Decian persecution (A.D. 250), fell asleep and awakened miraculously nearly two hundred years later.

P. 215. '*&c.*' This ending is in accord with the original text.

P. 218. *He lived amidst th' untrodden ways.* Mr. Walter Hamilton, whose large collection of parodies is well known, attributes this parody to Hartley Coleridge, but efforts to trace it have failed.

P. 219. *Peter Bell : a Lyrical Ballad.* When Wordsworth's *Peter Bell* was announced in 1819, John Hamilton Reynolds wrote—it is said in a single day—this *Lyrical Ballad* and hurried it out before Wordsworth's poem was issued. The fact that Reynolds used Wordsworth's measure suggests that he had seen a copy of the original. It was a criticism by Leigh Hunt of Wordsworth's *Peter Bell* and Reynolds' parody that moved Shelley to the writing of *Peter Bell the Third*. To his *Peter Bell* Reynolds attached a *Preface* and a short *Supplementary Essay*, also purporting to be written by W. W.

' It is now (the *Preface* began) a period of one-and-twenty years since I first wrote some of the most perfect compositions (except certain pieces I have written in my later days) that ever dropped from poetical pen. . . . It has been my aim and my achievement to deduce moral thunder from buttercups, daisies, celandines, and

(as a poet scarcely inferior to myself, hath it) " such small deer."
Out of sparrows' eggs I have hatched great truths, and with sextons'
barrows have I wheeled into human hearts piles of the weightiest
philosophy. . . . Of *Peter Bell* I have only thus much to say: It
completes the simple system of natural narrative, which I began so
early as 1798. It is written in that pure unlaboured style, which
can only be met with among labourers. . . . I commit my Ballad
confidently to posterity. I love to read my own poetry: it does
my heart good.'

In the *Supplementary Essay* 'W. W.' was made to declare
that he proposed 'in the course of a few years to write laborious
lives of all the old people who enjoy sinecures in the text or are
pensioned off in the notes of my Poetry.'

P. 221. *As clustering a relationship.* See *The Critic*, Act II.,
Scene 2 :

> And thou, my Whiskerandos, shouldst be father
> And mother, brother, cousin, uncle, aunt,
> And friend to me!

P. 228. *Blue Bonnets over the Border.* Scott's 'ditty to the
ancient air of " Blue Bonnets over the Border," ' *The Monastery*,
chap. xxv :

> March, march, Ettrick and Teviotdale,
> Why the deil dinna ye march forward in order ?

P. 231. *As Spencer had. ere he composed his Tales.* This probably refers to the Hon. W. R. Spencer, author of *Beth Gelert*, as
well as to the one-time fashionable tailless coat known as a
'spencer.'

P. 232. *This shall a Carder . . . Whiteboy . . . Rock's murderous commands.* The reference is to the secret associations
which were responsible for much agrarian crime in Ireland
during the early part of the nineteenth century.

P. 235. *If English corn should grow abroad.* Thus in fourth
edition of *Whims and Oddities* (1829), but ' go ' in some reprints.
The bull is probably intentional.

P. 237. *Huggins and Duggins.* Hood appears to have had
Pope's first Pastoral, *Spring*, especially in mind. In it Strephon
and Daphnis alternately sing the praises of Delia and Sylvia:

> In Spring the fields, in Autumn hills I love,
> At morn the plains, at noon the shady grove,
> But Delia always; absent from her sight,
> Nor plains at morn, nor grove at noon delight.

P. 237. *All things by turns, and nothing long.* 'Was everything
by starts, and nothing long.'—DRYDEN: *Absalom and Achitophel.*

P. 240. *We met.* T. H. Bayly's—

> We met—'twas in a crowd,
> And I thought he would shun me,
> He came—I could not breathe,
> For his eyes were upon me.

P. 241. *Those Evening Bells.* Moore's song begins:

> Those evening bells ! those evening bells !
> How many a tale their music tells
> Of youth, and home, and that sweet time
> When last I heard their soothing chime.

P. 241. *The Water Peri's Song.* Moore's *Lalla Rookh ;*

> Farewell—farewell to thee, Araby's daughter !
> (Thus warbled a Peri beneath the dark sea,)
> No pearl ever lay, under Oman's green water,
> More pure in its shell than thy Spirit in thee.

P. 242. *Cabbages.* The first verse of *Violets*, by L. E. L., runs:

> Violets ! deep blue violets !
> April's loveliest coronets:
> There are no flowers grow in the vale,
> Kissed by the sun, wooed by the gale,
> None with the dew of the twilight wet,
> So sweet as the deep blue violet.

P. 243. *Larry O'Toole.* Charles Lever: ' Did ye hear of the Widow Malone ?'

P. 243. *The Willow Tree.* In this Thackeray was parodying his own earlier treatment of the same theme, as Charles Lamb had parodied himself in the *Nonsense Verses* (see p. 154). Thackeray's serious version begins:

> Know ye the willow-tree,
> Whose grey leaves quiver,
> Whispering gloomily
> To yon pale river ?

P. 245. *Dear Jack.* In O'Keeffe's opera, *The Poor Soldier*, is the often-parodied song imitated from the Latin:

> Dear Tom, this brown jug that foams with mild ale,
> Out of which I now drink to sweet Nan of the Vale,
> Was once Toby Filpot, etc.

The Rev. Francis Fawkes, famous in his day as a translator of the classics, is the reputed author of the song.

P. 248. *The Almack's Adieu* and *The Knightly Guerdon.* These are varied parodies of a one-time popular song:

> Your Molly has never been false, she declares,
> Since the last time we parted at Wapping Old Stairs;
> When I vowed I would ever continue the same,
> And gave you the 'BACCO BOX marked with my name.
> When I passed a whole fortnight between decks with you,
> Did I e'er give a kiss, Tom, to one of the crew ?
> To be useful and kind with my Thomas I stayed,—
> For his trousers I washed, and his grog, too, I made.

P. 250. *W. E. Aytoun.* The contributions of Aytoun to the *Book of Ballads*, edited by ' Bon Gaultier,' that are here given are those which, on the authority of Sir Theodore Martin, were solely his own composition. Several of the *Ballads* had appeared in periodicals before they were collected and published in book form in 1845.

P. 252. *A Midnight Meditation.* Six poets are parodied in the ' Bon Gaultier' *Ballads* under the general heading, ' The Laureates' Tourney '—Wordsworth, the Hon. T— B— M'A—, the Hon. G— S— S—, T— M— RE, Esq., A— T—, and Sir E— B— L—, the last of which, by Aytoun only, is here given. The parodists, remembering *Rejected Addresses,* profess that the poems were sent to the Home Secretary when the Laureateship became vacant on the death of Southey.

P. 252. *These mute inglorious Miltons.* Hood had already used this pun connecting the poet and the oysters in his ballad of the blind *Tim Turpin :*

> A surgeon oped his Milton eyes,
> Like oysters, with a knife.

P. 254. *The Husband's Petition.* In this Aytoun was using to a ludicrous end the measure he had employed in *The Execution of Montrose :*

> Come hither, Evan Cameron !
> Come, stand beside my knee—
> I hear the river roaring down
> Towards the wintry sea.

P. 256. *Sonnet CCCI.* Martin Farquhar Tupper published a volume of *Three Hundred Sonnets* in 1860. *Punch* professed to have made an arrangement with him to continue the series, and boldly put the initials M. F. T. to this parody in the number for May 26, 1860.

P. 257. *You see yon prater called a Beales.* Edmond Beales (1803-1881) was President of the Reform League at the time of the Hyde Park riots. He thus figures in *Punch* in lines written apropos of tears shed by Walpole, Home Secretary, when he learnt of the riots:

> Tears at the thought of that Hyde Park affair
> Rise in the eye and trickle down the nose,
> In looking on the haughty Edmond Beales,
> And thinking of the shrubs that are no more.

P. 258. *The Lay of the Lovelorn.* This is one of the ' Bon Gaultier' *Ballads,* and is included by permission of Messrs. William Blackwood and Sons. Aytoun had no part in this parody. It was solely Sir Theodore Martin's, and in its author's opinion is the best he contributed to the collection. In the *Book of Ballads* Sir Theodore was at pains to explain that—

it was precisely the poets whom we most admired that we imitated the most frequently. This was certainly not from any want of reverence, but rather out of the fullness of our admiration, just as the excess of a lover's fondness often runs over into raillery of the very qualities that are dearest to his heart. 'Let no one,' says Heine, ' ridicule mankind unless he loves them.' With no less truth may it be said, Let no one parody a poet unless he loves him. He must first be penetrated by his spirit, and have steeped his ear in the music of his verse, before he can reflect these under a humorous aspect with success.

Some excellent parodists have succeeded very well in dissembling their love.

P. 266. *The Laureate's Bust at Trinity.* Parody of part of *Guinevere* in the *Idylls of the King :*

> So the stately Queen abode
> For many a week, unknown, among the nuns. . . .
> ' Late, late, so late ! and dark the night and chill!
> Late, late, so late ! but we can enter still.
> Too late, too late ! ye cannot enter now.'

The parody is from *Punch,* November 12, 1859.

P. 268. *Unfortunate Miss Bailey.* Tennyson's *The Lord of Burleigh.*

> In her ear he whispers gaily,
> ' If my heart by signs can tell,
> Maiden, I have watched thee daily,
> And I think thou lov'st me well.'

P. 270. *Cary.* Phoebe Cary wrote many parodies. One entitled *The Wife* is sometimes said to be a burlesque of Wordsworth:

> Her washing ended with the day,
> Yet lived she at its close,
> And passed the long, long night away
> In darning ragged hose.

> But when the sun in all his state
> Illumed the eastern skies,
> She passed about the kitchen grate
> And went to making pies.

As a matter of fact this only differs by the use of a few turns from

> Her suffering ended with the day,

by James Aldrich (1810-1856).

P. 271. *That very time I saw,* etc. See *Midsummer Night's Dream,* Act II., Sc. 1.

P. 272. *On a Toasted Muffin.* Sir E. L. B. L. B. L. B. Little was Edward Lytton Bulwer Lytton, afterwards Lord Lytton, who had written an anonymous satire, *The New Timon.*

P. 273. *In Immemoriam.* In connexion with these quatrains
it may be noted that Whewell (1794-1866), in one of his treatises,
published before *In Memoriam,* dropped into the following
sentence: ' No power on earth, however great, can stretch a cord,
however fine, into a horizontal line that shall be absolutely
straight.'

P. 274. *Bayard Taylor.* *The Diversions of the Echo Club* first
appeared in the *Atlantic Monthly,* 1872, and in book form in
1876. The poems here reprinted are given by permission of
the Houghton, Mifflin Company.

Taylor, writing to T. B. Aldrich, March 29, 1873, says:

> Story told me that Browning sent him the *Echo Club* last summer,
> with a note saying it was the best thing of the kind he had ever seen,
> and that if he had found the imitations of himself in a volume of his
> poems he would have believed that he actually wrote them.
>
> *Life and Letters of Bayard Taylor.*

P. 281. *All or Nothing.* While parodying Emerson's poetry
generally Bayard Taylor had probably chiefly in mind *The
Sphinx :*

> The Sphinx is drowsy,
> Her wings are furled:
> Her ear is heavy,
> She broods on the world.

Most of Bayard Taylor's parodies are obviously rather of the
poets' general styles than of particular poems.

P. 286. *If life were never bitter.* Parody of Swinburne's *A
Match :*

> If love were what the rose is
> And I were like the leaf.

P. 286. *Salad.* From *The British Birds* (1872):

> Enter three Poets, all handsome. One hath redundant hair, a
> second redundant beard, a third redundant brow. They present
> a letter of introduction from an eminent London publisher, stating
> that they are candidates for the important post of Poet Laureate to
> the New Municipality which the Birds are about to create.

P. 289. *I'm a Shrimp.*

> I'm afloat ! I'm afloat ! On the fierce rolling tide—
> The ocean's my home and my bark is my bride.
> Up, up, with my flag, let it wave o'er the sea,—
> I'm afloat ! I'm afloat ! and the Rover is free.

P. 290. *Dante Rossetti.* These poems are taken, by permission, from *The Works of Dante Gabriel Rossetti*—the single-

volume edition of 1911. ' MacCracken ' is a close parody of one of Tennyson's early poems, ' The Kraken ':

> Below the thunders of the upper deep;
> Far, far beneath in the abysmal sea,
> His ancient, dreamless, uninvaded sleep
> The Kraken sleepeth.

Mr. Francis MacCracken, of Belfast, was the purchaser of early works by the pre-Raphaelite artists.

P. 290. *The Brothers.* Another poem by Tennyson, ' The Sisters,' tells of the tragic love of twin girls for one man, and this duality suggested the verses to Rossetti when he found that the ' Thomas Maitland ' who had attacked his work in the *Contemporary Review* (' The Fleshly School of Poetry ') was really Robert Buchanan.

P. 292. *Ode to Tobacco.* This is in the Draytonian metre, ' Fair stood the wind for France,' but Calverley evidently had Longfellow in mind. Compare the second stanza of his Ode with the third stanza of Longfellow's *Skeleton in Armour :*

> I was a Viking old!
> My deeds, though manifold,
> No Skald in song has told,
> No Saga taught thee!

P. 294. *The real beverage for feasting gods on.* The allusion in the seventh stanza is to Jupiter and the Indian Ale:

> ' Bring it !' quoth the Cloud-Compeller,
> And the wine-god brought the beer—
> ' Port and Claret are like water
> To the noble stuff that's here.'

Calverley also parodied Byron in *Arcades Ambo.*

P. 297. *Wanderers.* Tennyson's ' The Brook,' with the song of the brook:

> I come from haunts of coot and hern,
> I make a sudden sally,

but ending in a parody of Tennysonian blank verse. In his *Collections and Recollections*, Mr. G. W. E. Russell has quoted the last six lines, ' which even appreciative critics generally overlook. . . Will any one stake his literary reputation on the assertion that these lines are not really Tennyson's ?' (The poem is from *Fly-Leaves*, 1872, by permission of Messrs. George Bell and Sons.)

P. 298. *Proverbial Philosophy.* Here are some typical lines by Martin Tupper:

A man too careful of danger liveth in continual torment,
But a cheerful expecter of the best hath a fountain of joy within
  him:
Yea, though the breath of disappointment should chill the sanguine
  heart,
Speedily gloweth it again, warmed by the live embers of hope;
Though the black and heavy surge close above the head for a
  moment,
Yet the happy buoyancy of Confidence riseth superior to Despair.

P. 300. *Read incessantly thy Burke—i.e.*, Burke's *Peerage*. *The Prince of Modern Romance—i.e.*, Lord Lytton.

P. 301. *The Cock and the Bull.* As Mr. Seaman truly remarks, this is a recognized masterpiece of the higher stage of parody, when an author's literary methods—in this case Browning's *The Ring and the Book*—are imitated. (From *Fly-Leaves.*)

P. 304. *Lovers, and a Reflection.* Calverley may have had in mind William Morris's 'Two Red Roses across the Moon,' which begins 'There was a lady lived in a hall,' but undoubtedly the source of his inspiration was Jean Ingelow's 'The Apple-Woman's Song,' from *Mopsa the Fairy*, the second line of which recurs: 'Feathers and moss, and a wisp of hay.' (From *Fly-Leaves.*)

P. 306. *Ballad.* Another burlesque of the same poet. Miss Ingelow attempted to retaliate in *Fated to be Free*, with feeble lines intended to pour scorn on ' Gifford Crayshaw '—*i.e.*, Calverley. (From *Fly-Leaves.*)

P. 309. *You are old, Father William.* An example of a parody known to everybody, although the original is known to few. The poem imitated is Southey's 'The Old Man's Comforts, and how he gained them,' beginning:

You are old, Father William, the young man cried,

and ending:

In the days of my youth I remember'd my God!
  And He hath not forgotten my age.

P. 314. *The Three Voices.* Tennyson's *The Two Voices :*

A still small voice spake unto me.

P. 322. *Beautiful Soup.* The authorship of ' Beautiful Snow,' which was immensely popular in this country as well as in its native America, cannot be verified. It has been attributed to an unhappy woman, to Major W. A. Sigourney, who was said to have written the verses in 1852, and who died in 1871, and to a James W. Watson.